E4

Dublin

The Travellers' Companion series

General editor: Laurence Kelly

St Petersburg: a travellers' companion
Selected and introduced by Laurence Kelly (1981)

Moscow: a travellers' companion
Selected and introduced by Laurence Kelly (1983)

Naples: a travellers' companion
Selected and introduced by Desmond Seward (1984)

Edinburgh: a travellers' companion
Selected and introduced by David Daiches (1986)

Florence: a travellers' companion
Selected and introduced by Harold Acton and Edward Chaney
(1986)

Istanbul: a travellers' companion
Selected and introduced by Laurence Kelly (1987)

Delhi and Agra: a travellers' companion
Selected and introduced by Michael Alexander (1987)

Vienna: a travellers' companion
Selected and introduced by John Lehmann and Richard Bassett
(1988)

View of the Four Courts looking down the Liffey;
aquatint by S.F. and H. Brocas from Coloured Views in Dublin, 1820 (*overleaf*)

DUBLIN

A Travellers' Companion

SELECTED AND INTRODUCED BY

Thomas and Valerie Pakenham

Constable London

First published in Great Britain 1988
by Constable and Company Limited
10 Orange Street London WC2H 7EG
Copyright © 1988 Thomas and Valerie Pakenham
Set in Monophoto Baskerville 11pt
by Servis Filmsetting Ltd, Manchester
Printed in Great Britain by
St Edmundsbury Press
Bury St Edmunds, Suffolk

British Library CIP data
Dublin: a travellers' companion.–(The
Travellers' companion series).
1. Dublin, to 1976
I. Pakenham, Thomas II. Pakenham, Valerie,
1939-   III. Series
941.8'35

ISBN 0 09 465810 2
ISBN 0 09 465820 X Pbk

In memory of Christine Longford

Contents

Illustrations   20

Acknowledgements   23

Introduction   27

Map of the city (*drawn by John Mitchell*)   48–9

DUBLIN: THE OLD CITY

1 The founding of the city; from *The Description of Ireland* by Richard Stanyhurst in Holinshed's *Chronicles*   53

2 A charter for Norman Dublin from Henry II; from *Strongbow's Conquest of Ireland* by F.P. Barnard   54

The Castle
3 King John commands the building of Dublin Castle in 1205; from *Strongbow's Conquest of Ireland* by F.P. Barnard   56

4 A Gaelic poet laments his lord, impaled on the walls of Dublin Castle; from *The Literary History of Ireland* by Douglas Hyde   56

5 The fate of Irish traitors – the unrepentant view of an Elizabethan Englishman; from Richard Stanyhurst's *Description of Ireland* in Holinshed's *Chronicles*   58

6 Trial by combat in the Castle Yard, 1584; from Holinshed's *Chronicles*   58

7 Hugh Roe O'Donnell escapes from Dublin Castle, Christmas Eve, 1592; from Lughaidh O'Clery's *Life of Hugh Roe O'Donnell*, in Constantia Maxwell's *Irish History from Contemporary Sources*   59

8 The defeat of the 'Old English' nobility; from a letter by Sir Christopher Plunkett to his son in 1612; in *Desiderata Curiosa Hibernica*   63

9 A ramble round the Castle in 1698; from John Dunton's letters quoted in Edward MacLysaght's *Irish Life in the Seventeenth Century*   64

10 A Castle ball in 1732; from the *Autobiography and Correspondence of Mrs Delany* 66

11 The wit and wisdom of Lord Chesterfield; from 'Sketches of Irish History' quoted in *Irish Cavalcade* by M.J. McManus 67

12 Custard-pies at the Lord Lieutenant's dinner, 1757; an unpublished letter (in the British Museum) from Chief Baron Willes to his friend, the Earl of Warwick 68

13 The United Irishmen fail to capture the Castle, 23 May 1798; from *The Rise and Fall of the Irish Nation* by Sir Jonah Barrington 69

14 The Castle guardroom; from *Jack Hinton, the Guardsman* by Charles Lever 72

15 George IV kisses the girls; from *The Croker Papers 1808–1857*, edited by R. Pool 74

16 The Vice-regal Court in the 1870s; from *Recollections of Dublin Castle and Dublin Society* (anon), 1902 75

Christ Church Cathedral
17 The miraculous crucifix at Christ Church Cathedral; from the *Topographia Hibernica* by Giraldus Cambrensis, in *Strongbow's Conquest of Ireland* by F.P. Barnard 77

18 The Normans rebuild Christ Church Cathedral, and a description of Strongbow; from *The Description of Ireland* by Richard Stanyhurst in Holinshed's *Chronicles* 78

19 Four Irish kings are knighted in Christ Church Cathedral in 1395; from *Froissart in Britain* by Sir Henry Newbolt 79

20 Lambert Simnel is crowned in Christ Church, 1487; from Holinshed's *Chronicles* 82

St Patrick's Cathedral
21 The Great Earl of Kildare makes peace with the Earl of Ormonde in St Patrick's; from Holinshed's *Chronicles* 84

22 The Great Earl of Cork's tomb is put in its place, 1635; from *The Life and Letters of the Great Earl of Cork* by Dorothea Townshend 87

23 Jonathan Swift describes his life as Dean of St Patrick's
   in 1733; from *The Correspondence of Jonathan Swift* edited
   by Elrington Ball   89

24 A visit to Swift's Deanery in the 1730s; from *The Memoirs
   of Letitia Pilkington*   90

25 Dean Swift's final descent into insanity; from *The
   Memoirs of Letitia Pilkington*   92

26 Swift's death and the rape of his locks, 19 October 1745;
   from *The Life of Doctor Swift* by Thomas Sheridan   93

27 Swift's epitaph; translated by W.B. Yeats   94

28 Sir Walter Scott visits St Patrick's; from *The Life of Sir
   Walter Scott* by J.G. Lockhart   94

29 Thackeray attends morning service in St Patrick's; from
   An Irish Sketchbook by W.M. Thackeray   96

Marsh's Library
30 Swift's epitaph on Archbishop Marsh; from *All Graduates
   and Gentlemen* by Muriel McCarthy   97

The Liberties
31 How the Liberties defend their boundaries; from the
   Recollections of John O'Keeffe   98

32 A plea for the weavers of the Liberties by Dean Swift;
   from *A Biography of Dublin* by Christine Longford   99

33 The cutting weavers take their revenge; from *Irish
   Varieties* by J.D. Herbert   99

34 A clergyman surveys the Liberties in 1798; from *Report on
   the Population of Ireland* by James Whitelaw, quoted in
   Constantia Maxwell's *Dublin Under the Georges*   100

35 A Trinity student attends a meeting of the United
   Irishmen in the Tailors' Hall, 1791; from *Ireland Sixty
   Years Ago* by J.E. Walsh   102

36 The arrest of Lord Edward FitzGerald in Thomas Street;
   from *Ireland, its Scenery, Character etc.* by Mr and
   Mrs S.C. Hall   104

37 Robert Emmett's rising in Thomas Street; from *Ireland in
    '98* by R.R. Madden   106

38 Emmett's execution outside St Catherine's church; from
    R.R. Madden's *Ireland in '98*   107

39 A 'thieves' kitchen' in the Liberties; from the
    Autobiography of William Carleton   109

40 An American doctor in the Liberties in 1844; James
    Johnson, quoted in *Dear, Dirty Dublin, A City in Distress*
    by Joseph O'Brien   111

41 A Frenchwoman in the Liberties in the 1880s, and a visit
    to the Guinness brewery; from *Three Months in Ireland* by
    Madame de Bovet   111

Kilmainham

42 The founding of the Royal Hospital at Kilmainham –
    Charles II's letter to James, Duke of Ormonde, 1679;
    from 'The Hospitals at Kilmainham' in *The Dublin
    Historical Record*, Vol. 20   115

43 The Duke of Ormonde's farewell toast; from *Ireland under
    the Stuarts* by Richard Bagwell   115

44 Extracts from the records of the Hospital at
    Kilmainham; from *The Dublin Historical Record*, Vol. 20   116

45 John Wesley visits Kilmainham Hospital in 1794; from
    Wesley His Own Biographer   117

46 Parnell in Kilmainham Jail; from *Recollections* by
    William O'Brien   118

47 Johnny Cassidy visits Kilmainham Jail with his uncle;
    from *Pictures in the Hallway* by Sean O'Casey   122

DUBLIN NORTH OF THE RIVER

Phoenix Park

48 The Duke of Ormonde saves Phoenix Park from
    Charles II's mistress, Lady Castlemaine, in 1663; from
    Thomas Carte's *Life of James, Duke of Ormonde*   127

49 The Phoenix becomes a people's park in the 1770s; from
    Dublin Old and New by Stephen Gwynn   128

50 A sham battle in Phoenix Park, in the 1820s; from
Charles Lever's novel, *Jack Hinton, the Guardsman*   128

51 A duel in the Phoenix; from the *Recollections* of Aubrey de
Vere   130

52 Queen Victoria writes to the King of the Belgians from
the Vice-regal Lodge; from *The Collected Letters of Queen
Victoria*, edited by G.E. Buckle   131

53 Thomas Carlyle calls at the Vice-regal Lodge, 1849;
from *Reminiscences of My Irish Journey* by Thomas Carlyle   132

54 A childhood memory of the Vice-regal Lodge; from *My
Early Life* by Winston Churchill   133

55 The Phoenix Park murders; from *The Illustrated London
News*, 13 May 1882   134

The Rotunda
56 A Charity breakfast for Dr Mosse's Lying-in Hospital,
1751; from *The Life and Correspondence of Mrs Delany*   137

57 A clergyman applauds Dr Mosse's hospital, 1777; from *A
Philosophical Survey of the South of Ireland* by the Revd
Thomas Campbell   138

58 The Irish Volunteers assemble in the Rotunda in 1778;
from *The Rise and Fall of the Irish Nation* by Sir Jonah
Barrington   140

Charlemont House (now the Municipal Art Gallery)
59 A judgement on Lord Charlemont by Sir Jonah
Barrington; from his *Historic Memoirs of Ireland*   143

60 A judgement on Lord Charlemont by Edmund Burke;
from Francis Hardy's *Memoirs of the Earl of Charlemont*   144

Belvedere House
61 After the hell-fire sermon at Belvedere College; from
Portrait of the Artist as a Young Man by James Joyce   145

O'Connell Street (Sackville Street)
62 Shelley preaches the revolution in Sackville Street in
1812; from *Letters to Elizabeth Hitchener* by Percy Bysshe
Shelley   147

63 George IV makes a royal progress down Sackville
(O'Connell) Street, 1821; from the journal of Colonel
William Blacker, in Constantia Maxwell's *History of
Trinity College*   147

64 The magnificent new Dublin Post Office and the postal
services of the time; described by William Curry in his
New Picture of Dublin, 1820   149

The Custom House
65 Building the Custom House – political problems; from
The Life of James Gandon by T.J. Mulvaney   151

66 Building the Custom House – constructional·problems;
Gandon's account from *The Life of James Gandon* by
T.J. Mulvaney   152

The Quays
67 Edmund Burke goes for a sail in the cellar; from *The
Early Life and Correspondence of Edmund Burke* by Arthur
Samuels   155

68 An English tourist admires the nearly completed Four
Courts, 1799; from *Letters on the Irish Nation* by George
Cooper   155

69 A soup kitchen on the Quays, 1847; from 'An open letter
to Lord John Russell' by John Mitchel, quoted in M.J.
McManus's *Irish Cavalcade*   156

St Mary's Pro-Cathedral
70 Death of the Liberator: Daniel O'Connell's body is
brought home to Dublin for burial, May 1847; from *The
Illustrated London News*   158

DUBLIN MOVES SOUTH

Trinity College
71 The founding of Trinity College in 1591 – Queen
Elizabeth I's letter to the Lord Deputy, the Lord
Chancellor and the Council of Ireland; from Constantia
Maxwell's *Irish History from Contemporary Sources*   165

72 Catholic fears at the founding of Trinity – a petition to
the Pope from Irish Catholics in exile, 1595; from
Constantia Maxwell's *Irish History from Contemporary
Sources* 165

73 Seventeenth-century student offences listed in the Book of
Censures; from *Trinity College, Dublin* by W. MacNeile
Dixon 166

74 The fate of the College under James II – extracts from
Trinity College Register; from *Trinity College, Dublin* by
W. MacNeile Dixon 167

75 Inventory of a Collegian's chamber; from *The Poems of
John Winstanley* 169

76 Edmund Burke is admitted to Trinity, 1744; from *The
Early Life and Correspondence of Edmund Burke* by Arthur
Samuels 170

77 A visit to the Trinity College cellars; from the *Recollections*
of John O'Keeffe 174

78 A visit to the Anatomy House in the 1770s; from
A Philosophical Survey of the South of Ireland by the
Revd Thomas Campbell 175

79 The Trinity students lose their Parliamentary privileges
in the 1790s; from *Ireland Sixty Years Ago* by J.E. Walsh 176

80 Student japes in the early 1820s – and an eccentric Vice-
Provost; from *Charles O'Malley* by Charles Lever 177

81 A tall story about Dr Barrett; from *The Dublin Penny
Journal*, 1840 180

82 Provost Mahaffy remembered; from *It isn't This Time of
Year at all* by Oliver St John Gogarty 180

Parliament House, College Green
83 The first Parliament on College Green; from *The History
of the Parliament House* by Sir John Gilbert 182

84 A diatribe against Parliamentary corruption in the
1730s; anonymous, from Sir John Gilbert's *History of the
Parliament House* 183

85 Benjamin Franklin admires the Irish Parliament; from a
    letter to Thomas Cushing in Sir John Gilbert's *The
    History of the Parliament House*   184

86 The Irish Parliament debates the Budget over dinner;
    from *Personal Sketches of His Own Times* by Sir Jonah
    Barrington   185

87 Henry Grattan hails the new Irish 'nation' in 1782; from
    Sir Jonah Barrington's *Rise and Fall of the Irish Nation*   186

88 Grattan returns to Parliament to vote against the Union;
    from *The Life and Times of Henry Grattan by his son*   189

89 The last hours of the Irish House of Commons; from *The
    Rise and Fall of the Irish Nation* by Sir Jonah Barrington   191

90 The last hours of the Irish House of Lords in 1799; from
    Thomas de Quincey's *Autobiographic Sketches*   192

91 An epitaph for the Parliament House; from *The Story of
    Dublin* by D.A. Chart   194

92 Daniel O'Connell salutes the Parliament House, 1844;
    from *The Life of Daniel O'Connell* by Michael MacDonagh   194

    St Stephen's Green
93 The early history of Stephen's Green; from *Picturesque
    Dublin* by Francis Gerard   198

94 Bishop Clayton's wife receives on Stephen's Green, 1731;
    from *The Autobiography and Correspondence of Mrs Delany*   198

95 Lord Orrery writes to congratulate Bishop Clayton on
    his new house and retails the Dublin gossip; from *The
    Orrery Papers*, edited by the Countess of Cork and Orrery   199

96 The poet Gerard Manley Hopkins arrives at Newman
    College on Stephen's Green; from *Letters of Gerard Manley
    Hopkins to Robert Bridges*   203

97 Stephen Dedalus calls on the Dean of Studies at the
    Jesuit University College; from *Portrait of the Artist as a
    Young Man* by James Joyce   204

98 W.M. Thackeray takes a grilled herring at the
    Shelbourne Hotel and explores the Green; from his *Irish
    Sketchbook*, 1843   205

99 George Moore stays at the Shelbourne and salutes the spring in Stephen's Green; from *Ave*, Volume I of his trilogy, *Hail and Farewell* 207

100 A nightly drama for Dubliners; from *The Shelbourne* by Elizabeth Bowen 210

101 George Moore dines at Ely House; from *As I was going down Sackville Street* by Oliver St John Gogarty 211

102 W.B. Yeats recites at Lady Ardilaun's tea-party; from *Bricks and Flowers* by Katherine Everett 214

103 A glimpse of Yeats and Maud Gonne on Stephen's Green; from *My Ireland* by Kate O'Brien 216

104 Brendan Behan's mother remembers Yeats; from *Brendan Behan's Island* by Brendan Behan 217

Kildare Street
105 The Kildare Street Club from *Parnell and his Island* by George Moore 219

Leinster House
106 A description of Leinster House; from *A Picturesque and Descriptive View of Dublin* by James Malton 220

107 A balloon ascent from Leinster House lawn, 1785; from Sir John Gilbert's *History of the City of Dublin* 221

108 A spy reports on Lord Edward FitzGerald in 1798; from Sir John Gilbert's *History of the City of Dublin* 224

109 Lady Sarah Napier describes Lord Edward FitzGerald's escape from Leinster House, March 1798; from Sir John Gilbert's *The History of the City of Dublin* 225

110 The 'greening' of Leinster House (Dáil Eireann), 1930; from *In Search of Ireland* by H.V. Morton 225

Merrion Square
111 Daniel O'Connell at home in Merrion Square, from *Sketches of the Irish Bar* by W.H. Curran 227

112 Dr William Wilde stands trial; from *The Life of Oscar Wilde* by Frank Harris 229

113 Dancing-parties in Merrion and Fitzwilliam Squares; by
Eilis Dillon, from *Victorian Dublin*, edited by Tom
Kennedy   230

DUBLIN THEATRE

114 Handel describes the rapturous reception of his *Messiah*
at its first performance in 1742; from *Autograph Letters of
Handel and Jennens*, edited by Edward, sixth Earl of Howe   235

115 The young Edmund Burke describes a fierce battle at
Smock Alley Theatre in 1747 between two factions of
Trinity students; from *The Early Life and Correspondence of
Edmund Burke* by Arthur Samuels   236

116 Mrs Siddons drowns a Dublin audience in tears, 1783;
from *The Kemble Era* by Linda Kelly   237

117 William Macready recalls the liveliness of a Dublin
theatre audience in the early nineteenth century; from
his *Reminiscences*, edited by Sir F. Pollock   238

118 The Dublin theatre in the doldrums in 1842; from
W.M. Thackeray's *An Irish Sketchbook*   239

The Abbey Theatre
119 Reviving the Irish Theatre – George Moore is taken by
W.B. Yeats to see 'the ghost of a theatre down by the
Quays'; the future Abbey Theatre; from George Moore's
Hail and Farewell   241

120 The battle for *The Playboy* – Lady Gregory's account;
from *Our Irish Theatre* by Augusta Gregory   243

121 The battle for *The Playboy* – an outraged citizen's
account; from *Joseph Holloway's Abbey Theatre*, edited by
Roger Hogan and Michael J. O'Neill   244

122 The battle for *The Playboy* – a schoolboy's memory; from
Walter Starkie's autobiography, *Scholars and Gypsies*   245

123 Backstage at the Abbey – Lady Gregory's journal, 1908;
from *Seventy Years* by Augusta Gregory   248

124 Downstage at the Abbey – a memory of Yeats; from
Austin Clarke's autobiography, *A Penny in the Clouds*   249

THE APPROACHES TO THE CITY
DUBLIN ON SEA

Ringsend
125 John Dunton arrives at Ringsend in 1698; from Edward
MacLysaght's *Irish Life in the Seventeenth Century* 255

Dublin Bay
126 Dublin Harbour in 1810; from *An Englishman's Descriptive
Account of Dublin* by Nathaniel Jeffreys 256

Dun Laoghaire
127 W.M. Thackeray lands at Kingstown (Dun Laoghaire)
in 1841; from his *Irish Sketchbook* 258

Sandycove
128 James Joyce at the Martello Tower in 1903; from *It isn't
This Time of Year at all* by Oliver St John Gogarty 261

129 Gogarty at the Martello Tower; from James Joyce's
Ulysses 263

130 James Joyce leaves the Martello Tower; from *Selected
Letters of James Joyce* edited by Richard Ellmann 267

Howth
131 A childhood in Howth, in the 1880s; from Maud Gonne
MacBride's autobiography, *A Servant of the Queen* 268

DUBLIN IN REVOLUTION

The Larkin Strike
132 A police baton charge in O'Connell Street, 1913; from
Sean O'Casey's *Drums under the Windows* 273

The Easter Rising
133 Easter Monday, 1916 in St Stephen's Green; from *The
Insurrection in Dublin* by James Stephens 276

134 Easter Monday, 1916 outside the GPO; from the
autobiography of Ernie O'Malley, *On Another Man's
Wound* 279

135 Easter Monday inside Trinity College; by John Joly, in
    Blackwoods Magazine, July 1916   281

136 Inside the GPO, Easter Week; from *Remembering Sion* by
    Desmond Ryan   284

137 The aftermath of the Rising – looting in Grafton Street
    and Sackville Street; from *The Sinn Fein Rebellion as I saw
    it* by Mrs Hamilton Norway   288

138 Part of Patrick Pearse's court-martial speech in 1916   290

139 The execution of James Connolly in Kilmainham; from
    Portrait of a Rebel Father by Nora Connolly   291

140 'Sixteen Dead Men'; from *The Collected Poems of
    W.B. Yeats*   293

141 A Dublin ballad by Dermot O'Byrne; from *An Anthology
    of 1916* by Edna Fitzhenry   294

142 O'Connell Street after the Rising; from Kate O'Brien's
    autobiography, *My Ireland*   294

143 The Chief Secretary's verdict on the Rising, 1932; from
    Augustine Birrell's *Things Past Redress*   295

144 'Was he out in Easter Week?'; from *Inishfallen, fare you
    well* by Sean O'Casey   295

LIFE, CUSTOMS AND MORALS IN DUBLIN

145 The wild Irish; from *Topographia Hibernica* by Giraldus
    Cambrensis, quoted in *Strongbow's Conquest of Ireland* by
    F.P. Barnard   299

146 The Ostomen; from Holinshed's *Chronicles*   301

147 Fortifying the city: a Royal Charter; from John Gilbert's
    Calendar of Ancient Records of Dublin   302

148 An Irish chieftain resists adopting English dress; from
    The Government of Ireland under Sir John Perrot.   303

149 A sixteenth-century Gaelic poet laments the betrayal of
    Irish ways; from Constantia Maxwell's *Irish History from
    Contemporary Sources*   303

150 The State of Dublin in 1620; from Luke Gernon's

Contents

Discourses, quoted in *Ireland 1607–1782* by James Carty — 304

151 The hospitable Mayor of Dublin, 1577, and how the Dublin citizens muster for their defence; from the *Description of Ireland* by Richard Stanyhurst in Holinshed's *Chronicles* — 307

152 An Elizabethan soldier complains of the price of Dublin ale in 1610; from Barnaby Rich's *New Description of Ireland* — 309

153 Sunday in Dublin, 1725, by D— S—; quoted in *Irish Cavalcade* by M.J. McManus — 310

154 Dublin society in the 1750s, and the virtuous Dublin ladies; manuscript of a letter from Chief Baron Willes in the British Museum — 314

155 The fighting Dubliners; from *Ireland Sixty Years Ago* by J.E. Walsh — 316

156 The Dublin footpads; from *Ireland Sixty Years Ago* by J.E. Walsh — 318

157 The eloquence of the Dublin beggar; from John Gamble's *Sketches of History, Politics and Manners taken in Dublin in the Autumn of 1811* — 318

158 Eloquence at the Viceroy's supper party in the early 1800s; from *Jack Hinton, the Guardsman* by Charles Lever — 320

159 An American tourist looks at splendour and misery in Dublin in the first years of the nineteenth century; from *Ancient & Modern Dublin* by William Curry — 321

160 William Cobbett visits the Dublin workhouse; from *Not by Bullets and Bayonets* by Molly Townsend — 322

161 Dining-out in Dublin in the 1840s; from W.M. Thackeray's *An Irish Sketchbook* — 323

162 Brass-plate Dublin; from *Seven Winters* by Elizabeth Bowen. — 324

163 Dublin after the 'crossness'; from *In Search of Ireland* by H.V. Morton — 326

Bibliography — 329

Index — 333

Illustrations

View of the Four Courts looking down the Liffey;
aquatint by S.F. and H. Brocas from *Coloured Views in
Dublin, 1820* (*by courtesy of the Board of Trustees of the
Victoria & Albert Museum*)   *frontispiece*

Henry II's seal   54

Sir Henry Sidney, Lord Deputy of Ireland, rides out from
Dublin Castle; detail from a late sixteenth-century
woodcut by John Derricke   57

The Great Courtyard at Dublin castle; aquatint by James
Malton from *Picturesque Views of Dublin, 1794* (*by courtesy of
the Board of Trustees of the Victoria & Albert Museum*)   71

Four Irish kings are instructed in English manners in
Dublin, 1395; illustration from Froissart's fifteenth-
century *Chronicle*   80

Richard Boyle, the Great Earl of Cork: engraving from a
portrait at Hardwick Hall   86

A tourist admires the monument to Dean Swift in St
Patrick's Cathedral; engraving from Walker's *Hibernian
Magazine*, 1802   95

The arrest of Lord Edward FitzGerald, 1798; cartoon by
George Cruikshank from W.H. Maxwell's *History of the
Irish Rebellion*   104

The execution of Robert Emmett, 1803; a contemporary
Dublin painting   109

Recreation time in Kilmainham Jail for Parnell and his
followers; from *The Illustrated London News*, 1882   119

The Phoenix Park murders; form *The Illustrated London
News*, May 1882   136

Dr Mosse's Lying-In Hospital and the Rotunda; aquatint
by S.F. and H. Brocas from *Coloured Views in Dublin, 1820*
(*by courtesy of the Board of Trustees of the Victoria & Albert
Museum*)   139

James Gandon's Custom House; aquatint by James
Malton, 1797   153

Daniel O'Connell's body lies in state in Marlborough Street Chapel (later the Pro-Cathedral); from *The Illustrated London News*, 1847   160–61

Interior of Trinity College Library; aquatint by James Malton, from *Picturesque Views of Dublin, 1794 (by courtesy of the Board of Trustees of the Victoria & Albert Museum)*   172–73

A Trinity student; engraving from Walker's *Hibernian Magazine*, 1774   178

The Speaker enters the Irish House of Commons, 1780s; from a painting by Francis Wheatley   185

Henry Grattan, addresses the Irish House of Commons, 1782; a contemporary engraving   187

Daniel O'Connell in his triumphal car salutes the Parliament House; from *The Illustrated London News*, 1844   197

The Beaux Walk on the north side of St Stephen's Green; aquatint by James Malton, 1797   200–01

'Mr W.B. Yeats presents Mr George Moore to the Queen of the Fairies' – cartoon by Max Beerbohm *(by permission of Mrs Eva Reichmann)*   208

Richard Crosbie and his balloon ascent from Leinster House lawn, 1785; a contemporary engraving *(by permission of the National Library of Ireland, Dublin)*   223

Daniel O'Connell at home in Merrion Square; from *The Illustrated London News*, 1843   228

W.B. Yeats lectures the audience at the Abbey Theatre; cartoon by Tom Lalor *(by permission of the National Library of Ireland, Dublin)*   250

The monument to George IV at Kingstown (Dun Laoghaire); an early nineteenth-century engraving   259

James Larkin at Liberty Hall during the Dublin workers' strike, 1913; pen and ink sketch by William Orpen   275

Inside the Dublin GPO, Easter Week, 1916; a contemporary reconstruction painted by Thomas Kiersey *(by permission of the National Library of Ireland, Dublin)*   287

An 'uncivilized' Irish chief banquets in the forest; from John Derricke's *Image of Ireland*   300

A group of Irish soldiers drawn by Albrecht Dürer   306

Dublin society amuses itself in the Rotunda pleasure-gardens; from Walker's *Hibernian Magazine*, 1790 315

A Dublin beggar plies his trade near Capel Street bridge; detail from an aquatint by James Malton, 1797 319

Acknowledgements

Anyone attempting the anthology of a city begins his search by consulting the historical experts who have gone before. In the case of Dublin, we were fortunate that many of them were also friends who offered generous bibliographical help. We would like particularly to thank the following: John Cowell, Maurice Craig, Owen and Ruth Dudley Edwards, Desmond Fitzgerald, William Garner and Anne Simmons of the Irish Architectural Archive, William Le Fanu, Desmond Guinness, Kevin Nowlan (who helped not only with historical background, but with selecting from a huge mass of undigested material), Terence de Vere White and Peter Walsh, Curator of the Guinness Museum. Most of the research for the book was done in the Irish National Library in Dublin or the London Library, whose librarians were unfailingly kind and patient with requests for obscure traveller's tales. For hospitality on many visits to Dublin, we would like to thank Moira Woods, Olda and Desmond Fitzgerald, and Desmond and Penny Guinness.

As in previous Travellers' Companions in this series, short biographical notes on writers or subjects of extracts have been included – or in the case of writers too well-known to need them, a note on the context of a particular extract. With a thousand years of Dublin history to choose from (or far longer if we are to take Richard Stanyhurst's date for the founding of the city, AD 155), it has been both pleasure and pain to compile this anthology: pain because so many extracts have had to be excluded on grounds of space or because the street or building to which they relate is now swept away. We have tried, as far as possible, to follow the brief for the series – that extracts should relate events rather than describe buildings; their architectural history can be found elsewhere. We have also chosen rather arbitrarily, with two or three exceptions, to end the timescale with Easter Week, 1916 and its immediate aftermath, an event which, for many Dubliners, as Sean O'Casey wrote, marked 'The Year of One in Irish History'.

We would like to make acknowledgement to the following for extracts used from their writings, editions, or where copyright permission was needed:

Associated Book Publishers (UK Ltd) and Methuen for H.V. Morton's *In Search of Ireland*; Curtis Brown and the Estate of Elizabeth Bowen for *The Shelbourne*, and Virago and the Estate of Elizabeth Bowen for *Seven Winters*; Sphere Books for Oliver St John Gogarty's *As I was Going Down Sackville Street* and *It Isn't This Time of Year at all*; Macmillan, London and Basingstoke, for Sean O'Casey's *Pictures in the Hallway*, *Drums Under the Window*, and *Inishfallen Fare Thee Well*; The Educational Company of Ireland for Nora Connolly's *Portrait of a Rebel Father*; The Bodley Head, Random House and the Executors of the James Joyce Estate for *Ulysses*; Johnathan Cape, Viking and the Executors of the James Joyce Estate for *Portrait of the Artist as a Young Man*; John Murray for Walter Starkie's *Scholars and Gypsies*; Katherine Everett and Constable for *Bricks and Flowers*; Kate O'Brien and Batsford for *My Ireland*; Brendan Behan and Hutchinson for *Brendan Behan's Island*; Tom Kennedy and the Dublin Arts Federation for *Victorian Dublin*; Macmillan USA for Lady Gregory's *Seventy Years*; Austin Clarke and Routledge & Kegan Paul for *Penny in the Clouds*; Richard Ellmann and Oxford University Press for *The Selected Letters of James Joyce*; R. Pool and Batsford for *The Croker Papers*; the South Illinois University Press, Roger Hogan and Michael J. O'Neill for *Joseph Holloway's Abbey Theatre*; Joseph O'Brien and the University of California Press for *Dear, Dirty Dublin, a city in distress*; Linda Kelly and The Bodley Head for *The Kemble Era*; Molly Townsend and Sheed & Ward for *Not by Bullets and Bayonets*; James Carty for *Dublin 1607–1872; The Dublin Historical Record*; Stephen Gwynn and Harrap for *Dublin Old and New*; Christine Longford and Methuen for *A Biography of Dublin*; Edward MacLysaght for *Irish Life in the Seventeenth Century*; Constantia Maxwell for *Irish History from Contemporary Sources, Dublin Under the Georges*, and *History of Trinity College, Dublin*; Christie's and the 6th Earl of Howe for the *Autograph Letters of Handel and Jennens*; A.P. Watt, Macmillan Publishing Company and Michael B. Yeats for 'Sixteen Dead Men' by W.B. Yeats; Sean MacBride for Maud Gonne Macbride's *Servant of the Queen*; Colin Smythe Ltd for James Stephens' *Insurrection in Dublin*; Hamlyn Publishing for Winston Churchill's *My Early Life*; Ernie O'Malley for *On Another Man's Wound*; and Desmond Ryan for *Remembering Sion*.

Last and most important, our thanks are due to the General Editor of this series, Laurence Kelly, for his help and encouragement, and to Prudence Fay who had the onerous task of editing the typescript in detail and keeping it within bounds.

T.P.
V.P.
1988

Introduction

Take the Holyhead ferry on a fine, summer morning, and you may be in for a surprise. Dublin or Naples? What are these calm blue waters, enclosed by the brown arms of two Italianate promontories, and that volcanic prong, sweeping up in two concave arcs two thousand feet from the bay?

Then you recognize it from its picture. The volcano is the Sugar Loaf, not Vesuvius, and the brown arms, freckled with white villas, are the arms of Killiney and Howth. Bay and mountain, they both belong to Dublin as Baiae and Vesuvius belong to Naples. How theatrical the setting, and how perfectly suited to the style of the city, even if Dublin turns out to have chosen the cool, north Italian stage-sets of Palladio, and shrunk from the exotic scenery of southern Baroque.

Soon the calm Palladian façades vanish in a fickle Celtic squall. That calmness is astonishing. Violence, as everyone knows, runs through Dublin's history like a jagged red seam in a carpet. How to reconcile the smooth eighteenth-century surface with the passions behind the brickwork – the passions bred by the invasions, rebellions, revolutions and counter-revolutions that have made the city what it is?

It was the narrow harbour, made secure by the generous bay and the sweep of the mountains that from the first attracted invaders. In the ninth century came Norse-speaking raiders from Norway, the Vikings. Theirs were the first long ships to come 'sniffing up the Liffey' (as a modern Irish poet puts it), ten days' hard sailing from bases in Bergen or Oslo. Apparently these Vikings found some kind of earlier settlements of wooden huts built by the Irish along the estuary: one at a Hurdle Ford (Ath Cliath) and the other at the Black Pool (Linn Dubh). Strung out on the coast either side of the Liffey were early Christian churches and monasteries, built and rebuilt in the previous three centuries, in the intervals between the fighting among local Irish chieftains. Their graveyards were punctuated with the high crosses and round towers that were a Celtic speciality. The Norwegians' speciality was a long ship and a battle-axe. For half a century they behaved like pirates, harrying the coastal plain from their lair beside the Liffey, looting for slaves and cattle, hunting for Irish souvenirs before burning the churches.

We know almost nothing about their pirate lair, the first Viking Dublin, except that they erected a great stone above the Black Pool, a stone about fourteen feet high, planted like a colonial standard. As the Steyne, it survived until the seventeenth century. Then in the early years of the tenth century, the Irish chieftains stopped fighting each other for long enough to make a successful counter-attack, and the Norwegian long ships sailed home with the survivors.

When the long ships returned they were manned by Danes, and this time the Viking toehold became a city. The Battle of Dublin gave them a permanent trading colony. It was a decisive battle fought in the harshness of midwinter, on 17 December 919. The Gaelic poet lamented:

Fierce and hard was the Wednesday
In which posts were strewn under the feet of the shields;
It shall be called until Judgement Day
The destructive memory of Ath Cliath.

If we took too seriously the laments of the medieval Irish scribes, we would think the whole of the next century was a Danish reign of terror. Brutal, ferocious, furious, untamed hordes: that is how the invaders were described. The invaders did not bother to leave their own version of events. Fortunately there is a mine of new archaeological evidence about Danish Dublin, and it is sober stuff. Day-to-day life in Dublin in the tenth century was doubtless brutish and short. It was also often dull. Commerce was the main preoccupation. There was more trading than raiding.

The most important archaeological discoveries were made from 1978 till 1980 and precipitated an unholy row. All the City corporation wanted to excavate was a hole for the foundations of a long-delayed new City Hall. This was to be a fashionable office complex in the shape of two eighty-foot-high pill boxes. They chose the best site in the heart of old Dublin, between Christ Church Cathedral and the Liffey, and stumbled on the core of the lost city of the Vikings. The row centred on whether the corporation should be allowed to destroy this core and go on with the pill boxes, or be told to look for a new site. They won the argument, unfortunately for posterity. But before the Viking city was lost again under the concrete (while the air was thick with missiles from the High Court) scholars had excavated thousands of artefacts, and added enormously to their knowledge of the way Viking Dublin and its successor – medieval Dublin – actually worked.

It turned out that the Vikings had built their walled city astride the ridge on the south bank of the Liffey. It was about a mile long and rather less than half a mile wide. The walls were built of stone about five feet thick and ten feet high. (One beautiful chunk was excavated along the line of the old river bank. Inside the masonry looked as fresh as when it was plastered.) Inside these imposing defences were hundreds of single-storey houses constructed of mud and wattle, with oak-framed doors and plastered walls. Even the floors were often made of plastered wickerwork. When the houses became insanitary, which they did very soon, they were levelled and replaced with new houses. It was a homely style of architecture, rather like the architecture of an African village today. There were no chimneys or windows. And it lasted in its essentials for several hundred years after the Danes had gone.

The narrow streets were full of workshops for craftsmen: bronzesmiths, tanners, weavers and blacksmiths. One possession that was most prized was a comb made from animal bone or antlers. Hundreds have been excavated, over two hundred in Wine Tavern Street alone. They were used for barter as well as for taming unruly Viking hair. Bronze working was also a speciality, and reached a very high technical standard. In the High Street area several hundred decorated bronze pins were excavated. Jewellery seems to have been common: bronze gilt brooches, gold armlets, gold and silver rings and so on. And the most striking evidence of the success of Dublin as a trading centre is the absence of weapons. Among all the tens of thousands of artefacts excavated, no arrows and only a few dozen weapons have been found.

By the eleventh century the local Danes had become half assimilated into the Gaelic world, and their power as an independent colony had ebbed away. (A similar fate overtook the Danish colonies at York, in Germany and elsewhere.) Increasing unity of religion – and a religion of one god – strengthened the bonds forged by the increasing diversity of trade. Norsemen took Irish wives. Gradually the terrifying Northern gods – Odin and Thor and Loki – lost their grip on Dublin's imagination, as Christianity came to dominate the whole of Europe. Squat wooden church spires rose on the southern bank of the Liffey, dedicated to both Irish and Danish saints. North of the river was built an outpost of the city, with a parish church dedicated to Danish Saint Michan, which was to be the only parish church north of the river for six hundred years. Two famous Danish kings of Dublin, Olaf Cuaran and Sitric Silkenbeard, retired to finish their days as holy men on the island of Iona.

One sympathizes with them. Odin or Thor or Jesus Christ: nothing seemed to alter the local appetite for fighting. Dublin was caught up in the three-way tug-of-war between Mael Sechnaill of Leinster, Brian Boru of the Midlands, and Ui Neill of the North. Brian claimed the high kingship but his armies were too weak to deliver it. The wars rumbled on, with Dublin periodically being captured and sacked. The contest reached its climax in 1014 when the combined forces of Leinster and the Danes were defeated by Brian Boru in the spectacularly bloody battle of Clontarf just outside the walls of Dublin. But it was a Pyrrhic victory for Brian. In Dublin it was soon business as usual. International trade had its ups and downs, and so did the city, sacked, rebuilt and sacked again with monotonous frequency.

When the Normans came in 1170, they came as a result of a local squabble, invited by a king of Leinster who had fled to England. Within a few years they had tidied up the confusion of centuries. Norman architecture and Norman institutions were imposed on Dublin and the Pale – the territory within about thirty miles. Two great stone cathedrals, Christ Church within the walls and St Patrick's just beyond, soon towered over the wooden houses of the city. Both were built in an uncompromising Anglo-Norman style, apt symbol that Dublin was and would be for the next seven hundred years a British garrison town in Ireland.

It is here that our Dublin tour should begin: on the dramatic ridge beside Christ Church Cathedral, averting our eyes from those concrete pill boxes now sitting on the site of the lost Viking city below us.

Picture this great colonial city in its heyday, the thirteenth century. The river has shrunk as the city has grown fat. Below us, at Cook Street, the medieval walls enclose new land reclaimed as the river has gradually silted up. The ships are moored further east. Streets have been laid out to assist trade, each with its own speciality: Fishamble Street for the fishmongers, and Wine Tavern Street for the wine merchants. Half a dozen stone churches have been built or rebuilt: St Audoen's, St Werburgh's, St Martin's, St Nicholas's and so on. Outside the walls there are ten abbeys or friaries, rich in tenant farms conferred on them by royal favour. But everything is dominated by these two cathedrals, and the great Castle commissioned by King John in 1204. Decorated with the heads of rebels, this must have been an awe-inspiring place, rather like an Irish Tower of London. There was a tower at each corner and a portcullis at the centre of the North Gate. In fact it was part fortress, part prison, part governor's palace, with a magnificent new hall modelled on Canterbury, and a fresco of the king and his barons, and other luxuries unheard of in Ireland, like piped water.

To get the colonial feeling of medieval Dublin, go to the north or south transept of Christ Church Cathedral. There, built in white stone imported from Dundry in Somerset and worked by the rough hands of English craftsmen, is Romanesque architecture as the English knew it. There are round arches and the ghost of a Gothic arch in the triforium (for this is the age of transition). The walls bare their teeth at you: those dogs' teeth – chevrons – loved by the Normans. Outside the south transept is an elegant doorway with more dogs' teeth and a pious portrait of some ruler thrown in. It is all very orderly and conventional. Then you descend to the crypt. Here the wild Celtic spirit has reasserted itself. The plan is a strange muddle, and the chapels are lying abreast instead of being separated behind the aisles.

By comparison, St Patrick's Cathedral has been scraped clean of all medieval feeling. It is rich with associations of many other periods. In fact, some would regard it as the principal national shrine (though the prize of the Protestant minority). Yet so zealous were the nineteenth-century restorers, that you can search in vain for a single medieval stone today.

After Dublin's emergence in the thirteenth century as an Early English colonial capital – a Gothic HQ for the governor of Britain's first colony – Dublin's later medieval history forms something of an anti-climax. There was no monumental building at this period. Not that trade failed to increase. The wooden cranes of Merchants Quay and Wood Quay creaked and rasped as they unloaded the bales of fine English wool and in return loaded Bristol ships with Irish hides and barrels of Irish butter. But Dublin was becoming increasingly isolated from the rest of the country, as Anglo-Norman immigrants elsewhere had become progressively Gaelicized – *ipsis Hibernis Hiberniores*. Only a few miles south of the city, in the foothills of the Dublin mountains, lived the wild Irish, O'Tooles and O'Briens, waiting to prey on the fat of the colony. Indeed the pattern of the Viking age was beginning to repeat itself. Making money demands different talents from making war. Dublin's businessmen were better at buying off enemies than fighting them.

When an unexpected crisis loomed early in the fourteenth century, they proved almost helpless. It took the form of the invasion of Robert Bruce with six thousand Scottish knights. Bruce landed at Carrickfergus in 1315 and fought his way south, looting the country as he went. By 1317 the campfires of his army at Castleknock were visible from the tower of St Audoen's church. Desperate efforts were made to rebuild the city walls. Gaps along the quayside were hurriedly repaired. Down came the only bridge across the Liffey, the one linking the old Danish city on the north bank with the main city to the south. The mayor of Dublin, Robert le Nottingham, lost his head and tried a policy of scorched earth. He set fire to part of the suburbs. The fire quickly spread across the walls and burnt part of Christ Church itself. Fortunately for the English, Bruce had forgotten to bring a siege train. Dublin was saved, surrounded by the blackened ruins of the suburbs.

Bruce's raid set off the decline of the political power of the colony. The next crisis nearly wiped it out. This was the series of famines, plagues and cattle moraines culminating in the Black Death of the mid-fourteenth century. Of course famine was endemic. (At one time people were only saved from starvation by the stranding of a school of whales at Clontarf.) How the Black Death reached Dublin is not known. Perhaps it came, like other invaders, from Bristol, or perhaps it came direct from France. At any rate the Black Death bacillus travelled by flea, carried in turn on the fur of a black rat. It proved so devastating that people thought the world was coming to an end. According to the estimate of an Irish friar, John Clyn, four thousand people died in Dublin between August and December 1348. No doubt John

Clyn, who died too, exaggerated the numbers. But Dublin, like all close-packed medieval communities, was especially vulnerable to disease. From England's point of view the plague had one good result. Dublin, wasted to a shadow, was more loyal than ever, more dependent on her powerful but over-burdened patron across the water.

Dublin's loyalty was not seriously tested till the end of the Middle Ages. It was then in 1534 that 'Silken Thomas' FitzGerald (actually, the hot-headed), son of the Earl of Kildare, raised the standard of revolt in Dublin. His father, the king's deputy and the head of the Anglo-Norman aristocracy in Ireland, had been summoned to London to answer charges of maladministration, but Silken Thomas heard a story that he had been executed. He stormed in to the meeting of the Council, being held at St Mary's Abbey across the river, and renounced his allegiance to the Crown. Understandably confusion resulted. There was a Geraldine faction, eager to follow Silken Thomas. There was also plague within the walls and the O'Tooles were lurking outside them. So the authorities played for time. The rebels were allowed within the walls, provided they agreed not to harm the townspeople. And loyal officials were allowed to withdraw to the Castle, well stocked with food and the city's supply of gunpowder. It was a daft bargain for Silken Thomas. The castle proved impregnable. In due course a new deputy arrived from England and made mincemeat of the Geraldines. Silken Thomas was dragged off in chains to England, where he and five of his uncles came to a gruesome end at Tyburn.

Dublin businessmen had proved their loyalty in a fashion. In fact, they sensibly tried to keep out of politics whenever they could. This was no longer an option in the Reformation which followed within a few years. Suddenly the city found itself in the front line of a major war. Inside the walls the symbols of Popery were broken or burnt. A great bonfire was lit outside Christ Church to dispose of holy statues and other dangerous images. (One pre-Reformation treasure, a sixteenth-century wooden statue of Our Lady, survives today in the Carmelites' church in Whitefriars Street. A priest rescued it from a junk shop in 1824.) The monasteries, nunneries and friaries outside the walls were demolished, their gold plate melted down, their farmland taken by the Crown or handed over to the king's men. The townspeople of Dublin accepted this orgy of destruction without protest. There were dutiful celebrations to honour Henry VIII as head of the Church, and little enthusiasm either when the pendulum swung back to Catholicism in Mary's reign or when the Reformation was resumed in all its vigour by Elizabeth.

It was the brutal wars of Elizabeth's reign that propelled the city forward to a new prosperity. Soldiers flooded over from England, led by ambitious English noblemen or low-born adventurers – both equally anxious to make their name by exterminating Irish rebels. Dublin supplied the army with everything it could not bring for itself. The city still clung to its medieval walls, punctuated by thirty-two towers and gateways, with the five-towered Castle looming over the south-east corner. But the city of wattle and daub was at last changing to a city of stone and slate and regular architecture. Tudor Dublin must have looked like other large British cities (Chester is the best known example today) with black and white the predominant style, the larger houses constructed in a cagework of darkened oak beams and white plaster.

Life could be merry if you were a merchant with a line in imported linen or wool or wine. Dublin was already famous for its hospitality. Fresh English settlers waxed indignant at the way the alehouses were open at all hours of the day and night, run by 'idle housewives' of dubious morals. On the other hand, no one seemed to care that many of the public buildings, including churches of the Reformed faith, were becoming ruinous. Only one new public building was erected, but it was one of the highest importance. In fact, its huge open site still dominates Dublin today. It was Trinity College, founded by Elizabeth I on the site of an old abbey, whose land had been given to the mayor and the people of Dublin as a reward for their loyalty after the Reformation.

After the hurricanes of the late sixteenth century – rebellions, massacres, pogroms – came calmer weather at the beginning of the seventeenth. Dublin recovered its breath. Under a powerful governor, Lord Wentworth (later Earl of Strafford) business expanded rapidly. So did the city. And this time the expansion was to some extent planned. Wentworth decided to preserve a kind of green belt on the east, south-east and north-west of the city: College Green, St Stephen's Green, and Oxmantown Green. They were to be 'kept for the use of citizens to walke and take the open air by reason this cittie is at this present growing very populous'. Time was running out for Wentworth. In London he was thought too big for his boots, and he soon ended on the scaffold. As for Dublin, its citizens were not long in the mood for promenades. They found themselves cringing in the front line – or close behind it – of a disastrous new war.

In the great Catholic rebellion of 1641 the city became the main refuge for loyal English Protestants fleeing from the North and Midlands. In 1650 Cromwell marched into Dublin, hell-bent on revenging himself against all Catholic rebels. The city had no doubts where its loyalty lay: with the winning side. Cromwell made it his base for his murderous sieges of Drogheda and Wexford. Then the smoke cleared. The agony of the civil war had opened the way for Dublin finally to slough off its medieval skin. The Restoration gave it back peace and prosperity. Of course that was the *sine qua non* for any conspicuous civic improvements. The city also needed someone with ideas to direct its expansion. And indeed it was now directed by the firm but benevolent hand of a great Viceroy, determined to reshape the city on a revolutionary new principle: splendour. Dublin would be the ceremonial capital of a centralized state, a symbol of power: his own, the King's and that of both peoples of Ireland, Protestant and Catholic.

The new Viceroy was an urbane Irish grandee, James Butler, first Duke of Ormonde, head of the great Anglo-Norman clan of Butler and no stranger to Continental ideas about replanning cities. He had learnt much, and suffered much, exiled in France with his royal master, Charles II. On 27 July 1662 he returned home like a Renaissance prince, Irish style. The Catholic peasantry came out to dance a welcome on the sands of Dublin Bay, singing *Thugamar féin an samhra linn* ('we have brought summer with us'). It was high time.

After a century of intermittent civil war, the people of Dublin must have felt as battered as their city. The Castle where Ormonde was supposed to live was described by one of his relations as 'the worst castle in the worst situation in Christendom'. Beside the Castle there were seventeen towers and gatehouses and two cathedrals, all verging on collapse. The population had shrunk to about nine thousand, most of whom lived in tumbledown cabins. From the distance the city might still sometimes look picturesque enough; it was a city of towers, decorated by the sails of windmills flickering in the sunlight.

Inside, the place was, literally, a shambles: dead animals choked the narrow alleys.

One can imagine Ormonde's first reaction. Away with this disgusting anachronism. Let us build a great Baroque city instead; an Irish Paris, with a Tuileries and a Luxembourg Gardens crowning the banks of the Liffey. But Ormonde's master, Charles II, had still less spare cash for embellishing Dublin than he had for London. So Ormonde had to make do and mend with the Dublin authorities. He must cut his own cloth to suit their pockets. It was only well beyond the limits of the city, where the corporation's writ did not run, and where land was cheap, that he could make a splash. Inside the city, splendour must give way to compromise.

Ormonde's first great splash was to buy up 1,500 acres of open fields west of the city. In Phoenix Park he gave the people a royal deer park, bigger and more splendid than any royal park in London. From the first it was conceived as a park for the public to enjoy. His second great splash complemented it. Just across the Liffey at Kilmainham he constructed the Royal Hospital, a home for old soldiers modelled on the Invalides in Paris and anticipating the Royal Hospital at Chelsea by a few years. So imposing is the style, so skilful the work of the architect, that people came to attribute this building to the hand of Sir Christopher Wren. In fact it is now known to be the work of an Irishman, of Sir William Robinson, the Irish Surveyor-General. The first stone was laid by Ormonde in 1680, after his return for a new term as governor, the second stone by another great Irish grandee, the first Earl of Longford. The vast building was completed in 1684. Restored recently (for the vast sum of £20 million, or nearly a thousand times what it cost to build) it is now open to the public, and remains the most splendid monument in the whole of Ireland.

Meanwhile, inspired by Ormonde, the city began to pull up its socks. Taking up where Wentworth left off, the Corporation decided to enclose the ancient commonage on the south-east, at St Stephen's Green, and create a municipally owned square. It was to be a public pleasure ground, surrounded by four terraces of houses whose ground was leased to the builders on long leases. Nothing now survives from this pioneering scheme but the vast scale of the layout. Each side of the square is nearly a quarter of a mile long, which makes Stephen's Green today larger than any square in London. The earliest and best houses on Stephen's Green now date from the eighteenth century.

But the foundations had been well laid: the broad, straight streets, and leafy public squares. They would be needed in Dublin's Golden Age, the eighteenth century. The guiding principle was Ormonde's: the cult of splendour. As the Corporation minutes put it, 'the whole designe of all persons concerned . . . is chiefly for the reputation, advantage and pleasure of the cittie'.

After pushing out to the south-east, the Corporation also channelled expansion in the opposite direction, to the open space across the Liffey on the north-west side, Oxmantown Green. Here their efforts were more prosaic. True, one fine public building was erected, the Bluecoat School (the forerunner of the current one which was built in the late eighteenth century). But there were no squares or gardens laid out on the north-west. It was here, on the muddy plain on the north bank of the Liffey, that the drovers' roads from the north and west converged on a new market called Ormonde Market. For centuries there had been only one bridge crossing the Liffey, so more bridges were now added: Bloody Bridge (named after the attempts to stop its construction), Ormonde Bridge, Essex Bridge and Arran Bridge.

Still more significant for the character of the city was Ormonde's decision to create a line of open quays beside the river. No doubt he was thinking of Paris again. The result was decisive. From Ormonde's Quay grew the main east-west axis that today bisects Dublin, a double line of roads and pavements along the river. So it was Ormonde who put the Liffey firmly in the foreground, and saved it (unlike so many rivers in British provincial cities) from being hidden away like a canal behind grimy factories and builders' yards.

Ormonde's long dazzling career finally ended with his recall in 1688, on the accession of James II, and soon the country was thrust on to the centre of the European stage. Civil war resumed, a civil war the Catholics this time seemed poised to win. Terrified Protestants fled to England, and the Fellows of Trinity tried to sell their plate on the English market. But it was seized in Dublin harbour and consigned to the King's stores.

In March 1689 King James landed at Kinsale and marched rapidly north to Dublin. His reception there moved him to tears of joy: 'the Papists shouting' according to one hostile observer, 'the soldiers' muskets, the bells ringing, and bonfires in all parts of the town'. But soon the contradictions of the King's position became apparent. How to reconcile the aims of loyal English Jacobites and wild Irish Catholics? His Patriot Parliament sat in Dublin exuding toleration. Naturally the Catholics wanted more: ascendancy. Meanwhile William of Orange had landed in England and sent over Schomberg hot-foot to repossess the sister kingdom. The Battle of the Boyne in 1690 and the Treaty of Limerick in 1691 extinguished the political hopes of the Catholics, whether English or Irish by origin. They were stripped of all public office, humbled and kept humble by the penal laws. Now followed the Golden Age of their enemies, the century of Protestant peace and Protestant triumph.

No one would now defend their political ideals, nor the methods they used to keep the Catholics out of power. Yet one thing has been recognized by even their bitterest opponents. They had a style and a sense of pride, a pride of community, colonial nationalism of a sort, bigoted and narrow as it was, that set them apart from a mere English garrison taking its orders from London. It was this relaxed colonial pride that gave – and gives – the eighteenth-century streets of Dublin their special feel. The self-confidence takes away one's breath. The men who shaped Dublin were not content to imitate London. They would go several times better. The streets would be wider, the squares larger, the great monuments – Parliament, the Four Courts, the Custom House – would all be more splendid. It took a century. And in the process the city became a masterpiece. For all its glaring faults, including the ghastly squalor of its slums, Dublin became one of the wonders of the eighteenth-century world.

Who were these men who found Dublin a shabby English-style city of narrow alleys and dirty lanes, and left it a great European capital of broad streets and leafy squares? There was no single mind focused on the great design. There was something just as good: unity of purpose. Unity may sound odd to find in Ireland. For one thing, ultimate political control still remained in London. For another, the backbone of Ireland, judged by wealth and political power, was a bunch of red-faced squires, notorious for drink and duelling, the kind of men satirized in Goldsmith's Tony Lumpkin. Among them were the few hundred country gentlemen whose ownership of land gave them much of the landed rental and almost all the seats in Parliament. The

Irish Tony Lumpkins seemed like a parody of their English counterparts. They came from the oddest backgrounds. Some could boast of hoary Catholic pedigrees; they were Gaelic like the O'Neills or 'Old English' like the FitzGeralds. They had adapted their religion, just as their English counterparts had done, to their political convictions. Others were pushy newcomers to Ireland, carpetbaggers of the recent wars and rebellions. Others again were Old Irish but new rich, men who had made a fortune out of pickled beef and bottled porter. Whatever their origin, they were now landowners and generally valued horse-flesh above books on Palladio or other architects.

But the rising tide of agricultural rents had aroused them all. With the possession of wealth came the desire to make it conspicuous. Few of them up till then had town houses. A wig and a velvet waistcoat, and 'improvements' to your country house and estate, were all very well. But what about a new house in Dublin for the season, that is when the rents were safely harvested, hunting was over, Parliament sat and no man of fashion would be seen dead among his prize sheep and cows?

As the red-faced squires flooded into Dublin, the same fashionable tide floated a whole new fleet of whey-faced professional men – lawyers, engineers, land agents, surveyors, civil servants, doctors, as well as traders, builders and businessmen of all kinds. Few of them could afford a country house, unlike the squires. But their Dublin houses must be convenient and fashionable enough to impress their clients. Here was a common purpose that would bridge the gap between the middle class and the upper gentry. To supply this new democracy a new Dublin of tall, elegant, compact, plain (inexpensive without looking cheap) red-brick terraces sprang into life.

The architects, planners and financial backers were as diverse a bunch as their clients. Some like the great Palladian architect, Sir Edward Pearce, died mysteriously young. Many, no doubt, like the great James Gandon, were rather too keen on the bottle. Most of these designers were of humble origin and emerged only briefly out of the shadows. The two largest estates were concentrated in the hands of two rival families, the *nouveau riche* Gardiners, based north of the Liffey, and the old-rich FitzWilliams, on the south side. It was to be a battle royal for the soul of fashionable Dublin, north versus south, that lasted for over a century.

At first it seemed that it would be a walk-over for Luke
Gardiner. He was a banker by profession, and had married well.
His wife was connected to the Mountjoys and Blessingtons. From
1714 he began to buy up the green fields north of the river, fields
which had once belonged to St Mary's Abbey. Eventually he
owned most of the building land north of the river. His first great
work was a short street of palatial houses laid out in the 1720s,
Henrietta Street, apparently named after the current Viceroy's
wife. Today it is a palatial slum, for the great three-bay and four-
bay terraced houses are marooned on the wrong side of Dublin.
(Early this century, a rascally Dublin alderman ripped out the
staircases and sold the fireplaces on the London market before
turning several houses into tenements.) But for a whole century
Henrietta Street was the fashionable place for bigwigs of every
kind, from gaitered bishops to gartered peers. No single street
(except perhaps Lower Dominick Street nearby) could boast
more magnificent plasterwork or richer panelling.

To the east, Luke Gardiner then launched an enormous tree-
lined mall called Sackville Street, similar to the mall in London's
Portland Place, built twenty years later. As O'Connell Street,
this is now Dublin's best known thoroughfare. Better, perhaps, if
it had been left forgotten in the background, to crumble away
like Henrietta Street. O'Connell Street has passed, as Dublin's
leading historian puts it, from neo-classic to neon classic. Ice-
cream parlours and ketchup restaurants now decorate the sites of
the houses of the hard-drinking squires. No doubt the street was
doomed. Only forty years after Gardiner gave up the ghost, his
quiet street was vandalized. The lower end was widened and
what is now O'Connell Bridge was built and later widened, to
turn the elegant mall into the main north-south axis, and
shopping centre.

Meanwhile, on the south side, still grander and more enduring
monuments – private and public – were being created. The
forerunners of this new wave of building south and east of the
historic centre were a pair of libraries, the gigantic library of
Trinity College (designed by Burgh, the Surveyor-General, and
finished by 1710) and the miniature library of Bishop Marsh,
finished about the same time. Neither has suffered from too little
– or too much – affection in the last 250 years, though Trinity's
airy loggia was drowned years ago in the torrent of new books.
The sardonic smile of the Great Dean floats over both – Swift,

who baited the Fellows of Trinity and mocked poor Bishop Marsh – (though he left him some of his own books, which you can still read, duly annotated in Swift's hand). Opposite the west façade of Trinity, dominating the traffic-choked oblong ironically called College Green, is Ireland's most spectacular monument after the Royal Hospital: the great Parliament House, designed by Captain (later Sir Edward) Pearce, in 1727.

Pearce was a dragoon officer by training, and a dilettante by temperament, a friend of Vanbrugh, who wandered round Italy in the footsteps of Grand Tourists like William Kent and Lord Burlington. His Parliament House was a great Palladian stage-set: a pantheon behind, with two elegant arcaded wings thrust forward to catch the fitful Irish sun. It was this Palladian temple that housed the rotten-borough owners of the Irish Parliament, Commons and Lords, two Chambers of landlords, haggling over jobbery and bribery like a pack of crooked shopkeepers. How incongruous that a building of such Palladian purity should house the venal Parliament! Yet its theatrical qualities suited it admirably. The Irish Parliament was more theatrical than most parliaments: from many points of view a political sham. For a century they talked of independence from Britain with the same panache with which they transformed Dublin. Yet they could not make common cause with their Catholic compatriots. In fact the Catholic peasantry were still waiting, out beyond the Poddle and the Dodder, as they had waited so long, brooding on their ancient wrongs. The Protestant Ascendancy needed Britain as much as Britain needed a loyal garrison. Soon enough the bluff of independence would be called and the theatre in College Green close its doors forever.

But this is to anticipate. By the mid-eighteenth century the city was pushing south-east, as the battle for the soul of fashionable Dublin was fought out over tea-cups and claret mugs. The pioneer of the drive south-east was the young James FitzGerald, Earl of Kildare and later first Duke of Leinster. He bought some cheap land east of Coote Lane, which he renamed Kildare Street, and here on the seedy eastern flank of the city built himself a great mansion in 1745. Town house or country house? It was both. Leinster House, as it became, was designed by Richard Cassels, Pearce's successor as the leading Palladian architect, and a specialist in country houses. Cassels made no bones about the fact that he preferred doing country houses. So

Leinster House is incongruous enough; a great long, stone-built Italian country house, with flanking wings and no 'back', marooned among the red-brick terraces and tall chimneystacks. Today it flies the tricolour and has a new role, no less incongruous than the one Cassels designed for it. This is the Dáil and Senate, the current Irish Parliament.

When the Duke of Leinster was asked whether this site was not somewhat remote, he is supposed to have replied, 'They will follow me wherever I go.' It was the cue for Lord Fitzwilliam of Merrion to begin his campaign to steal fashionable Dublin from the Gardiners. First Fitzwilliam built a magnificently broad street, Merrion Street, part of whose west side was kept open by the lawn of Leinster House. Then he launched into a still more magnificent square, Merrion Square, which took thirty years to fill with terraced houses. Some of these have rich plasterwork, and all their façades have been preserved more or less as designed. The great disaster occurred in Fitzwilliam Street, the street that leads southwards out of the east side of Merrion Square. This was once the most elegant piece of axial planning in Dublin, framing the blue Dublin mountains far to the south. But in 1958 the Electricity Supply Board insisted on replacing the thirty-two perfectly sound red-brick houses with a long pink concrete office block, making mockery of the vertical pattern of the windows in the rest of the terrace.

The eighteenth-century battle between two private landlords – Fitzwilliam and Gardiner – ended in victory claimed by both sides. By the 1790s fashionable Dublin was split roughly half and half between the north side and the south side. At the same time the State had been encouraged to help replan the city. Intervention took two forms: commissioning new public buildings and knocking out kinks in the city's street plan. The public buildings did not favour either side as they were built on the Quays: the Custom House (completed in 1791 for the unheard-of sum of £400,000) and the Four Courts (completed in 1802 for £200,000). Both these giants came from the drawing-board of James Gandon, the young English architect shipped over specially for the job. The choice of Gandon was inspired. He brought the new style of Palladianism pioneered by Sir William Chambers in England, a style where delicate neo-classical detail is used to contrast with massive Palladian modelling. Each of Gandon's public buildings is a masterpiece fit to challenge Pearce on his own ground. In fact Gandon ingeniously added a

new front door to the House of Lords on the east side of the
Parliament House. His great Corinthian colonnade shakes
hands with Pearce's great Ionic colonnade to the south. As for
the Custom House, this had a dramatic and permanent effect on
the direction of the city's growth. The old Custom House was at
Essex Bridge, below which the river was still open to shipping.
Now the ships were pushed firmly downstream, and a new
bridge (Carlisle Bridge, the future O'Connell Bridge) was built
just above the new Custom House, which was itself built on slob
land won back from the sea. It was this new bridge that gave the
Wide Street Commissioners the chance to create the main north-
south axis across the river.

In 1800 the Protestant Ascendancy finally got its come-
uppance. Dublin's Golden Age was over. Britain imposed a
legislative union, and Dublin's venal Parliament, bought out
from the red-faced squires, was sold very fittingly to be a bank, as
it remains today. The Union with Britain was precipitated by
the threat of a rival union, expressed in the United Irish
Rebellion of 1798. This in turn was inspired by the twin
revolutions in America and France. Protestant enthusiasts like
Wolfe Tone and Lord Edward FitzGerald (one of the younger
sons of the first Duke of Leinster) dreamt of an Irish republic, and
planned to use the ancient grievances of the Catholic peasantry
and the dissenters to break the British connection. The dream
evaporated on bloody battlefields from Antrim to Wexford.
Thirty thousand died. Dublin proved loyal enough, although
the United Irish had counted on a rising within the city co-
ordinated with attacks from outside.

After the Union some people predicted that grass would grow
in the streets of Dublin. The future was to be less theatrical.
Dublin continued to expand, but more slowly than before,
growing towards the two recently founded canals and filling the
squares, like Fitzwilliam Square in the south and Mountjoy
Square to the north. Some fine public monuments were added
on the north side: the GPO (completed in 1818) and Nelson's
Pillar (built in 1808–9, half a century before the London column,
and unfortunately dynamited in 1966 by Republicans to
celebrate the fiftieth anniversary of the Rising). There were also
some fine Catholic churches built, notably St Andrew's, St
Nicholas', and the Pro-Cathedral. But the city was no longer a
capital.

It was not so much the absence of the red-faced squires, some of whom now had seats in Westminster. Parliamentary reform would soon make them irrelevant. The Four Courts were not short of well paid lawyers, nor the city hospitals of well paid doctors. The most obvious effect of the Union and the 1798 Rebellion was that Dublin had lost its pride. The city began to look and feel as ordinary as an English commercial town.

At the same time fewer better-off people wanted to live in the centre, once the railway had brought the delightful southern seaside within half an hour of the city. Dublin's loss was the suburbs' gain: Donnybrook, Blackrock, Dun Laoghaire, Killiney and Howth. It was the north side that suffered worst. Here the fine houses were abandoned to the poor, and under the great plaster ceilings could be found some of the most shameful slums in Europe. On the south side of the core, the great houses suffered more from prosperity than neglect. Those in Grafton Street and Dawson Street were to become department stores, hotels and finally office blocks. Neon classic pays better than neoclassic. These were the forces of the market already identifiable in the nineteenth century. The city corporation, overwhelmed with social problems, and losing much of its rateable income to the independent boroughs in the suburbs, had neither the means nor the will to save Dublin.

But if nineteenth-century Dublin was running out of cash, it was to strike it rich in another field – literary talent. In October 1891 Ireland's great political chieftain, Charles Stewart Parnell, had died in England. On a day of lashing wind and rain his coffin was borne through the streets of Dublin, packed with vast silent crowds, to a final burial at Glasnevin. Ireland's hopes for political independence seemed at their nadir. It seemed at this moment, claimed the poet W.B. Yeats long after, that the national spirit burst out in a new channel, and Ireland's 'modern literature' began – the movement now known as the Irish Literary Renaissance.

Like many Irish movements, it began with a group of expatriates. Early in 1892, some of Yeats's friends gathered at his father's house in Chiswick, London, to found the Irish Literary Society. But what marked the real birth of the movement was an impassioned speech given by Douglas Hyde to its Dublin branch a few months later. Hyde was a Protestant clergyman's son, straight out of the old Ascendancy world, but he had spent his boyhood learning Irish and absorbing Gaelic myths and folklore from the peasant farmers around his father's rectory; and he had already made a reputation for himself as a poet and Gaelic scholar. Now he warned his Dublin audience that the only way Ireland would find her true self was by purging herself of English influence and going back to her own cultural roots. Yeats enthusiastically agreed. Between them then they soon recruited other enthusiasts – many of them, like Hyde, from the Ascendancy. How surprised the eighteenth-century red-faced squires would have been. There was Edward Martyn, a Catholic landowner from Galway; Lady Gregory, widow of another Galway landowner; and the novelist George Moore, who had left his estate in Mayo fifteen years before to live in Paris and London, but now returned to Dublin to play, he hoped, a key role in the new movement. Half a generation behind them was to emerge a string of equally talented young writers and poets: Sean O'Casey, James Stephens, Seamus O'Sullivan, Oliver St John Gogarty – and Dublin's most famous exile, James Joyce. (Joyce had no sympathy with Hyde's Celtic Revival, but he later described Dublin's literary gyrations of the period with sardonic humour.)

By 1899 the Irish Literary Society had become the Irish Literary Theatre; a few years later still it was to become the Irish National Theatre with a permanent home at the Abbey. Suddenly it seemed as if all Dublin was stage-struck. The Abbey's new productions became the focus of fierce political debates, with Yeats himself often rising white-faced, black hair thrown back, to lecture his audiences on their shortcomings. With the production of J.M. Synge's *Playboy of the Western World* in 1907, the theatre became a nightly battlefield between those who saw the play as an insult to Irish morals and the Trinity College students who defended the cast. Even a clash of cultures could end in broken heads.

In the next decade Dublin was to experience far more serious clashes. First, in 1913, there was the great tramway strike organized by Jim Larkin and James Connolly, which looked (to authority at least) like a Socialist revolution in embryo. It culminated in a bloody street battle in O'Connell Street, when the police charged strikers with batons and sabres. Sean O'Casey's account still makes harrowing reading, and a government enquiry into the strike revealed once again the appalling condition of the Dublin poor.

The Dublin Rising three years later caught everyone by surprise. On Easter Monday 1916, Dubliners woke to find the city centre taken over by Volunteers of the Irish Republican Army. They were only a few hundred men, ill armed and led by a strange mixture of poets, schoolmasters and one veteran of Larkin's strike, James Connolly. Their aim was to save the soul of Ireland, even if they had to sacrifice their own lives. At the time, the Rising seemed a forlorn hope. British troops were rushed across to Dublin and stamped it out within a week, gutting much of central Dublin – including the Post Office – in the process. But in the days that followed it was clear the insurgents had won a moral victory. And the execution of the leaders transformed them posthumously into national heroes.

In 1921, after several years of guerrilla warfare, Ireland finally won its independence. An official treaty was signed with England. Ireland became the Irish Free State. Even then the fighting was not over. In the Civil War that followed, a duel between the Free State army and the Republicans who would not accept the terms of the treaty, another of Dublin's finest public buildings was gutted by shell-fire: the Four Courts on the Quays. The Four Courts had housed the Irish State papers which made a spectacular bonfire, 'all the records of the country, processes, leases, testimonials . . . chronicled since Strongbow came to Ireland flying up', wrote Sean O'Casey, 'to come down scorched and blackened in every Dublin backyard and front garden!'

The new State, though desperately short of funds, then acted most generously. By the 1930s the damaged architectural masterpieces had been carefully restored in almost every detail. But by the '50s, prosperity had again begun to take its toll. The '60s saw many disasters. Far more buildings of the eighteenth century were destroyed by the planners and developers than were ever knocked down in the fighting. Soon it became apparent that some sort of miracle would be needed if Dublin were to be saved. And perhaps we are now seeing that miracle: the discovery that so many people in Dublin care about what is happening to their city and have enough pride – pride like that of their eighteenth-century forebears – to fight to try to preserve what is left.

THOMAS PAKENHAM
1987

Map of the City, locating the places described

1 The Castle
2 Christ Church Cathedral
3 St Patricks Cathedral
  & Marsh's Library
4 Guinness Brewery
5 Kilmainham Hospital
6 Kilmainham Jail
7 Aras an Uachtaran
  (The Vice-regal Lodge)
8 The Rotunda
9 Charlemont House
10 Belvedere College
11 The General Post Office
12 St Mary's Pro-Cathedral
13 The Custom House
14 The Four Courts
15 Trinity College
16 The Bank of Ireland
  (Parliament House)
17 Iveagh House; Newman House
18 The Shelbourne
19 Ely House
20 The Kildare Street Club
21 Dáil Eireann
  (Leinster House)
22 Abbey Theatre

Dublin
The old city

The old city

[1] The founding of the city; from *The Description of Ireland* by Richard Stanyhurst in Holinshed's *Chronicles*.

(Richard Stanyhurst (1547–1618) was the son of the Speaker of the Irish House of Commons. His *Description of Ireland* was written especially for Holinshed's *Chronicles*, first published in 1577, and like most Elizabethan history is firmly on the side of the English conquerors. Soon after, however, he became a Roman Catholic and fled to Spain, where he became one of Phillip II's advisers.)

Dublin the beautie and eie of Ireland, hath beene named by Ptolome, in ancient time, Eblana. Some terme it Dublina, others Dublinia, manie write it Dublinum, authors of better skill name it Dublinium. The Irish call it, Ballee er Cleagh, that is, a towne planted upon hurdels. For the common opinion is, that the plot upon which the ciuitie is builded, hath beene a marish ground; and for that by the art or invention of the first founder, the water could not be voided, he was forced to fasten the quake mire with hurdels, and upon them to build the citie. I heard of some that came of building of houses to this foundation: and other hold opinion that if a cart or waine run with a round and maine pase through a strcct called the high street, the houses on ech side shall be perceiued to shake. This citie was builded, or rather the buildings thereof inlarged, about the yeare of our Lord 155. For about this time there arrived in Ireland three noble Easterlings that were brethren, Avellanus, Sitaracus, and Yuorus. Avellanus being the eldest brother builded Dublin, Sitaracus Waterford, and Yuorus Limerike. Of the founder Avellanus, Dublin was named Avellana, and after by corruption of speach Eblana. This citie, as it is not in antiquitie inferiour to anie citie in Ireland, so in pleasant situation, in gorgious buildings, in the multitude of people, in martiall chivalrie, in obedience and loialtie, in the abundance of wealth, in largenesse of hospitalite, in maners and civilitie it is superiour to all other cities and townes in that realme. And therefore it is commonlie called the Irish or yoong London. The seat of this citie is of all sides pleasant,

Henry II's seal

comfortable, and wholesome. If you would traverse hils, they are not far off. If champion ground, it lieth of all parts. If you be delited with fresh water, the famous river called the Liffie, named of Ptolome Lybnium, runneth fast by. If you will take the view of the sea, it is at hand.

[2] A charter for Norman Dublin from Henry II; from *Strongbow's Conquest of Ireland* by F.P. Barnard.

(Henry II of England had taken formal possession of Ireland in 1172 from his vassal, Strongbow, Earl of Pembroke who had invaded Ireland three years before. The Norman settlement at Dublin was intended to follow the same pattern as Bristol, a

highly successful trading city, and many of the new settlers came
from there.)

Henry, king of England, duke of Normandy and Aquitaine, and
count of Anjou, to his archbishops, bishops, abbots, earls,
barons, justices, sheriffs, officers, and all liegemen, French,
English, and Irish, of all his land, greeting:

Know ye that I have given and granted and by the present
charter confirmed to my men of Bristol my city of Dublin to dwell
in.

Wherefore I will, and steadfastly enjoin, that they have and
hold it of me and of my heirs, well and in peace, freely and
undisturbed, entirely and fully and honourably, with all liberties
and free customs which the men of Bristol have in Bristol and
throughout all my land.

Witnesses: William de Braos, Reginald de Curtenai; Hugh de
Gundeville; William Fitz-Aldelm; Ralph de Glanville; Hugh de
Creissi; Reginald de Pavilli. At Dublin.

The Castle

[3] King John commands the building of Dublin Castle in 1205; from *Strongbow's Conquest of Ireland* by F.P. Barnard.

(The necessity for a stronghold in Dublin had become acute by the reign of King John, Henry II's son, partly owing to his own behaviour as a young prince. He had mortally offended the Gaelic lords by pulling their beards when they came to make their submission at Trim in 1185. From then on the Norman Pale was pushed back on Dublin. The original castle, encompassing the space of the present Upper Yard, was completed by 1220.)

To Meiler Fitz-Henry, Lord Justice of Ireland, – Greeting.

You have given us to understand that you have not a convenient place wherein our treasure may be safely deposited, and forasmuch, as well for that use as for many others, a fortress would be necessary for us at Dublin, we command you to erect a castle there in such competent place as you shall judge most expedient, as well to curb the city as to defend it if occasion shall so require, and that you make it as strong as you can, with good fosses and durable walls. But you are first to finish one tower, unless afterwards a castle and palace and other works that may require greater leisure may be more conveniently raised and that we should command you so to do: for which you have our pleasure, according to our desire – at present you may take to this use 300 marks from G. Fitz-Robert, in which he stands indebted to us.

GEDDINGTON, 21*st August* 1205.

[4] A Gaelic poet laments his lord, impaled on the walls of Dublin Castle; from *The Literary History of Ireland* by Douglas Hyde.

(The Gaelic poet is Angus O'Daly (1309–1350), bard to a Wicklow chieftain killed during one of the many battles against the Norman Pale. The beautiful English translation is by Douglas Hyde (1860–1949) who devoted his life to the restora-

Sir Henry Sidney, Lord Deputy of Ireland, rides out from
Dublin Castle. The heads of Irish 'traitors' are impaled above
the gate; detail from a late sixteenth-century woodcut by
John Derricke

tion of the Irish language and culture, was founder of the Gaelic
League, and, in old age, first President of Ireland.)

O body which I see without a head,
It is the sight of thee which has withered up my strength.
Divided and impaled in Ath-cliath,
The learned of Banba will feel its loss.
Who will relieve the wants of the poor?
Who will bestow cattle on the learned?
O body, since thou art without a head,
It is not life which we care to choose after thee.

[5] The fate of Irish traitors – the unrepentant view of an Elizabethan Englishman; from Richard Stanyhurst's *Description of Ireland* in Holinshed's *Chronicles*.

> These trunckles heddes do playnly showe
> Each rebelles fatall end
> And what a haynous crime it is
> The Queen for to offend.

[6] Trial by combat in the Castle Yard, 1584; from Holinshed's *Chronicles*.

During these continuall troubles in Mounster, the two lord iustices which laie at Dublin were much eased from all martiall affaires elsewhere, and were troubled but with the clamorings, exclamations, and brabling of the Irish people, not woorth the remembring: saving that a certeine combat was fought and tried before them in the castell of Dublin, betweene two Oconhours [*O'Conors*], verie neere coosens & kinsmen: the one was Teig mac Guill Patrike Oconhour appellant; the other was named Con mac Cormake Oconhour defendant. One of these appealed and charged the other for sundrie treasons in the late rebellion, and which could have no other triall but by combat, which was granted unto them. Whereupon, according to the lawes and orders of England for a combat to be tried, all things were prepared, the daie, time, and place appointed; and according to the same, the lord iustices, the iudges, and the councellors came and sat in the place appointed for the same, everie man in his degree and calling. And then the court was called, and the appellant or plaintife was brought in before the face of the court, being stripped into his shirt, having onlie his sword and target (which were the weapons appointed) and when he had doone his reverence and dutie to the lord iustices and to the court, he was brought to a stoole set in the one of the ends within the lists, and there sat. After him was the defendant brought in, in the like maner and order, . . . and . . . placed in the other end of the lists. Then were their actions and pleadings openlie read, and then the appellant was demanded whether he would averre his demand or not? . . . who did answer as did the other, that he would averre it by the swoord.

Upon this their severall answers, they were severallie called the one after the other, everie of them taking a corporall oth that their quarell was true, and that they would iustifie the same both with sword & blood. . . . And then when by the sound of a trumpet a signe was given unto them . . .; they arose out of their seats, and met ech one the other in the middle within the lists, and there with the weapons assigned unto them, they fought: in which fight the appellant did prevaile, and he not onlie did disarme the defendant, but also with the sword of the said defendant did cut off his head, and upon the point of the same sword did present it to the lord justices, and so with the victorie of his cnimic hc was acquittcd. Thus much I thought good to saic somwhat of much, of the maner of a combat, which . . . is now for want of use almost cleane forgotten, and yet verie necessarie to be knowne. And as for this combat it was so valiantlie doone, that a great manie did wish that it had rather fallen upon the whole sex [*sect*] of the Oconhours, than upon these two gentlemen.

[7] Hugh Roe O'Donnell escapes from Dublin Castle, Christmas Eve, 1592; from Lughaidh O'Clery's *Life of Hugh Roe O'Donnell*, in Constantia Maxwell's *Irish History from Contemporary Sources*.

(Hugh Roe O'Donnell, the fifteen-year-old son of the Prince of Tyrconnell, was kidnapped by a merchant ship from Lough Swilly and brought to Dublin as hostage for the Ulster Gaelic lords' good behaviour. He finally escaped from a cell in the Record Tower. After his ordeal and rescue in the Wicklow Mountains, he made his way back to Donegal, and duly succeeded his father as clan chieftain. He proved an able ally to Hugh O'Neill in the last uprising of the Gaelic lords, but after their defeat at Kinsale by Mountjoy in 1602, he fled to Spain and died of poison soon after. His escape route from Dublin Castle is still commemorated by Dubliners with an annual Christmas hike through the Wicklow Mountains.)

[1587.]   As for the ship of which we have spoken and her crew, when they had finished the business for which they had come, and taken with them the most desirable of the hostages . . . they sailed . . . after that with the strength of the north-west wind

along the shore of Ireland . . . till they landed in the harbour of
Dublin again. It became known immediately throughout the
whole city and to the Lord Justice and the Council, especially
that they had come after this manner, and that Hugh O'Donnell
was in their custody. They were glad of his coming, yet it was not
at all through love of him, and they summoned him to them
without delay so that he was face to face with them, and they
proceeded to converse with him and ask information of him, and
they were chiefly bent on searching out and discovering his
character. In the end they ordered him to be put in a strong stone
castle, where the nobles of the sons of Milesius were in chains and
captivity, expecting slaughter and death, together with some of
the nobles of the white foreigners who had come to the island
long before, and had entered into amity and friendship with the
Irish against the English who came last from the country of the
Saxons to take the island from both of them. It was their solace
and entertainment day and night in the close prison where they
were, to be lamenting over the intolerable hardships and relating
the great cruelty which was inflicted on them both, English and
Irish, and listening to the unjust sentences pronounced, and the
dishonour and ill-treatment done against the high-born nobles
of the sons of Milesius and of the white foreigners alike.

As for Hugh O'Donnell, he was, just like the rest, in chains for
the space of three years and three months, hearing of the ignoble
bondage in which the Irish were. It was anguish and sickness of
mind and great pain to him to be as he was, and it was not on his
own account, but because of the unbecoming helplessness of
his friends and kinsmen, his gentlemen (*urradha*) and leaders, his
sanctuaries and holy churches, his poets and learned men,
his subjects and people, expelled and banished to other territor-
ies throughout Ireland. He was always pondering and thinking
how he might find a way of escape. This was no easy thing for
him, for he was put every night into a well-closed apartment in
the castle for security, and until the hour of tierce on the morrow.
That castle was situated thus. There was a broad deep trench of
water all round it, and a compact bridge of boards over it,
opposite the door of the castle, and the grim-visaged host of the
English outside and inside the gate to guard it, so that no one
should pass them, in or out, without being challenged by the
foreign troop. However, there is no guard that is not taken
unawares at last. . . .

[1592.] When it seemed to the Son of the Virgin time that he should escape, he and some of his companions found the keepers off their guard in the very beginning of the night before they were taken to the refectory, and they took their fetters off. They went after that to the privy, having a long rope, and they let themselves down by means of the rope through the privy, till they came to the deep trench which was around the fortress. After that they climbed to the opposite bank, till they were on the edge of the trench at the other side. The hostages who escaped with Hugh were Henry and Art, the two sons of Shane, son of Con Bacach, son of Con, son of Henry, son of Eoghan. There was a certain faithful servant who visited them in the castle, in the guise of a horseboy, to whom they imparted their secret, so that he met them face to face when need was, and became their guide. They went off after that through the crowded street near the fortress, without being known or overheard by any one, for they were no more noticed than any one else of the city people, as no one stopped to converse with or visit any one in the houses of the stronghold at that hour, for it was the beginning of the night exactly, and the gates of the city were not yet closed. They went out beyond the city in that manner. They leaped over the rough and rugged parts of the huge moats and of the strong, firm palisades which were outside the city, until they came to the slopes of Slieve Roe [*the Three Rock Mountain*], over which Hugh had crossed at the time he first escaped. The darkness of the night and the hurry of the flight separated the oldest of the party from them. This was Henry O'Neill. Hugh was the youngest of the nobles. They were not pleased at the separation. They went on, however, their attendant leading the way. The night came on with a drizzle and downpour, and a venomous shower of rain and thick smooth snowflakes, so that it was not easy for the high-born nobles to walk on account of the storm and the scanty clothing, for they were without overmantles, having left them in the privy through which they had come.

This hurried journey, strange and unusual, was more severe on Art than on Hugh, and his gait was feebler and slower, for he was corpulent, thick-thighed, and he had been a long time confined in prison. It was not so with Hugh, for he had not passed the period of boyhood, and he had not ceased to grow in size and his gait was quick and nimble. When he perceived Art growing weak and his step heavy, what he did to him was to place one hand of his on his own shoulder and the other hand on the shoulder of the servant. They went on in this way across the upper part of the level mountain. They were tired and weary then, and they could not bring Art further with them. As they could not, they rested under the shelter of a lofty cliff on the moor which was in front of them. After halting there, they sent the servant with news of them to Glenmalure, the place where Fiach MacHugh was. This was a secure impregnable valley, and the English of Dublin were accustomed with their engines of war to besiege and assault it, in order to plunder and lay it waste. This Fiach maintained it valiantly against them, so that many heads were left behind with him, and they could do nothing against him . . . So, too, the hostages aforesaid made a tryst with him, and sent their servant to him. When [*the servant*] came to where Fiach was, he told his story to him and the state in which he left the youths who had escaped from the city, and that they would not be found alive if he did not go to their assistance quickly.

Thereupon Fiach selected a party of his picked men, and bade them go with the servant to the youths. They rose up at once as they were ordered, and went off, one having food and another ale and beer, until they came to the mountain, the place where the men had been left. Alas! truly the state and position of these nobles was not happy or pleasant when the soldiers who had come to seek them arrived. They had neither coverlets nor plaids nor clothing about their bodies to protect them from the cold and ice of the sharp winter season, but the only bedclothes around their fair skins, and pillows under their heads, were high-fenced bed-rails, white bordered of hail, freezing all round them, and attaching their light tunics and shirts of fine linen thread to their bodies, and their long shoes and sandals to their shins and feet, so that they seemed to the men that had come not to be human beings at all, but their shapes in sods of earth covered up by the snow; for they did not perceive a stir in their limbs, but just as if they were dead, and they were nearly so. Thereupon the soldiers raised them from where they lay and bade them take some of the food and ale, but they failed in this, for every drink they took they let it out of their mouths again. Even so, Art died at last and was buried in that place. As for Hugh, he retained the beer after that, and his strength was on the increase after drinking of it, except in his two feet, for they were like dead members without motion, swollen and blistered from the frost and snow.

[8] The defeat of the 'Old English' nobility; from a letter
by Sir Christopher Plunkett to his son in 1612; in *Desiderata
Curiosa Hibernica*.

(The 'Old English' were the descendants of the original Norman
settlers, most of whom had remained Catholic after the Reformation. At the first Parliament held in Dublin Castle since the
Elizabethan wars which had finally brought all Ireland under
English rule, they find themselves outnumbered by the new
settlers of the Tudor and Stuart plantations, and a ludicrous
struggle ensues. Christopher Plunkett, the letter-writer, later
became Earl of Fingal. His son, a Catholic, joined the 1641
rebellion and died a prisoner in Dublin Castle.)

And upon the 18th day of May, being Tuesday, the lord deputy,
with all the peers of the realm, and the noblemen, the clergy,
both bishops and archbishops, attired in scarlet robes very
sumptuously, with sound of trumpets; the lord David Barry,
viscount Buttevant, bearing the sword of estate; the earl of
Thomond, bearing the cap of maintenance: and after all these,
the lord deputy followed, riding upon a most stately horse, very
richly trapped, himself attired in a very rich and stately robe of
purple velvet, which the king's majesty had sent him, having his
train borne up by eight gentlemen of worth: and thus, in most
stately and sumptuous manner, they rode from the castle of
Dublin, to the cathedral church of St Patrick, to hear divine
service, and a sermon preached by the reverend father in God,
Christopher Hampton, D.D. archbishop of Armagh, and primate of all Ireland.

But as many of the nobility of Ireland, as were of the recusant
faction, went not into the church, neither heard divine service or
sermon, notwithstanding that they were lords of the parliament
house, and rode towards the church with other lords of estate, yet
they stayed without during the time of service and sermon. Now
when service was done, the lord deputy returned back to the
castle, those recusant lords joined themselves again with the rest
of the estate, and rode to the castle in manner as before they came
from thence.

Now the lord deputy, with all this honourable assembly, being
entered into the castle, ascended up into the high house of
parliament . . .

And when the whole high court of parliament was set, the lord chancellor made a grave and worthy speech, . . . and among many other things, his lordship declared the king's majesty's pleasure, concerning Sir John Davis, his majesty's attorney-general in Ireland; and how his highness was pleased, that he should be the speaker of the lower parliament house . . .

The next day, being the 19th of May, and the 2d of the parliament, the said Sir John Davis was brought into the parliament house, to be presented, and to take his place according to his majesty's good meaning, and was well allowed of and accepted of all men, except those which were infected with the opinions of recusancy, whereof were some there of all degrees, which took exceptions against Sir John Davis; and thereupon arose a great tumult, because there were two elections, *viz.* those of the recusants sect had chosen Sir John Everard knight, for the speaker, and therefore, would in no wise accept of Sir John Davis, and in this division grew an uncertainty who had most voices; whereupon Sir John Davis, with all those of the protestancy, went out to be numbered, and before they came in again those of the recusancy had shut the door, and had set Sir John Everard in the chair of the speaker; but when the protestants saw that, they quietly pulled Sir John Everard out of the chair, and held Sir John Davis therein; and thus, with great contention, the 2d and 3d days were spent: but the recusants prevailed not, for Sir John Davis was maintained in the place, according to his highness's good meaning. Then did the recusants of both houses of parliament withdraw themselves, and resorted not thither any more, notwithstanding that they were often sent for by the lord deputy. And now they began to invent new projects, whereupon they had sundry secret meetings among themselves. . . .

[9] A ramble round the Castle in 1698; from John Dunton's letters quoted in Edward MacLysaght's *Irish Life in the Seventeenth Century*.

(John Dunton (1659–1733) was a highly eccentric London bookseller, who had first tried emigrating to New England, then come to Dublin to escape domestic troubles. He later published an account of his rambles as *The Dublin Scuffle*.)

Another of my inquisitive rambles is to the castle, the place of residence for the chief governor. It is encompassed with a wall and dry ditch over which is a drawbridge and within that an iron gate, opposite to which in the inner court are two brass field pieces planted, as also some others on top of one of the towers, and yet it is no place of great strength, I mean such as is able to endure the battery of great guns, though it can command all the city from its towers. It has an handsome guardhouse for the soldiers and other rooms for the officers, for a foot company with three commissioned officers daily mount the guard, and whenever the government go out or come in they are received with colours flying and drums beating as the King is at Whitehall, and indeed the grandeur they live in here is not much inferior to what you see in London if you make allowances for the number of great men at court there. The building is handsome without much magnificence on the outside, you enter the house up a noble stairs and find several stately rooms one of which is called the Presence chamber and has a chair of state with a canopy over it. One part of the house stands over a large stone gallery supported by several pillars of stone.

At the back of the house lies a broad terrace walk the length of the building the walls covered with greens and flower pots, from hence on a stone arch over a little river you descend by two spacious pair of stone stairs into the garden, which is handsomely laid out into grass plots with green and gravel walks, and at the north side there are two rows of flourishing lime-trees, beneath which lies another grass walk. This garden was made by that great man the Lord Sidney, now earl of Romney, when he was chief governor. To the castle belongs an officer called the Constable of the Castle, who receives prisoners of state when committed, as the Lieutenant of the Tower does. To the north side lies the chapel to which the lord Galway goes constantly every morning to prayers, and at his return spends sometime in receiving petitions, which he answers with all the sweetness and readiness that any petitioner can wish for in so great a man.

Next the chapel is the office of the Ordinance, near which the King's gunsmiths and armourers work, before these buildings lies a large piece of ground called the Stable-yard, on one side of which are the King's stables, which as they are not extraordinary so they are no way despicable, but convenient and big enough; in this yard two companies of foot parade every morning, one of

which mounts the town guard and the other that of the Castle.
The little river which I now mentioned runs here, on the other
side of which stands the coach-houses, and biggest hay-stacks
that ever I saw.

[10] A Castle ball in 1732; from the *Autobiography and
Correspondence of Mrs Delany.*

(Mrs Delany, a niece of Lord Lansdowne, came to Dublin on a
prolonged visit as a young widow in 1730, and later returned to
marry Dr Delany, a famous Dublin preacher and close friend of
Dean Swift. Their house, Delville at Glasnevin, became a centre
of hospitality and her letters (mainly to her brother and sister in
England) give sparkling vignettes of eighteenth-century Dublin
society.)

Dublin, 7th March, 1731–32.

MY DEAR BROTHER,

May your assemblies increase at Wells, and every agreeable
entertainment that can give you any pleasure. A thousand
thanks to you for your last letter. I will not defer my answer,
though I am in a monstrous hurry.

'Tis fit in return for the account you give me of your
amusements, that I let you know what we do here. Why, on the
first of March we went to Court in the morning, heard a song of
Dubourg's, (not so pretty as the last,) after that compliment was
over and we had refreshed ourselves by dinner, we went again at
seven. The ball was in the old beef-eaters hall, a room that holds
seven hundred people seated, it was well it did, for never did I
behold a greater crowd. We were all placed in rows one above
another, so much raised that the last row almost *touched the ceiling!*
The gentlemen say we looked very handsome, and compared us
to Cupid's Paradise in the puppet-show. At eleven o'clock
minuets were finished, and the Duchess went to the basset table.

After an hour's playing the Duke [*of Dorset*], Duchess, and
nobility marched into the supper-room, which was the council
chamber. In the midst of the room was placed a holly tree,
illuminated by an hundred wax tapers; round it was placed all
sorts of meat, fruit, and sweetmeats; servants waited next, and

were encompassed round by a table, to which the company came by turns to take what they wanted. When the doors were *first* opened, the hurly burly is not to be described; squawling, shrieking, all sorts of noises: some ladies lost their lappets, others were trod upon. Poor Lady Santry almost lost her breath in the scuffle, and fanned herself two hours before she could recover herself enough to know if she was dead or alive. I and my company were more discreet than to go with the torrent; we staid till people had satisfied their curiosity and hunger, and then took a quiet view of the *famous tree*, which occasion'd more rout than it was worth.

[11] The wit and wisdom of Lord Chesterfield; from 'Sketches of Irish History' quoted in *Irish Cavalcade* by M.J. McManus.

The Earl of Chesterfield was a scholar and a man of wit, as well as an elegant courtier; his government of the country proves him not only a man of enlightened understanding, but of the most benevolent disposition. He came over in the year 1745, a period remarkable for the rebellion which raged in Scotland, and made it necessary to have an able and prudent statesman at the head of affairs in Ireland. By the wisdom and levity of his measures, the Catholics remained perfectly quiet; before his arrival, those in power had shut up their chapels in Dublin, and their priests were commanded to leave the country by proclamation. These severities were offensive to Lord Chesterfield; convinced that harsh treatment alienates the heart, but that gentle usage inspires confidence and gains the affections, he permitted them the undisturbed exercise of their religion. To accusations to their prejudice, resulting from dislike, he paid no regard; rumours of plots and insurrections were listened to by him with calm indifference.

One morning prior to the battle of Culloden, Mr Gardiner, the Vice-treasurer, abruptly entered his bedchamber with tidings that the Papists were rising. 'Rising?' said his lordship, yawning and looking at his watch; 'it is time for every honest man to rise; it is past nine o'clock, and I will rise myself.'

[12] Custard-pies at the Lord Lieutenant's dinner, 1757; an unpublished letter (in the British Museum) from Chief Baron Willes to his friend, the Earl of Warwick.

(Chief Baron Willes, originally from Warwickshire, rose through the Irish legal system to become head of the Irish Exchequer. He lived partly in Monkstown.)

Upon state days when some of the Nobility, Bishops, Privy Councils, and Judges dine with the Ld. Lieutn. he is attended with great state. Behind his chair stand his two pages. Behind them in the middle stands his Gentleman of the Bedchamber & on each side the steward and Controller of the Household with their white wands. When the 2nd course is set on the Table the King at Arms preceded by a pursevant at Arms & the King with his Crown on his head is attended into the Room & goes to the upper End & proclaims the Kings Stile in Latine, French, & English, & then the pursevant pronounces the words Largess Largess. And formerly the doors were then thrown open & the Crowd entered to see the Ld. Lieutenant at dinner. And the Company at the Table used to give the Sweetmeats &c to those that stood behind them. Some few years ago the Crowd grew troublesome & used to seize what was at Table [and throw it] over the Gentlemans heads. And it happening that a woman seized a large Custard in paste & in getting it over a Bishop's head it fell directly upon his face & robes, & he made so ridiculous a figure that it was thought proper to prevent such rudeness for the future that the Crowd would not be admitted till the Ld. Lieutenant was rose from Table. Accordingly now so soon as the Company rises from Table the Servants show all the Sweetmeats & Oranges &c on the Table & take away the Glass & Ornaments of the dessert & then the Mob enters & scramble for it. The Lord Lieutenant & Company retiring up one End of the room to see the diversion of the Scramble.

The ballroom upon the Kings Birthday is a prodigious fine sight. Tis a noble room Much larger than the Ballroom at St James. The Ld. Lieutenant & Lady duchess sit on two chairs of State at the upper end of the room, And behind them stand peers, Lord Justices & privy Councillors. There are 4 rowes of benches raised one above another the whole length of the room. A bar is made across the room about mid space between that &

the door stand the gentlemen. The four rows of Benches on each side are filled with Ladies only. And nobody dances but who the Gentleman Usher directs & takes out. As I stood by the side of the Lady Duchess Chair & had a fine view of the rows of Ladys I thought it the finest sight I ever saw. There were I believe about 400 Ladies, many of them extremely handsome. All of them very richly dressed, but not many that had any great quantity of Jewels, but the blaze of Beauty was superior to the sparkling of diamonds.

[13] The United Irishmen fail to capture the Castle, 23 May 1798; from *The Rise and Fall of the Irish Nation* by Sir Jonah Barrington.

(In 1798 the United Irishmen – a revolutionary movement largely inspired by the example of the American and French Revolutions – launched the first serious rising against English rule since the seventeenth century. Many of their leaders, including Lord Edward FitzGerald (see p. 104 and p. 225) were arrested before the rising, betrayed by the Castle's network of spies; and the attack on the Castle by rebel forces from the surrounding villages was confused and unco-ordinated. In this extract, the loyalist forces crouch in the cattlemarket north of the Castle.

Sir Jonah Barrington (1760–1834), who wrote this account ten years later, is a racy though highly unreliable historian of eighteenth-century Ireland. Son of a squire from Co. Leix, he sat as MP in Grattan's Parliament, which he later saw as the highpoint of the 'Irish Nation' (the Protestant Ascendancy version); he became an Admiralty judge after the Union; and was eventually deprived of office for embezzlement.)

The danger was considered imminent, the defence impracticable, yet there was a cheerful, thoughtless jocularity with which the English nation, under grave circumstances, are totally unacquainted; and plain matter-of-fact men can scarcely conceive that renovating levity which carries an Irish heart buoyantly over every wave, which would swamp, or at least water-log, their more steady fellow subjects. All the barristers, attorneys, merchants, bankers, revenue officers, shop-keepers, students of the University, doctors, apothecaries, and corporators, of an immense metropolis, in red coats, with a sprinkling of parsons, all doubled up together amidst bullock stalls and sheep pens, awaiting, in profound darkness (not with impatience), for invisible executioners to dispatch them without mercy, was not (abstractedly) a situation to engender much hilarity – scouts now and then came, only to report their ignorance – a running buzz occasionally went round, that the videts were driven in – and the reports of distant musketry, like a twitch of electricity, gave a slight but perceptible movement to men's muscles. A few (faintly-heard) shots on the north side also seemed to announce that the van-guard of the Santry men was approaching. In the mean time, no orders came from the general, and if there had, no orders could have been obeyed. It appeared, at break of day, that both Santry and Rathfarnham rebels had adjourned their assault to some other opportunity. . . .

The rebels had learned that the yeomanry were ready to receive them, and contented themselves with shooting some mail coachmen, and burning some houses, till morning dispersed them. The rebels on the south intended to take the castle by surprise, whilst the Santry men assailed the barracks; but their plan was disconcerted by Lord Roden, at the head of his dragoons (called the fox hunters, from their noble horses). His Lordship marched rapidly upon them, and surprised the few who had collected; and, being supported by a small number of light infantry, the attack completely succeeded. A few rebels were sabred, and some few made prisoners; but the body dispersed with little resistance. Lord Roden received a ball on his helmet, but was only bruised, and some dragoons were wounded; the other (county of Dublin) rebels retreated to join the Kildare men; the southern marched to unite themselves with those of Wicklow. Their plan had been excellent – had they acted steadily on it success was not improbable; however, the metropolis for some time had no further dread of molestation.

A new, disgusting, and horrid scene was next morning publicly exhibited; after which military executions commenced, and continued with unabating activity. Some dead bodies of insurgents, sabred the night before by Lord Roden's dragoons, were brought in a cart to Dublin, with some prisoners tied together; the carcasses were stretched out in the Castle yard, where the Viceroy then resided, and in full view of the

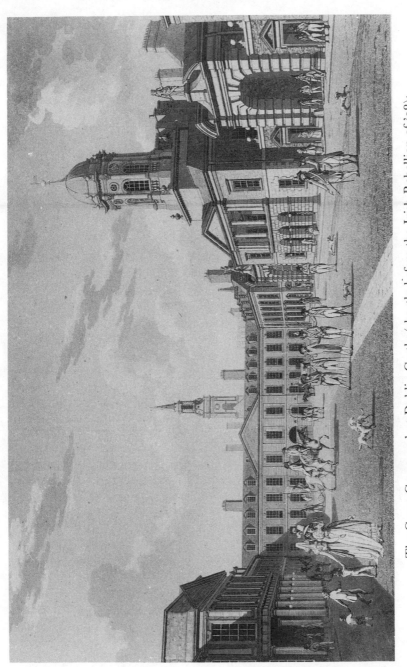

The Great Courtyard at Dublin Castle (shortly before the Irish Rebellion of '98); aquatint by James Malton from *Picturesque Views of Dublin*, 1794

Secretary's windows; they lay on the pavement, as trophies of the first skirmish, during a hot day, cut and gashed in every part, covered with clotted blood and dust, the most frightful spectacle which ever disgraced a royal residence, save the seraglio. After several hours' exposure, some appearance of life was perceived in one of the mutilated carcasses. The man had been stabbed and gashed in various parts, his body was removed into the guard-room, and means were taken to restore animation; the efforts succeeded; he entirely recovered, and was pardoned by Lord Camden; he was an extraordinarily fine young man, above six feet high, the son of a Mr Keogh, an opulent landholder of Rathfarnham; he did not, however, change his principles, and was, ultimately, sent out of the country.

[14] The Castle guardroom; from *Jack Hinton, the Guardsman* by Charles Lever.

(Charles Lever (1806–1872) originally studied medicine but in 1842 gave up work as a doctor to write and edit the *Dublin University Magazine*. He became one of the most popular writers of the Victorian age, producing a stream of rollicking novels mainly of Anglo-Irish life; *Jack Hinton* was one of his earliest. Set in the early 1800s, it is the story of 'an exceedingly young English guardsman coming over to Ireland at the time of the Duke of Richmond's viceroyalty when every species of rackety doings was in vogue'.)

When I next came to my senses, I found myself lying upon a sofa in a large room, of which I appeared the only occupant. A confused and misty recollection of my accident, some scattered fragments of my voyage, and a rather aching sensation in my head, were the only impressions of which I was well conscious. The last evening I spent at home was full in my memory, and I could not help thinking over my poor mother's direful anticipa-tions in my vain endeavours to penetrate what I felt had been a misfortune of some kind or other. The mystery was, however, too deep for my faculties; and so, in despair of unraveling the past, I set myself to work to decipher the present. The room, I have already said, was large; and the ceiling, richly stuccoed and ornamented, spoke of a day whose architecture was of a grand

and massive character. The furniture, now old and time-worn, had once been handsome, even magnificent. Rich curtains of heavy brocaded silk, with deep gold fringes, gorgeously-carved and gilded chairs, in the taste of Louis XV; marble consoles stood between the windows, and a mirror of gigantic proportions occupied the chimney-breast. Years and neglect had not only done their worst, but it was evident that the hand of devastation had also been at work. The marbles were cracked; few of the chairs were available for use; the massive lustre, intended to shine with a resplendent glare of fifty wax-lights, was now made a resting-place for shakos, bear-skins, and foraging-caps; an ominous-looking star in the looking-glass bore witness to the bullet of a pistol; and the very Cupids carved upon the frame, who once were wont to smile blandly at each other, were now disfigured with cork moustachoes, and one of them even carried a pair of spurs in his mouth. Swords, sashes, and sabretashes, spurs and shot-belts, with guns, fishing-tackle, and tandem whips, were hung here and there upon the walls, which themselves presented the strangest spectacle of all, there not being a portion of them unoccupied by caricature sketches, executed in every imaginable species of taste, style, and colouring. Here was a field-day in the park, in which it was easy to see the prominent figures were portraits: there an enormous nose, surmounted by a grenadier cap, was passing in review some trembling and terrified soldiers. In another, a commander-of-the-forces was seen galloping down the lines, holding on by the pummel of the saddle. Over the sofa I occupied, a levee at the Castle was displayed, in which, if the company were not villanously libelled, the viceroy had little reason to be proud of his guests. There were also dinners at the Lodge; guards relieved by wine-puncheons dressed up like field-officers; the whole accompanied by doggerel verses explanatory of the views.

The owner of this singular chamber had, however, not merely devoted his walls to the purposes of an album, but he had also made them perform the part of a memorandum-book. Here were the 'meets' of the Kildare and the Dubber for the month of March; there, the turn of duty for the garrison of Dublin, interspersed with such fragments as the following:–Mem.–To dine at Mat Kean's on Tuesday, 4th—Not to pay Hennesy till he settles about the handicap—To ask Courtenay for Fanny Burke's fan; the same Fanny has pretty legs of her own—To tell

Holmes to have nothing to do with Lanty Moore's niece, in regard to a reason!—Five to two on Giles' two-year-old, if Tom likes—N.B.–The mare is a roarer—A heavenly day, what fun they must have!–may the devil fire Tom O'Flaherty, or I would not be here now. These and a hundred other similar passages figured on every side, leaving me in a state of considerable mystification, not as to the character of my host, of which I could guess something, but as to the nature of his abode, which I could not imagine to be a barrack-room.

[15] George IV kisses the girls; from *The Croker Papers 1808–1857*, edited by R. Pool.

(King George IV made his visit to Dublin in August 1821 (in an unusually affable mood, having just heard the news of his wife's death) and was received with enormous enthusiasm – which soon evaporated when he failed to approve Catholic Relief.

John Wilson Croker (1780–1857) was a close friend of the King since Regency days. Born in Galway and educated at Trinity College, he wrote several drily satirical sketches of Irish life while in his twenties, and went on to found and edit the famous *Quarterly Review* and make a highly successful career in Tory politics. In old age, he was satirized himself as the unpleasant Rigby in Disraeli's novel *Coningsby*.)

August 20th. – The King held a *levée*, and previous to it received the addresses of the Synod of Presbyterians, the Quakers, and the Catholic bishops in the closet. He also had an investiture of St Patrick and the Bath. Lord Graves, proxy for the Duke of Cumberland, and Lords Donegal, Ormond, Meath, Roden, Fingal, and Courtown, were invested.

The address of the Catholic bishops was in bad taste; it talked too much politics, and said that they were four-fifths of the population. Everybody observed how unseemly this tone was at this time. Some days after, Lord Donoughmore told me that he had written this address, and he took great credit for having inserted these very passages. . . . I cannot conceive how a man can be so blinded by vanity or party as not see that his address is at least a thing not to boast of.

The *levée* which ensued was wonderfully crowded. I reckoned

1500 names, and was told there were 2000. I know not how many guineas were offered for the loan of a dress sword, and I know two people who were kept away by the want of this article of court dress. Some who came had most incongruous swords, and there were many ludicrous figures, but they were lost in the immense crowd, and many passed the King without seeing or recognising him.

August 21st . . . Dressed for the drawing-room. By opening a large suite of rooms, and by publishing the King's desire that no gentlemen should come except in attendance on ladies, the crowd was not so inconvenient as at the *levée* though the numbers were greater. I should suppose that above 1000 ladies were presented . . . and their dresses were both rich and in good taste. When the rooms began to thin, about twelve o'clock, I walked about with Lord Lovaine, making our observations, and we both agreed that it was a drawing-room quite equal, except as to jewels and titles, to any we had seen at St James's. By some interruption, about one-third of the company were cut off and prevented coming up with the stream. The attendants thought there were no more to be presented, so the door of the presence chamber was shut, and the King made his bows and retired. In a few minutes it was found that the ante-rooms were again full (the interruption in the train of carriages having been obviated). What was to be done? The King had retired and was undressed. On the other hand, the ladies were dressed and had no mind to retire; after a good deal of *pourparlers,* the King was told of the circumstance, and with great good nature he put on his fine coat, came back to the presence chamber, and went through the ceremony of kissing about 300 ladies more.

[16] The Vice-regal Court in the 1870s; from *Recollections of Dublin Castle and Dublin Society* (anon.), 1902.

The Castle, where this Card King lived, was a great centre of the city. In my childhood, boyhood, youth, manhood, I suppose no word rang out more loudly or more frequently in one's ears, or inspired such an awesome feeling. Often I passed it; often was I in it. There were held the 'levys,' 'draw'n rooms,' 'Patrick's balls,' dinners, concerts, and dances *galore.* You went from Westmoreland Street – often sounded West*more*land Street – to the Royal

Exchange, a rather stately building, which brought you to the steep 'Cark Hill,' *i.e.*, Cork Hill, on the top of which was the awful enclosure. It was rather an imposing place, with a great gateway and a guard-house adjoining, out of which – for what reason Heaven knows! – a large sort of church steeple rose. But everything in Dublin is more or less unaccountable. The older churches are mostly without steeples, while a guard-house *has* one. Within, there is a large and stately courtyard, and on the left an archway, opening on a second, viz., 'The Lower Kestle yard'; though it seems undignified to call these august enclosures 'yards.' Round the first court were the residences of the high and mighty officers – the Chamberlain (minus 'Lord') – Comptroller, all squeezed, sorely cribbed and cabined into little sets of rooms, much as those of smaller degree are at the Ambassadors' Court, St James's Palace. It was often a pitiable thing for those poor creatures, wives and children – who had all to 'cram' into these straitened apartments. Their wage was miserable enough, but there was free lodging, with occasional board, and it may be coals; consequently, these offices were much sought after by the broken-down peer or baronet, to whom such quarters were an object; while the Lord Lieutenant was glad to have persons of title about him. The aides-de-camp lived on their very position – on the strength of which they might have been at free board every day of their life. The *paid* aide – this was much insisted on – had, I believe, about £100 a year, with quarters; the extra, nothing.

And the household! – that awe-inspiring word! There was the 'Private Secretary,' the 'Additional Private Secretary,' and, odd to say, 'Assistant Private Secretary,' State Steward, Comptroller, Gentleman Usher, Chamberlain, and actually a 'Master of the Horse,' who looked after the job-master-hired animals mentioned already. Then came three paid aides and four unpaid ditto. There were also 'gentlemen at large,' and 'gentlemen-in-waiting.' There was the 'Physician in Ordinary,' 'Surgeon in Ordinary,' 'Surgeon to the Household,' 'Surgeon Oculist,' and 'Surgeon Dentist.' These last were entitled to appear at the levees and to be so announced, and, for aught I know, to walk in the tag, rag, and bob-tail procession.

A nice lady friend of my own, suffering from toothache, hurried to her dentist, and sent in her name. 'Is it see you to-day, Ma'am? It's quite impossible. Isn't he upstairs undressin' himself to go to the levy?

Christt Church Cathedral

[17] The miraculous crucifix at Christ Church Cathedral; from the *Topographia Hibernia* by Giraldus Cambrensis, in Strongbow's *History of Ireland* by F.P. Barnard.

(Giraldus Cambrensis (1146–1220) was the grandson of Nesta, a Welsh princess whose marriage was to found the famous Fitzgerald clan which dominated Norman Ireland. Giraldus accompanied Prince John (Henry II's ten-year-old son) to Ireland in 1184; and was offered but refused an Irish Archbishopric. His *Expugnatio* and *Topographia Hibernica* are the first and most influential Norman accounts of Ireland and Strongbow's conquest, and were designed as part of a grand (unfinished) history of Scotland, Wales and Ireland.

The church of Holy Trinity, or Christ Church, was at this time still the original Viking wooden structure.)

OF THE CROSS AT DUBLIN WHICH SPAKE AND BORE TESTIMONY TO THE TRUTH.

We come now to treat of occurrences in modern times. There is a cross possessed of great virtues in the church of the Holy Trinity at Dublin, and having the features of a crucifix. Not many years before the arrival of the English, namely, in the time of the Ostmen, this crucifix opened its sacred mouth and spoke in the presence of many persons who heard the words. The circumstances were these: one of the citizens had invoked the crucifix as the sole witness, and a kind of surety, in a contract which he had entered into. In process of time, however, the party with whom he had contracted repudiating his engagements, and persisting in denying his obligation for the money which the other had lent him on his credit, his fellow citizens, rather ironically than seriously, tried the case before the cross, and having assembled in the church for that purpose, the crucifix, on being adjured and called to witness, gave testimony to the truth in the presence of many persons who heard the words.

HOW THE SAME CROSS BECAME IMMOVEABLE

At the time that earl Richard [*Strongbow*] came first with an army to Dublin, the citizens, having a presage in their minds of the many evils which were impending, and fearing that the city would be taken, as they despaired of its defence, were contriving how they could make their escape by sea, and wished to carry away this cross with them to the islands. They used every effort in their power to effect this; but the whole population of the city failed to move it from its place either by force or contrivance.

[18] The Normans rebuild Christ Church Cathedral, and a description of Strongbow; from *The Description of Ireland* by Richard Stanyhurst in Holinshed's *Chronicles*.

(Strongbow was buried 'with great state', Giraldus relates, in the chancel of Christ Church in 1176. But the so-called Strongbow Monument is in fact a misnomer. His tomb was so badly damaged by a collapse of the Cathedral roof in 1562 that Sir Henry Sidney substituted the tomb of one of the Earls of Desmond.)

In the yeare one thousand two hundred and foure score, Robert Uffort came the third time to occupie the roome of lord chiefe iustice in Ireland, resuming that roome into his hands againe. . . . And about the same time, the citie of Dublin was defaced by fire, and the steeple of Christs church utterlie destroied. The citizens before they went about to repare their owne privat buildings, agreed togither to make a collection for reparing the ruines of that ancient building first begun by the Danes, and continued by Citrius prince of Dublin at the instance of Donat sometime bishop of that citie, and dedicated to the blessed trinitie.

At length Strangbow earle of Penbroke, Fitzstephans, & Laurence, that for his vertue was called saint Laurence arch-bishop of Dublin, and his foure successors, John of Evesham, Henrie Scortchbill, and Lucas, and last of all Iohn de saint Paule finished it.

The earle [Strongbow] was somewhat ruddie and of sanguine complexion and freckle faced, his eies greie, his face feminine, his voice small, and his necke little, but somewhat of a high stature: he was verie liberall, courteous and gentle: what he could not compasse and bring to passe in déed, he would win by good words and gentle spéeches. In time of peace he was more readie to yéeld and obeie, than to rule and beare swaie. Out of the campe he was more like to a souldior companion than a capteine or ruler: but in the campe and in the warres he caried with him the state and countenance of a valiant capteine. Of himselfe he would not adventure anie thing, but being advised and set on, he refused no attempts: for of himselfe he would not rashlie adventure, or presumptuouslie take anie thing in hand. In the fight and battell he was a most assured token and signe to the whole companie, either to stand valiantlie to the fight, or for policie to retire. In all chances of warre he was still one and the same maner of man, being neither dismaid with adversitie, nor puffed up with prosperitie.

[19] Four Irish kings are knighted in Christ Church Cathedral in 1395; from *Froissart in Britain* by Sir Henry Newbolt.

(This account in Froissart's famous fifteenth-century *Chronicles* comes from Henry Castide, an English squire who had been taken hostage as a youth while fighting in Ireland and married to his Irish captor's daughter. As a fluent Irish speaker, he is commanded by Richard II in 1394 to 'give attendance' on four Irish kings who had agreed to swear fealty to the English crown and bring them 'to reason and to the usage and customs of England'.)

They had a fair house to lodge in in Dublin, and I was charged to abide still with them, and not to depart; and so two or three days I suffered them to do as they listed, and said nothing to them, but they followed their own appetites; they would sit at the table and make countenance neither good nor fair; then I thought I should cause them to change that manner. They would cause their minstrels, their servants and varlets, to sit with them, and to eat in their own dish and to drink of their cups, and they shewed me that the usage of their country was good, for they said in all things (except their beds) they were and lived as common.

So the fourth day I ordained other tables to be covered in the hall after the usage of England, and I made these four kings to sit at the high table, and their minstrels at another board, and their servants and varlets at another beneath them; whereof by

Four Irish kings are instructed in English manners in Dublin
before being knighted in Christ Church Cathedral, 1395; from
Froissart's fifteenth-century *Chronicle*

seeming they were displeased, and beheld each other and would
not eat, and said how I would take from them their good usage
wherein they had been nourished.

Then I answered them, smiling to appease them, that it was
not honourable for their estate to do as they did before, and that
they must leave it and use the custom of England, and that it was
the king's pleasure they should so do, and how I was charged so
to order them.

When they heard that they suffered it, because they had put
themselves under the obeisance of the king of England, and
persevered in the same as long as I was with them. Yet they had
one use, which I knew well was used in their country, and that
was, they did wear no breeches. I caused breeches of linen cloth
to be made for them.

While I was with them I caused them to leave many rude
things, as well in clothing as in other causes. Much ado I had at
the first to cause them to wear gowns of silk furred with minnever

and gray; for before, these kings thought themselves well apparelled when they had on a mantle. They rode always without saddles and stirrups, and with great pain I made them ride after our usage.

And on a time I demanded them of their belief; wherewith they were not content, and said how they believed on God and on the Trinity, as well as we.

Then I demanded on what pope was their affection.

They answered me, on him of Rome.

Then I demanded if they would not gladly receive the order of knighthood, and that the king of England should make them knights according to the usage of France and England and other countries.

They answered how they were knights already and that sufficed for them.

I asked where they were made knights, and how, and when.

They answered that in the age of seven year they were made knights in Ireland, and that a king maketh his son a knight, and if the son have no father alive, then the next of his blood may make him knight; and then this young knight shall begin to joust with small spears, such as they may bear with their ease, and run against a shield set on a stake in the field, and the more spears he breaketh, the more he shall be honoured.

I knew their manner well enough, though I did demand it. But then I said that the knighthood that they had taken in their youth sufficed not to the king of England, but I said he should give them after another manner.

They demanded how.

I answered that it should be in the holy church, which was the most worthiest place. Then they inclined somewhat to my words.

Within two days after, the Earl of Ormond came to them, who could right well speak the language, for some of his lands lay in those parts: he was sent to them by the king and his council. They all honoured him, and he them: then he fell in sweet communication with them, and he demanded of them how they liked me.

They answered and said, 'Well; for he hath well shewed us the usage of this country; wherefore we ought to thank him and so we do.'

This answer pleased well the Earl of Ormond. Then he entered little and little to speak of the order of chivalry, which the king would they should receive: he shewed it them from point to point, how they should behave themselves, and what pertained to knighthood.

The Earl's words pleased much these four kings, whose names were these: first, the great O'Neal, king of Meath; the second, O'Brien of Thomond, king of Thomond; the third, Arthur MacMorrough, king of Leinster; the fourth, O'Connor, king of Connaught and Erne: they were made knights by King Richard of England in the cathedral church of Dublin, dedicate of St John Baptist [*Christ Church*]: it was done on our Lady Day in March; it fell on a Thursday.

These four kings watched all the night before in the church, and the next day at high Mass time with great solemnity they were made knights, and with them Sir Thomas Ourghem, Sir Jonathan Pado, and Sir John Pado his cousin.

These kings sat that day at the table with King Richard: they were regarded of many folks, because their behaving was strange to the manner of England and other countries, and ever naturally men desire to see novelties.

[20] Lambert Simnel is crowned in Christ Church, 1487; from Holinshed's *Chronicles*.

(England has just emerged from the Wars of the Roses, Henry VII is King, but his justiciar in Ireland, Garret More, the Great Earl of Kildare, chooses instead to crown a ten-year-old boy, claimed to be the Yorkist heir. The coup failed; Lambert Simnel was spared to turn spits in the royal kitchens, and Kildare – still safe on his own ground in Dublin – was granted an unconditional pardon. When Perkin Warbeck, the next Yorkist pretender, arrived in Cork, however, Henry VII took no chances . . . (see next extract).)

To (the) earle (Gerald, Earl of Kildare) came the wily priest, Sir Richard Simon, bringing with him a lad that was his scholar named Lambert, who he feigned to be the son of George, Earl of Clarence, lately escaped from the Tower of London. And the boy could reckon up his pedigree so readily and learned of the priest such princely behaviour that he greatly moved the said earl, and many of the nobles of Ireland . . . either to think, or to feign, that the world might believe they thought, verily this child to be

Edward, Earl of Warwick, the Duke of Clarence his lawful son.

And although King Henry more than half marred their sport in showing the right earl through all the streets of London, yet the lady Margaret, Duchess of Burgoyne, sister to Edward the Fourth, her nephew John de la Pole, the Lord Lovell, Sir Thomas Broughton, Knight, and divers other captains of this conspiracy, devised to abuse the colour of this young earl's name, for preferring their purpose.

Wherefore it was blazed in Ireland, that the King, to mock his subjects, had schooled a boy to take upon him the Earl of Warwick's name, and had showed him about London, to blind the eyes of the simple folk, and to defeat the lawful inheritor of the good Duke of Clarence, their countryman and protector during his life, with whose lineage they also derived title in right to the crown.

In all haste they assembled at Dublin and there in Christs Church they crowned this idol, honoring him with titles imperial, feasting and triumphing; raising mighty shouts and cries, carrying him from thence to the castle on tall men's shoulders that he might be seen and noted, as he was surely an honourable child to look upon.

Herewith assembling their forces together, they provided themselves with ships and embarking therein, they took to the sea and landing in Lancashire pressed forwards till they came to Newark upon Trent. Thereupon ensued the battle of Stoke commonly called Martin Stuarts Field, wherein Lambert and his master were taken, but yet pardoned of life and were not executed. The earl of Lincoln, the Lord Lovell, Martin Stuart, the Almail Captain and Maurice Fitzthomas, Captain of the Irish, were slain, and all their power discomfited as in the English history it may further appear.

St Patrick's Cathedral

[21] The Great Earl of Kildare makes peace with the Earl of Ormonde in St Patrick's; from Holinshed's *Chronicles*.

(When Perkin Warbeck, the Yorkish Pretender, arrived in Cork, King Henry VII, with the affair of Lambert Simnel in mind (see p. 82) sent James Butler, Earl of Ormonde, the Earl of Kildare's traditional enemy, to command an independent army in the south.

The hole cut in the chapterhouse door, as related below, can still be seen.)

Girald Fitzgirald earle of Kildare, son to Thomas Fitzgirald, of who mention hath beene made in the latter end of the former storie, a mightie man of stature, full of honor & courage, who had beene deputie & lord iustice of Ireland first & last 33 yeeres, deceased at Kildare the third of September, & lieth intoomed in the queere of Christes church at Dublin, in a chappell by him founded. Betweene him & Iames Butler earle of Ormond (their owne gelousies fed with envie & ambition, kindled with certeine lewd factious abettors of either side) as generallie to all noblemen, so especiallie to both these houses everie incident, ever since the ninth yeare of Henrie the seventh, bred some trouble in Ireland. The plot of which mutuall grudge was grounded upon the factious dissention, that was raised in England betweene the houses of Yorke & Lancaster, Kildare cleaving to Yorke, and Ormond relieng to Lancaster. To the upholding of which discord, both these noble men laboured with tooth and naile to overcrow, and consequentlie to overthrow one the other. And for somuch as they were in honour peeres, they wrought by hooke and by crooke to be in authoritie superiours. The governement therfore in the reigne of Henrie the seventh, being cast on the house of Kildare; Iames earle of Ormond a deepe and a farre reaching man, giving backe like a butting ram to strike the harder push, devised to inveigle his adversarie by submission & courtesie, being not then able to overmatch him with stoutnesse or preheminence. Whereupon Ormond addressed his letters to the deputie specifieng a slander raised on him and his, that he purposed to deface his governement, and to withstand his authorities. And for the cleering of himselfe and of his adherents, so it stood with the deputie his pleasure, he would make his speedie repaire to Dublin, & there in an open audience would purge himselfe of all such odious crimes, of which he was wrongfullie suspected.

To this reasonable request had the lord deputie no sooner condescended, than Ormond with a puissant armie marched towards Dublin, incamping in an abbeie in the suburbs of the citie, named saint Thomas court. The approching of so great an armie of the citizens suspected, and also of Kildares councellors greatlie disliked, lastlie the extortion that the lawlesse souldiers used in the pale by severall complaints detected: these three points, with diverse other suspicious circumstances laid and put togither, did minister occasion rather of further discord, than of anie present agreement. Ormond persisting still in his humble sute, sent his messenger to the lord deputie, declaring that he was prest and readie to accomplish the tenour of his letters, and there did attend (as became him) his lordship his pleasure. . . .

Kildare with this mild message intreated, appointed the meeting to be at saint Patrike his church: . . . the citizens and Ormond his armie fell at some iar, for the oppression and exaction with which the souldiers surcharged them. With whom as part of the citizens bickered, so a round knot of archers rushed into the church, meaning to have murthered Ormond, as the capteine and belwedder of all these lawlesse rabble. The earle of Ormond suspecting that he had beene betraied, fled to the chapiter house, put to the doore, sparring it with might and maine. The citizens in their rage, imagining that everie post in the church had beene one of the souldiers, shot hab or nab at randon up to the roodloft and to the chancell, leaving some of their arrowes sticking in the images.

Kildare pursuing Ormond to the chapiter house doore, undertooke on his honor that he should receive no villanie. Wherupon the recluse craving his lordships hand to assure him his life, there was a clift in the chapiter house doore, pearsed at a trise, to the end both the earles should have shaken hands and be reconciled. But Ormond surmising that this drift was intended for some further treacherie, that if he would stretch out his hand, it had beene percase chopt off, refused that proffer; until Kildare stretcht in his hand to him, and so the doore was opened, they

Richard Boyle, the Great Earl of Cork, who erected the splendid tomb to his wife in St Patrick's Cathedral (it was originally placed by the altar, until Thomas Wentworth forced its removal); engraving from a portrait at Hardwick Hall both imbraced, the storme appeased, and all their quarrels for that present rather discontinued than ended.

[22] The Great Earl of Cork's tomb is put in its place, 1635; from *The Life and Letters of the Great Earl of Cork* by Dorothea Townsend.

(Richard Boyle, the Great Earl of Cork, was the most successful of all the Elizabethans who came to Ireland to seek their fortune. He acquired vast estates and became Lord Treasurer of Ireland. In 1630 his 'dearest, dear wife' Catherine Fenton, who had borne him fifteen children, died suddenly and was buried in St Patrick's. The tomb he commissioned as her monument was to become the first battlefield in a power struggle between the aged Earl and the new Lord Deputy, Thomas Wentworth, later Earl of Strafford.)

In May the Pursuivant-at-arms completed a design for a magnificent tomb, which was to commemorate Lady Cork's parents and grandparents as well as herself. The stonecutter of Chapel Izod, who was already at work on the restoration of Maynooth Castle for the Earl of Kildare, was intrusted with this important piece of work, and it was estimated that the cost, including painting, gilding, and iron railings, would be £300. Eventually, between the cost of the iron supplied from the Earl's own forges, fees to the Dean and Chapter, and 'liberalities among the workmen,' the expense rose to £400. But the tomb was to cost him dearer than a few hundred pounds. By a strange irony of fate his troubles began at his wife's grave, and it was that stately marble erection that gave Strafford his much-desired opportunity to humiliate the Great Earl.

The tomb was not completed till January 1633; then the Earl wrote: 'This night the bones of my wife's grandfather, Dr Weston, sometime Lord Justice and Lord Chancellor of Ireland, of her father, Sir Geoffrey Fenton, Kt, principal secretary of state in Ireland, and the coffin wherein my lost wife's dead body was enclosed, were all removed out of the old tomb wherein they were all three buried in St Patrick's church, and all placed in the new vault of my wife's tomb by me made and erected at the upper end of the chancel of the said St Patrick's church, expecting a joyful resurrection.'

And then arrived the great Lord Deputy. . . . In the eyes of [*Strafford*] he [*the Earl of Cork*] was but a doting old Polonius, and not an honest dotard either. It was very convenient for Wentworth that Archbishop Laud had already a complaint against Cork which would be a good opening for the course of humiliation that the Deputy was preparing for the Great Earl, and would also give opportunities for a little plain speaking to several archbishops and deans.

To Laud's mind the black marble tomb which Cork had erected in St Patrick's Cathedral was nothing less than a scandal. Laud's trusted emissary Bramhall had written of it in horror as soon as he arrived in Dublin, telling that the tomb was 'erected in the proper place of the altar as if it were contrived to give it worship and reverence which the chapter and whole church are bound by special statutes to give towards the east.'

This commotion at first merely astonished the Earl of Cork, and he sent over letters to explain that his tomb, although it certainly stood at the east end of the cathedral, so far from standing on the site of the communion table, was placed in front of a blocked-up doorway. But protests and explanations were of no avail; Laud was determined that the tomb should be removed, and Wentworth was delighted to be the instrument of such a humiliation to Cork. . . .

It is true that commissioners were appointed to view the tomb before sentence was given, but the matter was really settled before they set foot in the cathedral. Lord Cork wrote that the commission examined some weak aged people as to where the altar had stood, but they spake by hearsay and to very little purpose. Wentworth, however, thought there was no need of human witnesses when the tomb itself spoke so much to the purpose. He wrote to Laud:

'I have issued a commission according to my warrant for viewing the Earl of Cork's tomb; the two archbishops and himself, with four other bishops and the two deans and chapters, were present when we met and made them all so ashamed that the Earl desires he may have leave to pull it down without reporting further with England; so I am content if the miracle be done, though Mahomet do it, and there is an end of the tomb before it came to be intombed indeed.'

And then the next spring, March 1635, Wentworth wrote triumphantly:

'The Earl of Cork's tomb is now quite removed: how he means to dispose of it I know not, but up it is put in boxes, as if it were marchpanes and banquetting stuffs going down to the christening of my young master in the country. The wall is closed again, and as soon as it is dry and fit to be wrought upon, it shall be decently adorned or else—! It costs me at least one fifty pounds for my share.'

Cork could but submit with the best grace he could muster up. Even in his diary he only records that it cost him £68 to remove the tomb to the side of the cathedral, and so the struggle ended, and the first triumph was scored to the Lord Deputy.

[23] Jonathan Swift describes his life as Dean of St Patrick's in 1733; from *The Correspondence of Jonathan Swift* edited by Elrington Ball.

(Jonathan Swift (1667–1745), poet, satirist and philanthropist, was born in Dublin, and returned there to live full-time in 1713 when he was appointed dean of St Patrick's. In black moods he regarded the post as banishment: during his years in London he had irretrievably offended the Whigs with his lampoons. In this extract he is writing more philosophically to one of his oldest friends, Alexander Pope.

Only a fragment of his Deanery remains, as part of the police station opposite the Cathedral.)

I am told, to my great misfortune, that a very convenient offer happening of a coach with one gentleman and his sister coming to Ireland from their elder brother, your friend and neighbour, you waived the invitation pressed on you, alleging the fear you had of being killed here with eating and drinking; by which I find that you have given some credit to a notion of our great plenty and hospitality. . . .

If you had ventured to come over you should have had a very convenient warm apartment more open than usual in great cities, with a garden as large as your green plot that fronts the Thames, and another about two hundred yards further, larger than your great garden and with more air, but without any beauty. You should have small dinners of what you liked, and good wine, and you eat and drink so little that I could well afford it, considering how often you would be invited either with me or without me. The conveniences of taking the air, winter or summer, do far exceed those in London; for the two large strands just at two edges of the town, are as firm and dry in winter, as in summer. There are at least six or eight gentlemen of sense, learning, good humour and taste, able and desirous to please you, and orderly females, some of the better sort, to take care of you. These were the motives that I have frequently made use of to entice you hither; and there would be no failure among the best people here, of any honours that could be done you.

As to myself, I declare my health is so uncertain that I dare not venture among you at present. I hate the thoughts of London, where I am not rich enough to live otherwise than by shifting, which is now too late. Neither can I have conveniences in the country for three horses and two servants, and many others which I have here at hand. I am one of the governors of all the hackney coaches, carts and carriages, round this town, who dare not insult me like your rascally wagoners or coachmen, but give me the way; nor is there one Lord or squire for a hundred of yours, to turn me out of the road, or run over me with their coaches and six. Thus, I make some advantage of the public poverty, and give you the reasons for what I once writ, why I choose to be a freeman among slaves, rather than a slave among freemen. Then, I walk the streets in peace without being justled, nor ever without a thousand blessings from my friends the vulgar. I am Lord Mayor of one hundred and twenty houses, I am absolute lord of the greatest Cathedral in the kingdom, am at peace with the neighbouring Princes, the Lord Mayor of the city and the Archbishop of Dublin; only the latter, like the King of France, sometimes attempts encroachments on my dominions, as old Lewis did upon Lorraine.

[24] A visit to Swift's Deanery in the 1730s; from *The Memoirs of Letitia Pilkington*.

(Letitia Pilkington (1712–1750), the pretty young wife of a penniless Irish parson, met Dean Swift when his eccentricities had already become marked. Swift befriended the young couple generously and found Letitia's husband a job in England. The marriage soon broke up, Letitia returned to Dublin, destitute, and was supported by Swift's friend, Dr Delany. Her memoirs were published in 1748, three years after Swift had died, probably from Menière's disease which had produced his apparent insanity.)

On our return to the Deanery House, we found there waiting our coming Dr Delany and Mr Rochford, to whose wife *A Letter of Advice to a new-married Lady* (published since in the Dean's works) was written, and which, by the by, the lady did not take as a compliment, either to her or the sex, Mr Pilkington, Dr Sheridan, author of *The Art of Punning*, with two or three other clergymen (who usually passed Sunday evening with the Dean). Mr Pilkington, and I were for going home, but the Dean told us: 'He gave us leave to stay to supper'; which from him was a sufficient invitation. The Dean then pulled out of his pocket a little gold runlet, in which was a bottle-screw, and, opening a bottle of wine, he decanted it off; the last glass being muddy, he called to Mr Pilkington to drink it: 'For', says he, 'I always keep some poor parson to drink the foul wine for me.' Mr Pilkington, entering into his humour, thanked him, and told him: 'He did not know the difference, but was glad to get a glass at any rate.' 'Why then', says the Dean, 'you shan't, for I'll drink it myself: why p—x take you, you are wiser than a paltry curate whom I asked to dine with me a few days ago; for upon my making the same speech to him, he told me he did not understand such usage, and so walked off without his dinner. By the same token, I told the gentleman who recommended him to me that the fellow was a blockhead, and I had done with him.'

The Dean then missing his golden bottle-screw, told me, very sternly: 'He was sure I had stolen it.' I affirmed, very seriously, I had not. Upon which he looked for it, and found it where he himself had laid it. ''Tis well for you', says he, 'that I have got it, or I would have charged you with theft.' 'Why, pray, Sir, should I be suspected more than any other person in the company?' 'For a very good reason', says he, 'because you are the poorest.' . . .

The Dean shewed me into a little street-parlour (where sat his housekeeper, a matron-like gentlewoman, at work). 'Here', says he; 'Mrs Brent, take care of this child (meaning me) and see she does no mischief, while I take my walk out within doors.' The

Deanery House has I know not how many pair of back-stairs in it, the preceding Dean who built it, being it seems extremely fearful of fire, was resolved there should be many ways to escape in case of danger.

The Dean then ran up the great-stairs, down one pair of back-stairs, up another, in so violent a manner that I could not help expressing my uneasiness to the good gentlewoman lest he should fall and be hurt. She said: 'It was a customary exercise with him, when the weather did not permit him to walk abroad.'

I told Mrs Brent 'I believed the Dean was extremely charitable.' 'Indeed, Madam', replied she, 'nobody can be more so; his income is not above six-hundred pounds a year, and every year he gives above the half of it in private pensions to decayed families; besides this, he keeps five-hundred pounds in the constant service of the industrious poor: this he lends out in five pounds at a time, and takes the payment back at twelve-pence a week; this does them more service than if he gave it to them entirely, as it obliges them to work and at the same time keeps up this charitable fund for the assistance of many. You cannot imagine what numbers of poor tradesmen, who have even wanted proper tools to carry on their work have by this small loan been put into a prosperous way and brought up their families in credit. The Dean (added she) has found out a new method of being charitable, in which however, I believe, he will have but few followers; which is, to debar himself of what he calls the superfluities of life, in order to administer to the necessities of the distressed: you just saw an instance of it; the money a coach would have cost him he gave to a poor man, unable to walk. When he dines alone, he drinks a pint of beer, and gives away the price of a pint of wine; and thus he acts in numberless instances.'

[25] Dean Swift's final descent into insanity; from *The Memoirs of Letitia Pilkington*.

The first proof he gave of his incivility was affronting the Lord Lieutenant at the Lord Mayor's table, who, because he had not paid his compliments to him in due form, he very civilly accosted by the extraordinary title of 'You fellow with the Blue String'. Some little time after this he invited two clergymen to take the air

with him, and when he got them into a coach, he did so belabour
them and knock their heads together, that they were obliged to
cry out for assistance.

From this he fell into a deep melancholy and knew nobody. I
was told the last sensible words he uttered were on this occasion:
Mr Handel, when about to quit Ireland, went to take his leave of
him. The servant was a considerable time before he could make
the Dean understand; which, when he did, he cried, 'Oh, a
German and a genius! A prodigy! Admit him.' The servant did
so, just to let Mr Handel behold the ruins of the greatest wit that
ever lived along the tide of time, where all at length are lost.

[26] Swift's death and the rape of his locks, 19 October
1745; from *The Life of Doctor Swift* by Thomas Sheridan.

(Thomas Sheridan (1719–1788) was Swift's godson and the first
to publish his collected writings. He made his name as actor-
manager of Dublin's Smock Alley Theatre (see p. 226). His son,
Richard Brinsley Sheridan, brilliantly continued the family
tradition in London.)

The behaviour of the citizens on this occasion [*Swift's death*],
gave the strongest proof of the deep impression he had made on
their minds. Though he had been, for so many years, to all
intents and purposes dead to the world, and his departure from
that state seemed a thing rather to be wished than deplored, yet
no sooner was his death announced, than the citizens gathered
from all quarters, and forced their way in crowds into the house,
to pay the last tribute of grief to their departed benefactor.
Nothing but lamentations were heard all around the quarter
where he lived, as if he had been cut off in the vigour of his years.
Happy were they who first got into the chamber where he lay, to
procure, by bribes to the servants, locks of his hair, to be handed
down as sacred relicks to their posterity. And so eager were
numbers to obtain at any price this precious memorial, that in
less than an hour, his venerable head was entirely stripped of all
its silver ornaments, so that not a hair remained. He was buried
in the most private manner, according to directions in his will, in
the great aisle of St Patrick's Cathedral . . .

[27] Swift's epitaph; translated by W.B. Yeats.

(Swift's epitaph on himself is the Latin inscription in St Patrick's, above his tomb. Yeats called it 'the greatest epitaph in history'.)

> Swift has sailed into his rest;
> Savage indignation there
> Cannot lacerate his breast.
> Imitate him if you dare,
> World-besotted traveller; he
> Served human liberty.

[28] Sir Walter Scott visits St Patrick's; from *The Life of Sir Walter Scott* by J.G. Lockhart.

(The famous Scottish novelist visited Dublin in 1825 accompanied by his son-in-law and future biographer Lockhart (who is here writing to his wife). Scott was enthusiastically lionized by Dubliners, and reported to his friend, Maria Edgeworth, that he found the city 'splendid beyond my expectations'.)

... one thinks of nothing but Swift there – the whole cathedral is merely his tomb. Your papa [*i.e. Scott*] hung long over the famous inscription, which is in gilt letters upon black marble; and seemed vexed there was not a ladder at hand that he might have got nearer the bust (apparently a very fine one), by Roubilliac, which is placed over it. This was given by the piety of his printer, Faulkener. According to this, Swift had a prodigious double chin; and Peveril remarked that the severity of the whole countenance is much increased by the absence of the wig, which, in the prints, conceals the height and gloom of the brow, the uncommon massiveness and breadth of the temple-bones, and the Herculean style in which the head fits in to the neck behind. Stella's epitaph is on the adjoining pillar – close by. Sir Walter seemed not to have thought of it before (or to have forgotten, if he had), but to judge merely from the wording that Swift himself wrote it. She is described as 'Mrs Hester Johnson, better known to the world by the name of Stella, under which she is celebrated in the writings of Dr Jonathan Swift, Dean of this cathedral.' 'This,' said Sir Walter, 'the Dean might say – any one else would

A tourist admires the monument to Dean Swift in St Patrick's Cathedral; engraving from Walker's *Hibernian Magazine*, 1802

have said more.' She died in 1727, Swift in 1745. Just by the entrance to the transept, is his tablet in honour of the servant who behaved so well about the secret of the Drapier's letters.

[29] Thackeray attends morning service in St Patrick's; from *An Irish Sketchbook* by W.M. Thackeray.

(William Makepeace Thackeray, who had not yet made his name as a novelist, wrote his *Irish Sketchbook* in 1842 as a sequel to a *Paris Sketchbook*. The gaunt ruin he found was soon afterwards to be restored to its present form by the munificence of Sir Benjamin Guinness, later Lord Ardilaun.)

The service at Saint Patrick's is finely sung; and the shameless English custom of retreating after the anthem, is properly prevented by locking the gates, and having the music after the sermon. The interior of the cathedral itself, however, to an Englishman who has seen the neat and beautiful edifices of his own country, will be anything but an object of admiration. The greater part of the huge old building is suffered to remain in gaunt decay, and with its stalls of sham Gothic, and the tawdry old rags and gimcracks of the 'most illustrious order of Saint Patrick,' (whose pasteboard helmets, and calico banners, and lath swords, well characterize the humbug of chivalry which they are made to represent,) looks like a theatre behind the scenes. 'Paddy's Opera,' however, is a noble performance; and the Englishman may here listen to a half-hour sermon, and in the anthem to a bass singer whose voice is one of the finest ever heard.

Marsh's Library

[30] Swift's epitaph on Archbishop Marsh; from *All Graduates and Gentlemen* by Muriel McCarthy.

(The beautiful library adjoining St Patrick's, which contains many of Swift's books, was founded in 1700 by Narcissus Marsh, Provost of Trinity College and later Archbishop of Armagh, to provide a free library for scholars and dispel the dismal ignorance he found among his own Trinity students. Though one of Swift's earliest patrons, he did not earn his affection. Swift wrote this spiteful character study three years before Marsh's death.)

Marsh has the reputation of most profound and universal learning; this is the general opinion, neither can it be easily disproved. An old rusty iron-chest in a banker's shop, strongly lockt and wonderful heavy, is full of gold; this is the general opinion, neither can it be disproved, provided the key be lost, and what is in it be wedged so close that it will not by any motion discover the metal by the clinking. Doing good is his pleasure; and as no man consults another in his pleasures, neither does he in this . . . without all passions but fear, to which of all others he hath least temptation, having nothing to get or to lose; no posterity, relation or friend to be solicitous about; and placed by his station above the reach of fortune or envy . . . He is the first of human race, that with great advantages of learning, piety and station ever escaped being a man . . . He is so wise to value his own health more than other men's noses, so that the most honourable place at his table is much the worst, especially in summer . . . No man will be either glad or sorry at his death, except his successor.

The Liberties

[31] How the Liberties defend their boundaries; from the *Recollections* of John O'Keeffe.

(The Liberties had belonged originally to the Great Abbey of Thomas Court, but after its suppression by Henry VIII they were granted to his Chancellor, William Brabazon. His descendant, the Earl of Meath, settled large numbers of Huguenot weavers there, and it quickly became Dublin's most prosperous quarter, though not for long.

John O'Keeffe (1747–1835) was a Dublin actor and later an immensely popular London playwright. His *Recollections*, published in his extreme old age, give a delightfully rambling picture of his early Dublin life.)

In what is called the Earl of Meath's Liberty, the Lord Mayor of Dublin has no jurisdiction, this quarter of the town having a court of its own. This Liberty consists of some of the largest, finest, and richest streets in Dublin; for instance, Meath-street, Francis-street, and the Coombie. In the latter was the Weavers' Hall: over the gate a pedestrian gilt statue, as large as life, of George the Second. The Lord Mayor walked the boundaries, his sword-bearer before him; but when arrived at the point where the Liberty begins, he was met by a certain chosen number of people, who stopped his progress, and in a kind of seeming scuffle took the sword from the sword-bearer: if not thus prevented, and the Lord Mayor permitted to go on, wherever he went, with his sword of office borne before him, the power of his warrant would reach; but this ceremony is done without the least riot or ill-will, being part of the business previously well prepared. All this affair took place in one day, the first of August, every third year. To this grand triennial festival people flocked to Dublin from all parts of Ireland, England, Scotland, and even from the Continent: it was always looked to with great joy. The Regatta at Venice was something in this way.

[32] A plea for the weavers of the Liberties by Dean Swift; from *A Biography of Dublin* by Christine Longford.

(Some of the Liberties formed part of Swift's little 'kingdom' at St Patrick's. He wrote this poem for a benefit performance for the weavers who were already suffering the ruin of their trade by foreign imports. He also (as Letitia Pilkington shows on p. 92) practised charity from his own pocket to help them. After his death, their situation became increasingly desperate and they took drastic steps (see next extract) to discourage the wearing of foreign cloth.)

> We'll dress in manufactures made at home,
> Equip our kings and generals at the Combe.
> We'll rig in Meath Street Egypt's haughty queen,
> And Antony shall court her in rateen.
> In blue shalloon shall Hannibal be clad
> And Scipio trail an Irish purple plaid.
> In drugget dressed, of thirteen pence a yard,
> See Philip's son amidst his Persian guard;
> And proud Roxana, fired with jealous rage,
> With fifty yards of crape shall sweep the stage.

[33] The cutting weavers take their revenge; from *Irish Varieties* by J.D. Herbert.

Another party of lawless myrmidons were allowed frequently to commit the greatest enormities, with no further punishment than dispersion by a magistrate and soldiers; . . . These delinquents were weavers out of work, and they considered their want of employment proceeded from the fashion of wearing India nankeens, muslims and French silks. For the purpose of deterring persons from the wear of these articles of dress, they assembled in numerous bodies, and with knives made for the occasion, cut every foreign dress worn by man or woman, no matter of what rank, if they were walking, and, in some cases, have stopped carriages, and destroyed ladies' dresses, putting every one to the knife, and in terror and fear of their life; for they were so infuriate, that description faints in giving an adequate idea of the horror and alarm many suffered under this wild and savage-like operation. It was a fine field for the doctors: nervous fevers produced them an abundant harvest.

Another mode of revenge taken by the lads of the loom was seizing on some mercer, haberdasher, or tailor, who might have been the vendor or maker of these objectionable dresses; and when they got such a well-known character in their possession they hurried him along, to utter dismay or hope of escape of him or friends, until they had done with him. After dragging him through miry channels – for this practice was followed in muddy weather generally – they brought him perhaps to the Weaver's Square . . . in the Liberties of Dublin . . . There they stripped him naked; then with a brush, not camel's hair, they daubed him over with warm tar; then a bag of feathers was got, and everyone who could get at the victim stuck the feathers over him: then they led him in mock triumph through the Liberties, and, when saturated, let him get home if he was able . . .

[34] A clergyman surveys the Liberties in 1798; from *Report on the Population of Ireland* by James Whitelaw, quoted in Constantia Maxwell's *Dublin Under the Georges*.

(The Reverend James Whitelaw (1749–1813) was the rector of St Catherine's church in the Liberties, and spent his life working among the Dublin poor. He died of fever, caught from his parishioners, in 1813.)

The streets [in this part of the City] are generally narrow; the houses crowded together; the rears or back-yards of very small extent, and some without accommodation of any kind. Of these streets, a few are the residence of the upper class of shopkeepers or others engaged in trade; but a far greater proportion of them, with their numerous lanes and alleys, are occupied by working manufacturers, by petty shopkeepers, the labouring poor, and beggars, crowded together to a degree distressing to humanity. A single apartment in one of these truly wretched habitations, rates from one to two shillings per week, and to lighten this rent two, three, or even four families become joint tenants. As I was usually out at very early hours on the survey I have frequently surprised from ten to sixteen persons, of all ages and sexes, in a room not 15 feet square, stretched on a wad of filthy straw, swarming with vermin, and without any covering, save the wretched rags that constituted their wearing apparel.

This crowded population wherever it obtains is almost universally accompanied by a very serious evil – a degree of filth and stench inconceivable except by such as have visited these scenes of wretchedness. Into the backyard of each house, frequently not 10 feet deep, is flung from the windows of each apartment, the ordure and other filth of its numerous inhabitants; from which it is so seldom removed, that I have seen it nearly on a level with the windows of the first floor; and the moisture that, after heavy rains, oozes from this heap, having frequently no sewer to carry it off, runs into the street, by the entry leading to the staircase. One instance out of a thousand that might be given, will be sufficient. When I attempted in the summer of 1798 to take the population of a ruinous house in Joseph's Lane near Castle market, I was interrupted in my progress by an inundation of putrid blood, alive with maggots, which had from an adjacent slaughter yard burst the back door, and filled the hall to the depth of several inches. By the help of a plank and some stepping stones which I procured for the purpose (for the inhabitants without any concern waded through it) I reached the staircase. It had rained violently, and from the shattered state of the roof a torrent of water made its way through every floor, from the garret to the ground. The sallow looks and filth of the wretches who crowded round me indicated their situation, though they seemed insensible to the stench, which I could scarce sustain for a few minutes. In the garret I found the entire family of a poor working shoemaker, seven in number, lying in a fever, without a human being to administer to their wants. On observing that his apartment had not a door, he informed me that his landlord, finding him not able to pay the week's rent in consequence of his sickness, had the preceding Saturday taken it away, in order to force him to abandon the apartment. I counted in this style 37 persons; and computed, that its humane proprietor received out of an absolute ruin which should be taken down by the magistrate as a public nuisance, a profit rent of above £30 per annum, which he extracted every Saturday night with unfeeling severity. . . .

In July 1798 the entire side of a house 4 storeys high, in School-House Lane, fell from its foundation into an adjoining yard, where it destroyed an entire dairy of cows. I ascended the remaining ruin, through the usual approach of shattered stairs, stench and filth. The floors had all sunk on the side now unsupported, forming so many inclined planes; and I observed with astonishment, that the inhabitants, above 30 in number, who had escaped destruction by the circumstance of the wall falling outwards, had not deserted their apartments. I was informed, that it had remained some months in this situation, and that the humane landlord claimed, and actually received for it, the usual rent. . . .

[35] A Trinity student attends a meeting of the United Irishmen in the Tailors' Hall, 1791; from *Ireland Sixty Years Ago* by J.E. Walsh.

(John Walsh (1816–1865) was the Irish Attorney General and Master of the Rolls. His account of eighteenth-century Dublin, especially its underworld (pp. 316–8), was first published in 1849 and reprinted again and again. Here an anonymous student penetrates the so-called Back Lane Parliament set up by the United Irishmen, before they turned to revolution (see p. 69). The three men described all became leaders in the Rebellion of 1798: Hamilton Rowan fled, Tandy was sent to prison, and Wolfe Tone cut his throat with a penknife to escape execution.)

I entered college in the year 1791, a year rendered memorable by the institution of the society of the United Irishmen. They held their meetings in an obscure passage called Back-Lane, leading from Corn Market to Nicholas-street. The very aspect of the place seemed to render it adapted for cherishing a conspiracy. It was in the locality where the tailors, skinners, and curriers held their guilds, and was the region of the operative democracy. I one evening proceeded from college, and found out Back-lane, and having inquired for the place of meeting, a house was pointed out to me, that had been the hall in which the corporation of tailors held their assemblies. I walked in without hesitation – no one forbidding me – and found the society in full debate, the Hon. Simon Butler in the chair. I saw there, for the first time, the men with the three names, which were now become so familiar to the people of Dublin – Theobald Wolfe Tone, James Napper Tandy, and Archibald Hamilton Rowan.

The first was a slight effeminate-looking man, with a hatchet face, a long aquiline nose, rather handsome and genteel-looking, with lank, straight hair combed down on his sickly red cheek, exhibiting a face the most insignicant and mindless that could be imagined. His mode of speaking was in correspondence with his face and person. It was polite and gentlemanly, but totally devoid of any thing like energy or vigour. I set him down as a worthy, good-natured, flimsy man, in whom there was no harm, and as the least likely person in the world to do mischief to the state.

Tandy was the very opposite looking character. He was the ugliest man I ever gazed on. He had a dark, yellow, truculent-looking countenance, a long drooping nose, rather sharpened at the point, and the muscles of his face formed two cords at each side of it. He had a remarkable hanging-down look, and an occasional twitching or convulsive motion of his nose and mouth, as if he was snapping at something on the side of him while he was speaking.

Not so Hamilton Rowan. I thought him not only the most handsome, but the largest man I had ever seen. Tone and Tandy looked like pigmies beside him. His ample and capacious forehead seemed the seat of thought and energy; while with such an external to make him feared, he had a courtesy of manner that excited love and confidence. He held in his hand a large stick, and was accompanied by a large dog.

I had not been long standing on the floor, looking at and absorbed in the persons about me, when I was perceived, and a whisper ran round the room. Some one went up to the president, then turned round, and pointed to me. The president immediately rose, and called out that there was a stranger in the room. Two members advanced, and taking me under the arm, led me up to the president's chair, and there I stood to await the penalty of my unauthorized intrusion. I underwent an examination; and it was evident, from the questions, that my entrance was not accredited, but that I was suspected as a government spy. The 'battalion of testimony,' as it was called, was already formed, and I was supposed to be one of the corps. I, however, gave a full and true account of myself, which was fortunately confirmed by a member who knew something about me, and was ultimately pronounced a harmless 'gib,' and admitted to the honour of the sitting.

The arrest of Lord Edward FitzGerald in Thomas Street, 1798; cartoon by George Cruikshank, from W.H. Maxwell's *History of the Irish Rebellion*. Both Lord Edward and Major Sirr (firing) are buried in St Werburgh's church nearby

[36] The arrest of Lord Edward FitzGerald in Thomas Street; from *Ireland, its Scenery, Character etc.* by Mr and Mrs S.C. Hall.

(Anna Maria Hall, née Fielding, was born in Dublin in 1800, was taken to live in London aged fifteen, and became an immensely popular novelist and playwright especially for her stories and sketches of Irish society.

Lord Edward FitzGerald, described, here, was the son of the Duke of Leinster (see p. 69) and another of the leaders of the 1798 Rebellion. The mysterious theft of his dagger was explained long afterwards in Sheridan Lefanu's memoirs *Seventy Years of*

Irish Life (1893): his mother, Emma Lefanu, had stolen it on a patriotic impulse as a child from Major Swan's house in North Great George Street, and hidden it in her feather mattress.)

Many matters of melancholy interest are associated with 'the Liberties' of Dublin. The records of Thomas-street, and the streets in its immediate vicinity, might fill a volume. It was in this street that the gallant and unhappy Lord Edward Fitzgerald was taken, on the 19th of May, 1798. Major Sirr (town-major of the city), having received information that he was concealed in the house of a man named Murphy, a feather-dealer, in Thomas-street, proceeded, with a sufficient force, to arrest him. He was accompanied by Mr Ryan and Mr Swan, both officers of Yeomanry. The two burst into the small bedroom in which Lord Edward was sleeping, partly dressed. He was armed with a dagger, with which he mortally wounded Mr Ryan, having stabbed him in fourteen places, and severely injured Mr Swan. Mr Sirr entered while Mr Ryan and Lord Edward were struggling on the floor, and fired a pistol at his lordship; the ball entered the shoulder, and a short time afterwards, on the 3rd June, caused his death in the prison of Newgate. 'The dagger,' says Mr Moore, 'was given, by Lord Clare, a day or two after the arrest, to Mr Brown, a gentleman well known and still living in Dublin, who has by some accident lost it. He describes it to me, however, as being about the length of a large case-knife, with a common buck-handle, the blade, which was two-edged, being of a waved shape.' Of the room in which this tragic scene occurred, Mr McManus made a drawing, in 1838. He informs us that no change has taken place in its furniture or character since 1798, except that it has received a coat of whitewash – one part of it, however, having been left untouched; this spot is of about a foot square, nearly three feet from the ground. It is covered with large drops of faded blood. The room is small and square, with two windows and a fire-place projecting into one of the angles, – common in old Irish houses. Even the political enemies of Lord Edward Fitzgerald have rendered justice to his memory; and few men had more, or warmer friends. He was a brave enthusiast; who had unhappily imbibed republican principles by his connexion with France; but it is not too much to say that no 'traitor' ever more honestly believed in the justice of a cause or more conscientiously considered that 'rebellion' was duty to his country. With his sad fate, we trust, the evil genius of 'the Geraldines' for ever disappeared. The history of the family, from their first foot-tread in Ireland to the melancholy year '98, might form a volume more full of wonders than a folio of romance.

[37] Robert Emmett's rising in Thomas Street; from *Ireland in '98* by R.R. Madden.

(The abortive Emmett rising of 1803 provided a tragic coda to the 1798 Rebellion. Emmett, aged twenty-four, was captured in his hiding-place at Harolds Cross a few weeks later, and executed outside St Catherine's church in Thomas Street (see next extract). His famous speech at his trial, 'Let no man write my epitaph', earned him a place in the pantheon of Irish revolutionary heroes.)

On the morning of the appointed day, June 23, 1803, the Kildare men were seen directing their steps towards the capital. They had collected round one of the depots in Thomas Street in unusual crowds, when about five o'clock they were persuaded by their officers to return home. Here treachery began. It is highly probable that its full extent was never known to Emmett, who was of a trusting, sanguine nature, constitutionally opposed to suspecting his fellow-men, and so single-minded that he regarded others with whom he was acting as like himself. The defection of the Wicklow and Wexford followers would have deterred a less ardent spirit than Emmett's from proceeding. He never quailed under the disappointment, though he bitterly felt the pain of their disloyalty. Towards dusk he directed the distribution of pikes to the waiting crowds in Thomas Street, and proceeded to make the necessary arrangements for the contemplated attack. The different leaders received their instructions; the forces were assembled in their respective places. These were to act on the signal of a rocket, which Emmett was to send up when he considered the time had arrived for the commencement of hostilities; Emmett and two of his followers were to head the attack on the Castle. At eight o'clock they sallied out of the depot in Thomas Street, and were met by ringing cheers from the insurgents. The consternation excited by their presence was vivid: every avenue was thronged, every window had its inquisitive heads; shopkeepers ran to their doors and beheld with amazement a lawless band of armed insurgents in the midst of a peaceable city, an hour at least before dark. The scene at first might have appeared amusing to a careless spectator, but when a rocket ascended and burst over the heads of the people, the aspect of affairs underwent a wonderful change. The impulse of the moment was self-preservation; those who a few moments before seemed to look on with vacant wonder, now assumed a face of horror and fled with precipitation. The wish to escape was simultaneous, and the eagerness with which the people retreated impeded their own flight, as they crowded upon one another down alleys, courtways and lanes, while the screams of women and children were heartrending. 'To the Castle!' shouted the enthusiastic leader, drawing his sword, while his followers clustered at his heels. On they went, but on reaching the Market-house his adherents visibly diminished. On looking round him, he found hardly fifty to sustain him in his reckless attempt to storm the citadel. Among those who were left, a thirst for outrage and revenge had destroyed all discipline and supplanted patriotism. He hastened from front to rear, from man to man, in vain endeavours to quell disorder. Their worst passions, inflamed by the whisky with which they had plied themselves, had brutalised them. 'Our cause is lost!' exclaimed Emmett, snatching a rocket which a man was about to send up, and trampling it under his foot; 'let our friends at a distance escape; comrades, provide for your own safety.'

[38] Emmett's execution outside St Catherine's church; from R.R. Madden's *Ireland in '98*.

The scaffold on which the young martyr [*Emmett*] suffered was a mere temporary arrangement, consisting of a few boards laid across a number of empty barrels, that were placed for this purpose nearly in the middle of the street. Through this platform rose two posts, fifteen feet high, and a traverse beam was placed across them. Underneath the beam, about three feet from the platform, was a single narrow plank supported on two ledges, on which the prisoner was to stand at the moment of being launched into eternity. The platform was about six feet from the ground, and was ascended by a ladder.

When Emmett alighted from the carriage, and was led to the foot of the scaffold, his arms being tied, he was assisted to ascend by the executioner, but he mounted quickly and with apparent alacrity. He addressed a few words to the crowd in a firm, sonorous voice, avoiding any reference to political matters, or to the events with which his fate was connected. He merely said: 'My friends, I die in peace, and with sentiments of universal love and kindness towards all men.' He then shook hands with some friends who were near, presented his watch to the executioner, and removed his stock. The immediate preparations for execution were then carried into effect; he assisted in adjusting the rope round his neck, and was then placed on the plank underneath the beam, with the cap drawn over his face; but he contrived to raise his hand and partly remove the cap, and spoke a few words in a low tone to the executioner. The cap was replaced, and he stood with a handkerchief in his hand, the fall of which was to be the signal for the last act of the finisher of the law. After standing on the plank for a few seconds, the executioner asked, 'Are you ready, sir?' One of his friends who stood close by distinctly heard Robert Emmett say in reply, 'Not yet.' There was another momentary pause – no signal was given; again the executioner repeated the question, and the reply 'Not yet,' was given. The question was put a third time, and the same gentleman who gave the report, heard Emmett pronounce the word 'Not–'; but before he had time to utter another word, the executioner tilted one end of the plank off the ledge, and a human being, full of genius, patriotism, and truth, was dangling like a dog, writhing in the agonies of the most revolting and degrading of all deaths. . . .

After hanging for a moment motionless, life terminated with one convulsive movement of the body. At the expiration of the usual time the remains were taken down, and extended on the scaffold. The head was struck from the body, grasped by the hair, and paraded along the front of the gallows by the hangman, proclaiming to the multitude, 'This is the head of a traitor!' Near the scaffold, where the blood had fallen on the pavement from between the planks of the platform, some dogs collected, lapping up the blood; more than one spectator loitered about, and, when the soldiers drove the dogs away, dipped their handkerchiefs in the blood. . . .

The execution of Robert Emmett outside St Catherine's church, 1803;
a contemporary Dublin painting

[39] A 'thieves' kitchen' in the Liberties; from the *Autobiography* of William Carleton.

(William Carleton (1794–1869), later famous for his stories and novels of Irish peasant life, arrived in Dublin in 1804 to seek his fortune, lost his job and his lodgings and, almost penniless, was directed to an unusual refuge for the night.)

The man put threepence into my hand, and desiring me to follow him, went to the door of a cellar exactly over the way; at this he kicked and, on its being opened, told me I might pass the night there.

'I am putting you into very respectable company,' said he, 'so be sure and conduct yourself like a gentleman.'

The cellar was very spacious; I should think that the entrance into Dante's Inferno was paradise compared with it. I know and have known Dublin now for about half a century, better probably than any other man in it. I have lived in the Liberty and in every close and outlet in the City of the Panniers, driven by poverty to the most wretched of its localities, and I must confess that the scene which burst upon me that night stands beyond anything the highest flight of my imagination could have conceived. Burns must have witnessed something of the sort, or he could never have written the most graphic and animated of all his productions – 'The Jolly Beggars'.

When I got down to the cellar and looked about me, I was struck, but only for an instant, by the blazing fire which glowed in the grate. My eyes then ran over the scene about me, but how to describe it is the difficulty. It resembled nothing I ever saw before or since. The inmates were mostly in bed, both men and women, but still a good number of them were up, and indulging in liquors of every description, from strong whiskey downwards. The beds were mostly what are called 'shakedowns' – that is, simple straw, sometimes with a rag of sheet, sometimes with none. There were there the lame, the blind, the dumb, and all who suffered from actual and natural infirmity; but in addition to these, there was every variety of impostor about me – most of them stripped of their mechanical accessories of deceit.

If not seen, the character of those assembled and their conduct could not possibly be believed. This was half a century ago, when Dublin was swarming with street beggars and impostors of every possible description. This, I understood afterwards, was one of the cellars to which these persons resorted at night, and there they flung off all the restraints imposed on them during the course of the day. I learned afterwards that there were upwards of two dozen such nightly haunts in the suburban parts of the city. Crutches, wooden legs, artificial cancers, scrofulous necks, artificial wens, sore legs, and a vast variety of similar complaints were hung up on the walls of the cellars, and made me reflect upon the degree of perverted talent and ingenuity that must have been necessary to sustain such a mighty mass of imposture. The songs and the gestures were infamous, but if one thing puzzled me more than another, it was the fluency and originality of blackguardism as expressed in language. In fact, these people possessed an indecent slang, which constituted a kind of language known only to themselves, and was never spoken except at such orgies as I am describing. Several offered me seats and were very respectful, but I preferred standing, at least for a time, that I might have a better view of them. While I was in this position, a couple of young vagabonds – pickpockets, of course – came and stood beside me. Instinct told me their object, but as I knew the amount in my purse – one penny – I felt little apprehension of having my pockets picked. On entering the cellar I had to pay twopence for my bed, so that I had just one penny left.

How the night passed I need not say. Of course I never closed my eyes; but, so soon as the first glimpse of anything like light appeared, I left the place and went out on my solitary rambles through the city.

[40] An American doctor in the Liberties in 1844; James Johnson, quoted in *Dear, Dirty Dublin, A City in Distress* by Joseph O'Brien.

Dublin – rent and split – worm-eaten, mouldering, patched and plastered – unsightly to the eye, unsavoury to the taste, and not very grateful to the olfactories – here there is but one step from magnificence to misery, from the splendid palace to the squalid hovel. . . .

. . . [And on the Liberties] winds and rain have *liberty* to enter freely through the windows of half the houses – the pigs have *liberty* to ramble about – the landlord has *liberty* to take possession of most of his tenements – the silk-weaver has *liberty* to starve or beg.

[41] A Frenchwoman in the Liberties in the 1880s, and a visit to the Guinness brewery; from *Three Months in Ireland* by Madame de Bovet.

(Anne Marie de Bovet, daughter of a famous French general, made her name as a literary critic and travel-writer. Her *Lettres d'Irlande* were first published in 1889.)

To see the abject squalor of Dublin in its very depths one has only to walk along by St Patrick's, and particularly the street which joins the two cathedrals – a street consisting of two rows of tumbledown, mouldy-looking houses, reeking of dirt, and oozing with the disgusting smell of accumulated filth of many generations, with old petticoats hung up instead of curtains, and very often instead of glass in the dilapidated windows. On each ground floor, shops with overhanging roofs, and resembling dirty cellars, expose for sale sides of rancid bacon, bundles of candles and jars of treacle – a delicacy as much sought after as soap is neglected – greens, cauliflowers, musty turnips and bad potatoes; while at every three doors is a tavern, which in the midst of these hovels resembles a palace. Every other house is an old-clothes' shop, where the sale of the above-mentioned rags is combined with money-lending at large interest. Shoes that are taken out of pawn there on Saturday night for Sunday mass are pledged again on Monday morning. Business is as brisk there all Sunday as it is during the week. . . .

On the pavements, strewn with vegetable-refuse and other mess, a permanent market is held. There are barrels of red herrings, pickled in brine: flat baskets, in which are spread out the most disgusting bits of meat that one can possibly imagine; stale cows' feet; overkept sheeps' heads, bits of flabby pink veal, tripe, intestines, skins, and fat of every animal eatable and otherwise – refuse that no well-trained dog would touch. . . . But all these ragged and vermin-covered people are most affable; there are none of those fierce looks, those looks of hatred with which in other countries the poor welcome 'the rich' who happen to have missed their way among them; on the contrary, they are very pleased when ladies and gentlemen think it worth while to visit them. They look at them with a curiosity which is neither low-bred nor insolent, require very little encouragement to be made to talk, and willingly shake hands with the good-natured stranger who will sacrifice his gloves. Far from being ashamed of their rags, they are proud of being looked at; pretty, fair, or red-haired girls, whose freshness has not yet been spoilt by bad air, insufficient food, or drinking to excess, nudge each other, laughing and blushing; cheeky children come and stare at you, under your very nose, and vanish like a flock of sparrows if you pretend to be angry; mothers smile at you gratefully if you glance tenderly at the baby.

One should not leave the Liberties without visiting the immense industrial establishment which, on the confines of this miserable quarter, represents the fortune of Dublin. I mean the Guinness Brewery, where is manufactured the black beer called stout, or porter, which looks like bottled blacking, and in every part of the world where the English language is spoken is the rival of Bass and Co's pale ale. Founded in 1750, the Guinness Brewery has, during the last fifty years, grown to such proportions that in 1885 its business transactions were five times greater than in 1837. One can form some idea of what this is from the fact that three years ago the business was sold for six millions sterling to a company, Sir Edward Cecil Guinness, Bart, remaining Chairman of the Board. By way of a joke, people say that Dublin beer is black because it is made with the water of the Liffey. The truth is, that its colour as well as its peculiar taste is due to the malt having been first roasted.... To reduce [the barley] to malt it is soaked for two or three days in vats, then it is left in the air to sprout, after which it is dried and baked in an oven. The malt is then warehoused in air-tight rooms till the moment it is wanted. The brick building used for this purpose is the largest in Dublin, and can hold a million bushels. After being carefully winnowed, the malt is crushed by metal rollers, and then macerated with warm water. From this process comes an insipid and colourless must, removed by suction pumps into copper boilers that hold nearly twenty-two thousand gallons, where it is boiled with hops which give a bitter taste to the malt liquor.... The mixture then passes through pipes into refrigerators, whence, once reduced to a proper temperature, it is again poured into vats, where it comes into contact with yeast. It is then that fermentation is produced, the result being the decomposition of the saccharine matter into alcohol. This operation, which lasts from three to four days, is overlooked by excise-men, and the sum received by the Treasury in this way comes to a daily amount of 1200*l*. The vats are twenty-seven in number, and together hold over a million gallons.

The visitor who has the curiosity to poke his nose through one of the openings made in the side may have a very good idea of the feelings the Duke of Clarence experienced when he was drowning in the butt of Malmsey, with this difference, that if he fell headlong into this seething frothy mixture, he would be asphyxiated by the carbonic acid gas it gives off, before he could arrive at the surface. It would be a very pleasant way of committing suicide. Before one has experienced it one can form no idea of the strength of the fermenting fumes of stout, nor of the delicious perfume that emanates from it – absolutely different from that of any other spirituous liquor. After a vat is emptied the washers are obliged to wait four and twenty hours before they can enter it. One second of it is enough to turn you dizzy, and two to make you insensible. . . .

Kilmainham

[42] The founding of the Royal Hospital at Kilmainham –
Charles II's letter to James, Duke of Ormonde, 1679; from
'The Hospitals at Kilmainham' in *The Dublin Historical
Record*, Vol. 20.

(The first Duke of Ormonde, who ruled Ireland as Lord
Lieutenant on and off from 1661 to 1684, was responsible for
many of Dublin's greatest improvements: Kilmainham, Phoenix
Park, King's Hospital (originally for old men and boys), the
layout of the Quays.)

Whereas many of the soldiers in our army in Ireland, who are
grown aged, or otherwise unserviceable, are yet continued in our
pay for want of some fitting provision for their livelihood and
maintenance — Our will and pleasure, therefore, is, and we do
hereby authorize and require you to cause deduction of sixpence
in the pound to be from time to time made out of all the pay that
from and after the 29th day of March last, shall grow due by the
present, or any future establishment, to any person or persons
whatsoever upon our military list in our said Kingdom.

And we do hereby give unto you full power and authority from
time to time, to issue and employ the same towards the building
and settling an hospital for such aged and maimed officers and
soldiers as shall be dismissed out of our army as unserviceable
men, and for making provision for their future maintenance, in
such way and manner as you shall think fit.

[43] The Duke of Ormonde's farewell toast; from *Ireland
under the Stuarts* by Richard Bagwell.

(James, Duke of Ormonde (see previous extract) was a devoted
servant of Charles II whom he had followed into exile; but he was
dismissed as Lord Lieutenant by James II in 1785, and gave this
farewell toast in Kilmainham.)

As soon as the bad news reached him, Ormonde called the
Council together. All leave was stopped, officers were ordered to

their quarters, and on the following day King James was proclaimed with great pomp, but with many gloomy forebodings among the Protestants of Dublin. The Lord Lieutenant's commission expired with Charles II, Lord Granard and Archbishop Boyle remaining Lords Justices. But Ormonde gave a dinner to all the officers then in Dublin, at the Royal Hospital, just built most appropriately upon the site once occupied by the Priory of St John and dedicated to the use of worn-out soldiers. Raising his glass, he said. 'Look here, gentlemen! They say at Court that I am now become an old doating fool; you see my hand doth not shake, nor does my heart fail, nor doubt but I will make some of them see their mistake,' and so drank the new King's health. He then left Ireland for the last time. On the road he chanced to see in the *Gazette* that his regiment of horse had been given to Richard Talbot without any notice to him. Many of those Protestants who were in a position to do so, followed their protector to England, many sought the colonies, and the shadow of coming change was over those that remained.

[44] Extracts from the records of the Hospital at Kilmainham; from *The Dublin Historical Record*, Vol. 20.

1693 Apr. 7 – Ordered that each soldier in the Hospital be allowed 2d. every week for buying tobacco.

1700 Dec. 16 – Ordered – That it be an established rule, that if any soldier of the Hospital shall presume to marry, he be immediately turned out of the house and the Hospital clothes taken from him.

1703 Sep. 22 – The Governors are of the opinion that Sir Patrick Dun, Physician of the Hospital and Mr Peter Goodwin, the Providore, be directed to settle a particular table for more suitable diet for such soldiers, who by reason of their age or other infirmities or distempers, cannot eat the common food . . .

1706 Dec. 17 – For the better preservation and attendance of the soldiers, many having been lost for want of a surgeon being at hand to bleed them or apply other remedies, the Master appointed Robert Curtis, Surgeon's Mate, Resident Surgeon of the Hospital.

1710 Dec. 11 – The Governors taking into consideration the

clothing of the decayed officers, and what particulars will be fit to be provided for them in order to their decent appearing at the Hospital as Commissioned Officers – Resolved – That each Officer be furnished with a scarlet coat, an Athlone hat laced with gold lace, and a pair of blue worsted stockings, to be paid out of the pay of each officer.

1769 Nov. 29 – It appearing that numbers of the soldiers (especially those who come from abroad) are violently afflicted with scorbutic disorders – being advised, we also approving of the same, that Lucan Spa Water may be of great service to them, and therefore of opinion that a car with proper vessels and a horse, should be immediately provided and maintained at the hospital for this sanitary purpose.

1802 Jan. 12 – Ordered that on Christmas Day, St Patrick's Day and the King's Birthday, each man should receive a double allowance of rations and two quarts of ale in lieu of beer.

[45] John Wesley visits Kilmainham Hospital in 1794; from *Wesley His Own Biographer* (extracts from his *Journals*).

(John Wesley, the famous evangelical preacher and founder of Methodism, visited Ireland more than twenty times between 1747 and 1768, but made little impact on the religious views of its citizens.)

Thursday, 20. – I saw Dr Stephen's Hospital, far cleaner and sweeter than any I had seen in London, and the Royal Hospital for old soldiers, standing on the top of an hill overlooking Phoenix Park. All the buildings are kept not only in good repair, but likewise exactly clean. The hall is exceeding grand: the chapel far better finished than anything of the kind in Dublin. O what is wanting to make these men happy? Only the knowledge and the love of God.

[46] Parnell in Kilmainham Jail; from *Recollections* by William O'Brien.

(Charles Stewart Parnell led the Irish Parliamentary Party in the great struggle for Home Rule at the end of the nineteenth century. He was arrested in 1881 for his part in the Land League Agitation, and sent to Kilmainham. William O'Brien (1852–1928) was one of Parnell's most militant supporters, editor of the Land League's journal, *The United Irishman*, and arrested along with him. He later voted against Parnell in the great party split of 1891, but after Parnell's death helped to reunify the party. He wrote several books of reminiscence in his old age.)

The period of repose, in the hope of which I welcomed the cells of Kilmainham, proved thus to be one of the most laboriously active passages of a pretty active life. But it was sweetened by an exhilaration of combat and a companionship with revered and trusty men, and, it must be added, a rugged courtesy on the part of our captor, which leave me scarcely a single memory of those six prison months that it is not a personal luxury to recall. . . . Mr Forster's prison arrangements were unquestionably humane. All the prisoners were allowed to mingle together freely in the prison yards during the abundant hours of exercise; to smoke their pipes, to read their newspapers, to play at hand-ball, or, if their tastes were more sedentary, at chess or dominoes, and to have their meals supplied by a friendly restaurateur (or, as it happened, restaurateuse).

There was, indeed, one element of serpentlike calculation mixed with Mr Forster's dovelike prison arrangements. The exultant remark he let drop about the prodigal expenditure of the League funds by the Ladies' Land League lets out the secret. As the suspects were allowed to get in their meals from outside, the privilege cost the League funds £1 a week per suspect, and Forster had only to fill his jails with a sufficient number of prisoners to deplete the League exchequer by over £1000 a week, which was the figure the support of the prisoners had actually reached in the November of 1881. But there once more Mr Forster challenged an encounter with an antagonist against whom he was but poorly matched. Parnell at once saw the game, and with an unswerving instinct made his move. He passed the word through all the jails that the suspects, after a date named, would go back to prison fare, in order to spare the Land League funds the crushing burden of their support. Needless to say, he himself set the example. The food question was, indeed, with him at all times of a profound unconcern worthy of the traditional Irish contempt for 'the dirty belly.' It was the mechanically

Recreation time in Kilmainham Jail for Parnell and his followers;
from *The Illustrated London News*, 1881

ingenious view of the prison fare question, as of most other things, that chiefly interested him. The prison fare included twice a week a lump of inferior beef per man, and Parnell conceived the project of pooling all our lumps of beef together in a common pot, from which, with the aid of broken bread and of the vegetables fished out of the prison soup of the previous day's dietary, he concocted a famous dish of Irish stew. He and Dr Kenny collaborated in producing this curious mess, over which, I am afraid, we grimaced more than over the unadorned prison food, but which was to the cooks a source of never-failing joy and pride . . .

It has been mentioned that six or eight of us were lodged together in 'a concentration camp,' of which Parnell's room was the dining-room and the club-window. It has often been a matter of bitter regret that I took no notes of our *noctes coenaeque* around the Chief's frugal table. At the time and for many a year after, anything I might put in writing was liable to seizure and official scrutiny, with the unfortunate result that my diaries were kept mostly in uneventful periods when they were least useful. Not, indeed, that Parnell was in the smallest degree a professor of table-talk. He would have been the last to understand Dr Johnson's passion for 'talking for victory.' He was much more truly an admirer of Biggar's immortal axiom of obstruction: 'Never talk except in Government time.' At table, as everywhere else, he was simple, genial, unpretentious. But he was in the habit of dropping pregnant sayings, for any record of which surer than my own memory I would now give much. . . .

There was no subject on which Parnell better loved to chat than America and the American Revolution. He would delight to trace Washington through his constant retreats and devices for avoiding battle, holding that to his willingness to decamp and play an inglorious waiting-game it was due that the insurrection was not promptly suppressed by the troops. 'Washington would be a highly unpopular leader in Ireland,' he would say, with a smile. For the United States of our day, bursting with youthful energy and rude strength, he had the admiration of one who was half American by blood and five-sixths in sympathy. He would always topple over Mr O'Kelly's calculations of disaster to England from France or Russia with the observation: 'Pooh! The United States are the only people that could smash England.

They may even be the means of freeing Ireland without the smashing.' . . .

Parnell's superstitions have been frequently and unduly dwelt upon. They always seemed to me whimsicalities that amused him, rather than beliefs that had any real influence. His objection to the colour green was genuine, and often laughable; but arose, in my judgment, chiefly from a fear of arsenical poisoning. 'How could you expect a country to have luck that has green for its colour!' he once said. When I reminded him that green, as the National colour, dated no farther back than the United Irishmen, and that until then the Irish ensign was supposed to be blue, he responded smiling: 'It's just the same – blue is more than half green.' A lady worked for him, while he was in prison, a superb eider-down quilt, covered with green satin, with his monogram worked in gold bullion – a present worthy of a king. I am sure he must have sent a sweet and gracious acknowledgement, but the gorgeous quilt never rested on his bed. It was hidden away carefully underneath a press, where, I am afraid, the mice soon tarnished its glory. Lady devotees sent him innumerable other marks of homage worked in the dangerous colour – embroidered smoking-caps, tea-coseys, and even bright green hosiery. The latter he insisted resolutely on destroying; the others he distributed freely among his brother-prisoners, until almost every man in the prison, except himself, had his green tasselled turban and green woollen vests. . . .

His terror of contagious disease was very real indeed. One evening, I happened to mention at dinner that I had got a note informing me that two of my sub-editor's children were down with scarlatina. 'My God! O'Brien,' he cried, almost in a panic, 'what did you do with the letter?' When I told him it was still in my pocket, he begged of me instantly to throw it into the fire. Seeing how genuine was his concern, I did so. 'Now,' said he, 'wash your hands.' This time I found it difficult to avoid smiling. He bounded from the dinner-table, and with his own hands emptied the water ewer into the basin on the wash-hand-stand. 'For God's sake, O'Brien, quick!' he cried, holding out the towel towards me, with an earnestness that set the whole company in a roar. He returned to his dinner in a state of supreme satisfaction. 'Buckshot,' he said, 'is not going to get rid of us so cheaply as that.'

[47] Johnny Cassidy visits Kilmainham Jail with his
uncle; from *Pictures in the Hallway* by Sean O'Casey.

(Sean O'Casey (1880–1964) came from a lower-middle-class
Protestant Dublin family, which fell into acute poverty after his
father's early death. This episode comes from the second book
of his six-volume autobiography, which charts his sickly childhood, his work as a Dublin labourer, his involvement in the
trade-union struggles led by Larkin (see p. 273) and his final
emergence as the Abbey Theatre's most brilliant playwright
since John Synge. His avowed aim in writing his autobiography
was 'to make gold embroidery of dancin' words'.)

There it was. A great, sombre, silent stone building, sitting like a
toad watching the place doing its ragged middle-aged minuet. A
city of cells. A place where silence is a piercing wail; where
discipline is an urgent order from heaven; where a word of
goodwill is as far away as the right hand of God; where the
wildest wind never blows a withered leaf over the wall; where a
black sky is as kind as a blue sky; where a hand-clasp would be
low treason; where a warder's vanished frown creates a carnival;
where there's a place for everything, and everything in its
improper place; where a haphazard song can never be sung;
where the bread of life is always stale; where God is worshipped
warily; and where loneliness was a frightened, hunted thing.

His uncle pulled his coat open showing the Crimea medal
shining on his waistcoat, with two bars striding across the
coloured ribbon. They went through the iron gateway leading to
the main door of the jail, the ready way in and the tardy way out,
a heavy thick iron gate set deep, desperately deep, into solid
stone, with a panel of five scorpions wriggling round each other
carved out of the stone that formed the fanlight that gave no light
to the poisoned city of Zion inside. As Johnny and his uncle came
near, the heavy thing swung open, and a warder stood there,
with the Crimea medal glittering on his breast, and a hand
stretched out to greet Tom, who seized it and held it for a long
time.

– Come along in, Tom, me son, and your young friend, said
the warder. You're welcome, he's welcome, you're both as
welcome as the rooty call blowing for dinner.

They went inside to the courtyard, the heavy thing swung

back again, and Johnny was installed as a freeman among the prisoners and captives.

They went into the central hall, and, standing on the flagged floor, gazed at the three tiers of cells, with narrow railed lobbies on the first and second floors, and a narrow steel stairway leading to each of them.

– It's a great sight, said the warder, to see the prisoners coming in, in single file, step be step, hands straight be their sides, over a hundhred of them, quiet an' meek, marching right, left, right, left, each turning into his own little shanty when he comes to it; with half a dozen warders standing on the alert, and the sound of the steel doors clanging to, like the sound of waves on a frozen sea, all shut up safely for the night, to read their Bible or stretch themselves down and count the days to come before the Governor dismisses them and wishes them godspeed. Here, me lad, he said, opening a cell door, have a decko at the nice little home we provide for them who can't keep their hands from pickin' an' stealin' . . . Go on in, me lad – no fear o' the door closing on them who are the friends of those sent by the Queen for the punishment of evildoers.

Johnny went a little way into the cell, with his heart beating. It was spick and span, the little stool scrubbed till it was shining like a dull diamond, and the floor spotless. A slop-pail stood to attention in a corner; over it a tiny shelf holding a piece of yellow soap and a black-covered Bible, showing that cleanliness was next to godliness; and a tiny grating to the side of the door, letting the air through to keep the cell fresh and wholesome; all, in the night, lighted up by a baby-tongued flicker of gas in a corner . . .

– Here's something to see, said the warder, showing a fairly-sized room, lighted with two arched windows, for this is the room where Parnell was kept when we had him prisoner here. A man, he went on, if ever there was one, a sowl man. The least little thing you done for him, it was always thank-you, thank-you, from him even when you opened the door before you locked him up for the night. A sowl man, I'm tellin' you, Tomas, an honour to do anything for him, he was that mannerly, even to us, mind you, that you'd fall over yourself in thryin' to please him; and never the icy glint in his eye, unless the name of some big bug in the opposite camp was mentioned; oh, be Jasus, then the flame in his eye 'ud freeze you, ay, man, an' shook hands when he was leaving, too; imagine that, Tom, shook hands with us that was busy holdin' him down, though no-one in this world, ay, or in the next either, could really hold Parnell down; for even in here he was more dangerous than he was roamin' about outside, a deal more dangerous, for, with Parnell a prisoner, the Irish 'ud stop at nothin', ay, an' well he knew it – an' one of us, too, Tom, me boy.

  – How one of us? asked Uncle Tom.

  – Why a protestant, man, makin' him fair an' equally one of ourselves. Not fit to do anything for themselves, the roman catholics must have a protestant to lead them. Looka at them now, an' Parnell gone! Gulpin' down the sacrament while they're tryin' to get at each other's throats; furiously tetherin' themselves to the roar o' ruin; twistin' into a tangle everything that poor Parnell had straightened out, with the hope of ever standing up against a single law that England likes to make gone for ever!

Dublin
North of the River

Phoenix Park

[48] The Duke of Ormonde saves Phoenix Park from Charles II's mistress, Lady Castlemaine, in 1663; from Thomas Carte's *Life of James, Duke of Ormonde.*

(Thomas Carte (1696–1754) was a highly controversial Jacobite historian whose defence of Charles I and the later Stuarts brought him into frequent conflicts with the Whigs. At one point he fled to France. His great *Life* of Ormonde was an extension of his Stuart sympathies – and he collected a vast mass of original documents for it. In Dr Johnson's view, however, he 'diffused the matter in too many words'.)

The Countess of *Castlemaine*, whose understanding bore no proportion to her power, . . . had occasion of resentment against the Duke of *Ormonde*, and at this time, as well as at all others, whenever an opportunity offered, did him all the ill offices that were in her power. She had obtained of the King a warrant for the grant of the *Phoenix* park and house near *Dublin*, which was the only place of retirement in the summer season for a chief Governor; and the more necessary at that time, when his Grace coming over, found the castle of *Dublin* so out of repair, and in such a miserable condition, after the neglect of it during the late usurpation, that it did not afford him sufficient accommodations. The Lord Lieutenant refused to pass this warrant, stopped the Grant, and prevailed with his Majesty to enlarge the park by the purchase of 450 acres of land adjoining in *Chapel Izod* of the Lord Chancellor *Eustace*, and to fit up the house for the convenience of himself and his successors in the government of *Ireland*. This incensed the Lady *Castlemaine* so highly, that upon his Grace's return to *England*, meeting him in one of the apartments about Court, she without any manner of regard to the place or company, fell upon him with a torrent of abusive language, loaded him with all the reproaches that the rancour of her heart could suggest, or the folly of her tongue could utter, and told him in fine, that she hoped to live to see him hanged. The Duke heard all unmoved, and only made her this memorable reply; 'that he was not in so much haste to put an end to her days, for all he wished with regard to her was, that he might live to see her old.'

[49] The Phoenix becomes a people's park in the 1770s; from *Dublin Old and New* by Stephen Gwynn.

(This complaint from the *Freeman's Journal* recalls the strict reign of Nathaniel Clements as Ranger of Phoenix Park. Clements designed and built the handsome classical Ranger's Lodge (1751) which later was expanded to become the Vice-regal Lodge, and is now Aras an Uachtaran, the residence of the Irish President.)

Under the rule of Mr Clements every impropriety was rigorously expelled from that beautified spot. Ill-looking strollers of either sex could never get admittance at the gate except on public occasions. Cars and noddies [the cheapest form of shay] were refused passage. But now the gates are opened wide to Tag, Rag and Bobtail. The Sabbath is abused by permitting a hurling match to be played there every Sunday evening, which is productive of blasphemous speaking, riot, drunkenness, broken heads and dislocated bones, among ten thousand of the lower class; and meanwhile the deer are hunted by detached parties of these vagrants and their dogs.

[50] A sham battle in Phoenix Park, in the 1820s; from Charles Lever's novel, *Jack Hinton, the Guardsman*.

(The Fifteen Acres – now playing-fields – opposite the Vice-regal Lodge were the venue for military drill and manoeuvres in the eighteenth and nineteenth centuries, which provided an immensely popular spectacle for Dubliners. Here a manoeuvre gets out of hand.)

Winding along the quays, we crossed an old and dilapidated bridge; and after traversing some narrow and ruinous-looking streets, we entered the Park, and at length reached the Fifteen Acres.

The carriages were drawn up in line; his Grace's led horses

were ordered up, and staff-officers galloped right and left to announce the orders for the troops to stand to arms. . . . The manoeuvres of the day included a sham battle; and scarcely had his excellency passed down the line, when preparations for the engagement began. The heavy artillery was seen to limber up, and move slowly across the field, accompanied by a strong detachment of cavalry; columns of infantry were marched hither and thither with the most pressing and eager haste; orderly dragoons and staff-officers galloped to and fro like madmen; red-faced plethoric little colonels bawled out the word of command, till one feared they might burst a blood-vessel; and already two companies of light infantry might be seen stealing cautiously along the skirts of the wood, with the apparently insidious design of attacking a brigade of guns. As for me, I was at one moment employed carrying despatches to Sir Charles Asgill, at another conveying intelligence to Lord Harrington; these, be it known, being the rival commanders, whose powers of strategy were now to be tested before the assembled and discriminating citizens of Dublin. Not to speak of the eminent personal hazard of a service which required me constantly to ride between the lines of contending armies, the fatigue alone had nigh killed me. Scarcely did I appear breathless at head quarters on my return from one mission, when I was despatched on another. Tired and panting, I more than once bungled my directions, and communicated to Sir Charles the secret intentions of his lordship, while with a laudable impartiality I disarranged the former's plans by a total misconception of the orders. Fatigue, noise, chagrin, and incessant worry, had so completely turned my head, that I became perfectly incapable of the commonest exercises of reason. Part of the artillery I ordered into a hollow, where I was told to station a party of riflemen. Three squadrons of cavalry I desired to charge up a hill, which the seventy-first highlanders were to have scrambled up if they were able. Light dragoons I posted in situations so beset with brushwood and firs, that all movement became impossible; and, in a word, when the signal-gun announced the commencement of the action, my mistakes had introduced such a new feature into tactics, that neither party knew what his adversary was at. . . .

In the midst of all this confusion, a new element of discord suddenly displayed itself. That loyal corps, the Cork militia, who were ordered up to attack close to where the Duke and his staff were standing, deemed that no better moment could be chosen to exhibit their attachment to church and state than when marching on to glory, struck up with all the discord of their band, the redoubted air of 'Protestant Boys.' The cheer burst from the ranks as the loyal strains filled the air; but scarcely had the loud burst subsided, when the Louth militia advanced with a quick step, their fifes playing 'Vinegar-hill.'

For a moment or two the rivalry created a perfect roar of laughter; but this very soon gave way, as the two regiments, instead of drawing up at a reasonable distance for the interchange of an amicable blank cartridge, rushed down upon each other with the fury of madmen. So sudden, so impetuous was the encounter, all effort to prevent it was impracticable. Muskets were clubbed or bayonets fixed, and in a moment really serious battle was engaged; the musicians on each side encouraging their party, as they racked their brains for party-tunes of the most bitter and taunting character; while cries of 'Down with King William!' 'To hell with the Pope!' rose alternately from either side.

[51] A duel in the Phoenix; from the *Recollections* of Aubrey de Vere.

(Aubrey de Vere (1814–1903), Limerick landowner, poet and essayist, published his memoirs in 1897. Here he is recalling the Ireland of his grandfather's days.)

In those days a duel was the most mirthful of pastimes, and in Dublin there still remains a tradition of two lawyers, – one the biggest, and the other the smallest, man in Irish society – who met in the Phoenix Park, just after sunrise, to indulge in that amusement. As they approached each other, the big man set his glass to his eye, and exclaimed: 'But where is my honourable opponent? For I really cannot see him.'

'What's that he's saying?' demanded the little man.

'I just remarked,' replied the big man, 'that I am so large that if you miss me, you are like the man who, when he took aim at the parish church, never succeeded in hitting the parish.'

'What is that big "Golumbus" of a man babbling about?' was his small antagonist's rejoinder. 'That I can't miss him and he cannot see me? Let his second get a bit of white chalk, and draw my exact size and shape on that huge carcass of his; and any bullet of mine that hits outside that white line shall not count.'

[52] Queen Victoria writes to the King of the Belgians from the Vice-regal Lodge; from *The Collected Letters of Queen Victoria*, edited by G.E. Buckle.

(Queen Victoria paid her first visit to Ireland in 1849 when Ireland was still reeling from the great Famine, but her letters make no mention of it. On her third visit – in 1861 – stones were thrown at Prince Albert through the Kildare Street Club windows. She did not return for forty years.)

LODGE, PHOENIX PARK, 6th August, 1849. My dearest uncle, – Though this letter will only go tomorrow, I will begin it today and tell you that everything has gone off beautifully since we arrived in Ireland, and that our entrance into Dublin was really a magnificent thing. . . . We came in with ten steamers, and the whole harbour, wharf, and every surrounding place was *covered* with *thousands* and thousands of people, who received us with the greatest enthusiasm. We disembarked yesterday morning at ten o'clock, and took two hours to come here. The most perfect order was maintained in spite of the immense mass of people assembled, and a more good-humoured crowd I never saw, but noisy and excitable beyond belief, talking, jumping and shrieking, instead of cheering. There were numbers of troops out, and it really was a wonderful scene. This is a very pretty place and the house reminds me of dear Claremont. The view of the Wicklow mountains from the windows is very beautiful and the whole park is very extensive and full of fine trees.

We drove out yesterday afternoon and were followed by jaunting-cars and riders and people running and screaming, which would have *amused* you. In the evening we had a dinner party, and so we have tonight. This morning we visited the Bank, the Model School (where the Protestant and Catholic Archbishops received us), and the College; and this afternoon we went to the Military Hospital. Tomorrow we have a Levee, where 1700 are to be presented, and the next day a Review, and in the evening the Drawing-Room, when 900 ladies are to be presented.

George [the Duke of Cambridge] is here, and has a command here. He rode on one side of our carriage yesterday. You see more ragged and wretched people here than I ever saw anywhere else. *En revanche*, the women are really very handsome – quite in the lowest class – as well at Cork as here; such beautiful black eyes and hair and such fine colours and teeth.

I must now take my leave. Ever your most affectionate Niece, VICTORIA R.

[53] Thomas Carlyle calls at the Vice-regal Lodge, 1849; from *Reminiscences of My Irish Journey* by Thomas Carlyle.

(Unlike Queen Victoria, the great historian Thomas Carlyle came to Ireland especially to study the 'Irish problem' in the wake of the Famine, as a painful duty. His comments on Dublin were particularly dyspeptic – perhaps partly as the result of a bad sea-crossing – and he showed little patience with Dublin social etiquette.)

Of Thursday I can remember only a dim hurly-burly, and whirlpool of assiduous hospitable calls and proposals, till about 4 o'clock when a 'Sir Philip Crampton,' by no means the most notable of my callers, yet now the most noted in my memory, an aged, rather vain and not very deep-looking Doctor of Physic, came personally to 'drive me out,' –drive me to the Phoenix Park and Lord Lieutenant's, as it proved. *Vapid-inane* looking streets in this Dublin, along the quays and everywhere; sad defect of waggons, real *business* vehicles or even gentleman's carriages; nothing but an empty whirl of street cars, huckster carts and other such 'trashery.' Sir P's talk, of Twistleton mainly – Phoenix Park, gates, mostly in grass, monument a pyramid, I really don't remember in 'admonition' of what, – some victory perhaps? Frazer's Guide-Book would tell. Hay going on, in pikes, coils, perhaps swaths too; patches of potatoes even: a rather dimmish wearisome look. House with wings (at right angles to the body of the building) with esplanade, two sentries, and utter solitude, looked decidedly dull. Sir Ph, some business inside, tho' Ldship. *out*, leaves me till that end; I write my name, with date merely, not with address, in his Lordship's *book* ('haven't the honor to know her Ladyship,') am conducted through empty galleries, into an empty room in the western (or is it *northern?*) wing, am there to wait. Tire soon of waiting; walk off leaving message.

[54] A childhood memory of the Vice-regal Lodge; from *My Early Life* by Winston Churchill.

When does one first begin to remember? When do the waving lights and shadows of dawning consciousness cast their print upon the mind of a child? My earliest memories are Ireland. I can recall scenes and events in Ireland quite well, and sometimes dimly, even people. Yet I was born on November 30, 1874, and I left Ireland early in the year 1879. My father had gone to Ireland as secretary to his father, the Duke of Marlborough, appointed Lord-Lieutenant by Mr Disraeli in 1876. We lived in a house called 'The Little Lodge,' about a stone's throw from the Viceregal. Here I spent nearly three years of childhood. . . .

My nurse, Mrs Everest, was nervous about the Fenians. I gathered these were wicked people and there was no end to what they would do if they had their way. On one occasion when I was out riding on my donkey, we thought we saw a long dark procession of Fenians approaching. I am sure now it must have been the Rifle Brigade out for a route march. But we were all very much alarmed, particularly the donkey, who expressed his anxiety by kicking. I was thrown off and had concussion of the brain. This was my first introduction to Irish politics!

In the Phoenix Park there was a great round clump of trees with a house inside it. In this house there lived a personage styled the Chief Secretary or the Under Secretary, I am not clear which. But at any rate from this house there came a man called Mr Burke. He gave me a drum. I cannot remember what he looked like, but I remember the drum. Two years afterwards when we were back in England, they told me he had been murdered by the Fenians in this same Phoenix Park we used to walk about in every day. Everyone round me seemed much upset about it, and I thought how lucky it was the Fenians had not got me when I fell off the donkey.

It was at 'The Little Lodge' I was first menaced with Education. The approach of a sinister figure described as 'the

Governess' was announced. Her arrival was fixed for a certain day. In order to prepare for this day Mrs Everest produced a book called *Reading without Tears*. It certainly did not justify its title in my case. I was made aware that before the Governess arrived I must be able to read without tears. We toiled each day. My nurse pointed with a pen at the different letters. I thought it all very tiresome. Our preparations were by no means completed when the fateful hour struck and the Governess was due to arrive. I did what so many oppressed peoples have done in similar circumstances: I took to the woods. I hid in the extensive shrubberies – forests they seemed – which surrounded 'The Little Lodge.' Hours passed before I was retrieved and handed over to 'the Governess.' . . .

I revisited 'The Little Lodge' when lecturing on the Boer War in Dublin in the winter of 1900. I remembered well that it was a long low white building with green shutters and verandahs, and that there was a lawn around it about as big as Trafalgar Square and entirely surrounded by forests. I thought it must have been at least a mile from the Viceregal. When I saw it again, I was astonished to find that the lawn was only about sixty yards across, that the forests were little more than bushes, and that it only took a minute to ride to it from the Viceregal where I was staying.

[55] The Phoenix Park murders; from *The Illustrated London News*, 13 May 1882.

(The murder of Lord Frederick Cavendish (Gladstone's nephew) and Thomas Burke by a Fenian splinter group, the Invincibles, caused widespread horror among Irish nationalists. Parnell (who had just been released from jail after making the so-called Kilmainham pact with Gladstone) offered his resignation, but Gladstone dissuaded him. Most of the Invincibles were caught, and five were eventually executed.)

A twofold murder, perpetrated last Saturday evening in Phoenix Park, Dublin, has furnished a new example of the atrocious wickedness of that foul conspiracy of the enemies of civilised society – Nihilists or Anarchists, or Fenians, by whatever name they may be called in Europe or America, the same in Ireland, under cover of an agitation for different political objects – who are plotting everywhere to subvert all regular Government, for the purpose doubtless of Communistic plunder – by evoking the terrorism of assassination . . .

Saturday last was the day upon which the new Lord Lieutenant of Ireland, Earl Spencer, KG, succeeding to that great office upon the retirement of Earl Cowper, arrived from England, and made his public entry into Dublin, receiving a formal address from the Lord Mayor and Corporation of that city, and loudly cheered by the people as he rode on horseback through the streets. On arriving at the Castle the new Viceroy . . . was conducted . . . to the Privy Council Chamber, where the ceremony of swearing him in took place. Mr Burke, the Under-Secretary, bore the sword of State, and afterwards Earl Spencer took his seat at the council board, with his head covered, as Lord Lieutenant. Lord Frederick Cavendish was then sworn as Chief Secretary by the Clerk of the Council. A rocket from the Castle yard announced the completion of the ceremony, and a salute of fifteen guns was fired in the adjacent Phoenix Park. . . . The new Chief Secretary, Lord Frederick Cavendish, remained in the offices of his own department, engaged in business, till past seven o'clock, when he set out for his lodge in Phoenix Park, which is about the centre of that inclosure. His Lordship went on foot. He knew the way well, for he had been there before when his brother, Lord Hartington, was Chief Secretary. He had arrived from England but at noon of that fatal day.

Mr Burke, the Under-Secretary, left the Castle on a car some minutes later, and overtook Lord F. Cavendish about the Park gate. The Under-Secretary then got off the car, which he dismissed, and the Under-Secretary and Chief Secretary walked together on the left-hand path. It is presumed that Lord Cavendish was going merely to look in at his own house, for he and the Under-Secretary were to dine with Earl Spencer at the Viceregal Lodge. About two hundred yards from the Phoenix Column, they were murderously attacked. It was then nearly half-past seven o'clock, but it was still broad daylight. The attack was so sudden and silent that it scarcely attracted any notice. A common hackney car appears to have driven up and four fellows jumped off it, the driver remaining in his seat. Lord Frederick Cavendish was on the outside of the path, and Mr Burke was

The Phoenix Park murders – a sketch of the scene outside the
Vice-regal Lodge; from *The Illustrated London News*, May 1882

next the grass. The assailants rushed upon them with daggers,
and a fierce struggle for life took place. But the murderers killed
their victims in a few moments, and then drove off by a side road
in the direction of Chapelizod, and rapidly disappeared.

The Rotunda

[56] A Charity breakfast for Dr Mosse's Lying-in Hospital, 1751; from *The Autobiography and Correspondence of Mrs Delany.*

(Bartholomew Mosse (1712–1759) was one of Dublin's most remarkable benefactors. After studying surgery and midwifery in Europe, he returned to Ireland to found the first free lying-in hospital in the British Isles. Originally it was sited in George's Lane, but in 1748 he leased five acres of waste ground north of Gardiner's Mall (the future O'Connell Street) and began to build a magnificent new hospital to the designs of Richard Cassells. At the same time he laid out a walled pleasure garden with refreshment rooms whose entrance fee would help support the hospital. The hospital, its tower topped with a golden cradle, was finally completed in 1757. A Rotunda or concert room (now the Gate Theatre) was added soon after, giving the hospital its modern name. Mosse planned several other great philanthropic projects for Dublin, but died, worn out and in debt, aged only 45. His successor, Sir Fielding Ould, was celebrated in the following Dublin rhyme:

Sir Fielding Ould is made a knight.
He should have been a Lord by right,
For then the ladies' cry would be,
'O Lord, good Lord, deliver me!')

Went to Dr Moss's *gratis breakfast*, Mrs F. Hamilton with us . . . Dr Moss, you must know, is the chief manager and operator of the Lying-in Hospital, and has gardens laid out for the entertainment of company in the manner of Vauxhall and Ranalagh; and in order to gather together subscribers for the next season he gave a *gratis breakfast* and a fine concert of music in a large room which was not opened before, and is in the gardens. The music allured us, and we went, D.D. [Dr Delaney] with us, at about half an hour after eleven, the concert to begin at 12. When we came, with some difficulty we squeezed into the room, which they say is 60 feet long, and got up to the breakfast-table, which had been well pillaged; but the fragments of cakes, bread and butter, silver coffee-pots, and tea-kettles without number, and all sorts of spring flowers strewed on the table, shewed it had been set out plentifully and elegantly. The company, indeed, looked as if their principal design of coming was for a breakfast. When they had satisfied their hunger the remains were taken away, and such a torrent of rude mob (for they deserved no better name) *crowded in* that I and my company *crowded out* as fast as we could, glad we escaped in whole skins, and resolving never more to add to the throng of a *gratis* entertainment. We got away with all speed, without hearing a note of the music.

[57] A clergyman applauds Dr Mosse's hospital, 1777; from *A Philosophical Survey of the South of Ireland* by the Revd Thomas Campbell.

(Thomas Campbell (1738–1795) was a rather sententious clergyman from the North of Ireland. A friend of Dr Johnson, he was the author of several 'philosophical' travel books in the Johnsonian manner.)

In my last, I mentioned to you Mosse's Hospital; which, I think, deserves particular notice, whether we consider it as a specimen of architecture, or, as an example to prove, that every principle of our nature may be rendered subservient to the interests of humanity.

As a building, it is magnificent, and, being the most faultless I ever beheld, is a lasting monument of the abilities of Mr Castels, who was also the designer of the duke of Leinster's, and the Parliament House. In other respects, the structure must do eternal honour to the founder, Dr Mosse, a physician of this city; who, by the mere effort of his own genius, in defiance of avowed opposition, and contempt of popular clamour, erected this stately fabric, for the purpose of relieving lying-in-women; the first charity of the kind in these kingdoms, and in which, above 10,000 poor females have been delivered within twenty years. His only resources were lotteries, and the emoluments arising from the concerts and gardens. The benevolence of the public was at length awakened; the king gave stability to the institution by a charter, and parliament bestowed a bounty on the widow of

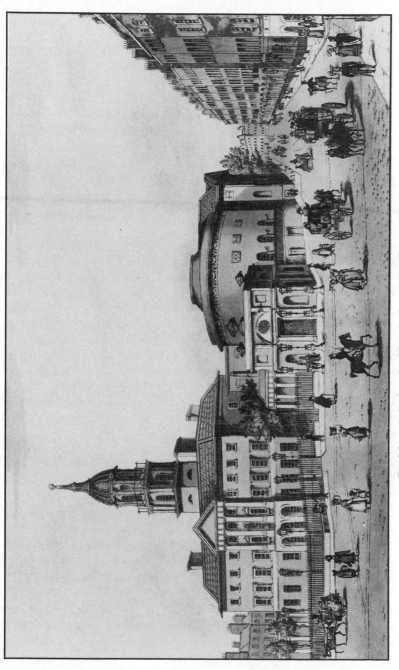

Dr Mosse's Lying-In Hospital and the Rotunda;
aquatint by S.F. and H. Brocas from *Coloured Views in Dublin*, 1820

him, who had devoted his life to the service of his fellow-creatures.

The present master of this hospital, is a Doctor Jebb, a gentleman of fine parts; whose acquaintance, I am sure, you would be pleased with. He tells me, that except some beds given, and endowed by private donors, the fund for support of this charity, is raised from musical entertainments, and from subscriptions to a right of walking in the gardens at all times. They have lately built a large circular room, called the Rotunda, of an area, as I guess, about a third of that of Ranelagh, but without any pillar in the centre. Here they have an organ and orchestra for concerts, in the wet evenings of summer, and for balls in winter. So that, upon the whole, this is the Vauxhall, Ranelagh, and Pantheon of Dublin.

Nay, it is something more than all these, it is a polite place of public resort on Sunday evenings. Whether this entertainment be strictly defensible, in a religious point of view, I shall not determine; but, if the goodness of the end may in any instance be pleaded in justification of the means, I think it may in this. However, it seems rather a matter of wonder, that London, so fond of amusement, and so ready to adopt new fashions of dissipation, has not struck out something similar . . . On these nights, the rotunda and gardens are prodigiously crowded, and the price of admission being only sixpence, every body goes.

[58] The Irish Volunteers assemble in the Rotunda in 1778; from *The Rise and Fall of the Irish Nation* by Sir Jonah Barrington.

(The Volunteer movement had sprung up in the late 1770s, ostensibly to provide a defence for Ireland against France while the British had their hands full fighting the American colonists. In fact they soon became a proto-Nationalist movement of their own, taking their ideas from the Americans and demanding free trade and legislative independence. Eventually their more moderate leaders, notably the Earl of Charlemont (see next extract), became alarmed, fearing a head-on clash with the English government, and persuaded their regiments to disband – much to Barrington's disapproval.)

The Royal Exchange of Dublin was first selected for the meeting of the volunteer delegates. Whoever has seen the metropolis of Ireland, must admire the external architecture of that building; but, as it was constructed solely for mercantile purposes, it would have been inadequate to the accommodation of a very large deliberative assembly. It was therefore determined that the Rotunda (being the finest room in Ireland) was best adapted for the meeting of the National Convention. This was, and continues to be, the great assembly-room of Dublin, and it consists of a circular salon of very large dimensions, connected with numerous and very spacious chambers, and terminates Sackville Street, the finest of the Irish metropolis. It is surmounted by a dome, exceeding in diameter the Irish House of Commons, and was perfectly adapted to the accommodation of a popular assembly.

This salon, and the connected chambers, had been fitted up for the important purpose to which they were to be appropriated. But little did the Irish people conceive, that what they then considered as the proudest day the nation had ever seen, only preceded by a little time her final dissolution, and even prepared the grave in which her new-gained independence was to be inhumated.

The firing of twenty-one cannon announced the first movement of the delegates from the royal Exchange to the Rotunda; a troop of the Rathdown cavalry, commanded by colonel Edwards, of Old-court, county of Wicklow, commenced the procession; the Liberty brigade of artillery, commanded by Napper Tandy, with a band, succeeded. A company of the barristers' grenadiers, headed by colonel Pedder, with a national standard for Ireland, borne by a captain of grenadiers, and surrounded by a company of the finest men of the regiment came after, their muskets slung, and bright battle-axes borne on their shoulders. A battalion of infantry, with a band, followed, and then the delegates, two and two, with side arms, carrying banners with motto and in their respective uniforms – broad green ribands were worn across their shoulders. Another band followed playing the special national air alluded to. The chaplains of the different regiments, in their cassocks, marched each with his respective corps, giving solemnity to the procession, and as invoking the blessing of heaven on the surrounding multitude. Several standards and colours were borne by the different corps of horse and foot; and another brigade of artillery, commanded by councillor Calbeck, with labels on the cannons' mouths, was escorted by the barristers' corps in scarlet and gold (the full dress uniform of the kings' guards); the motto on their buttons being 'Vox populi suprema lex est.'

The procession itself was interesting, but the surrounding scene was still more affecting. Their line of march, from the Exchange to the Rotunda, was through the most spacious streets and quays of the city, open on both sides to the river . . . an immense body of spectators, crowding every window and house-top; . . . every countenance spoke zeal, every eye expressed solicitude, and every action proclaimed triumph: green ribands and handkerchiefs were waved from every window by the enthusiasm of its fair occupants; crowds seemed to move on the house-tops; ribands were flung on the delegates as they passed. . . . Those who did not see or who did not recollect that splendid day, must have the mortification of reflecting, that (under all its circumstances) no man did before, and no man ever will, 'behold its like again.'—

The entrance of the delegates into the Rotunda was most interesting and awful. Each doffed his helmet or his hat, as if he felt the influence of that sacred place where he was about to sacrifice at the Shrine of Freedom.

Charlemont House
(now the Municipal Art Gallery)

[59] A judgement on Lord Charlemont by Sir Jonah Barrington; from his *Historic Memoirs of Ireland*.

(James Caulfield (1728–1799), first Earl of Charlemont, was the designer and builder of the magnificent house in Parnell Square which now houses the Municipal Art Gallery. After extensive travels in Asia and Europe, he had returned to Ireland to devote himself to his country, and emerged as a cultural and political leader of Dublin society in the 1770s and 1780s. He died, disillusioned, just before the Union which abolished the Irish Parliament. His beautiful summer-house or Casino, built on his estate at Marino, Clontarf, also survives as a public monument.)

From the first moment that James Earl of Charlemont embarked in Irish politics, he proved himself to be one of the most honest and dignified personages that can be traced in the annals of Irish history; – the love of his country was interwoven with his existence – their union was complete – their separation impossible; but his talents were rather of the conducting class, and his wisdom of a deliberative nature – his mind was more pure than vigorous – more elegant than powerful – and his capacity seemed better adapted to counsel in peace, than to command in war.

Though he was not devoid of ambition, and was devoted to popularity, his principles were calm, and his moderation predominant; – for some years at the head of a great army – in the heart of a powerful people – in the hand of an injured nation – and during the most critical epocha that a kingdom ever experienced – he conducted the Irish nation with incredible temperance – and, in the midst of tempests, he flowed on, in an unruffled stream of constitutional patriotism, fertilizing the plains of liberty, and enlarging the channel of independence – but too smooth and too gentle to turn the vast machinery of radical revolution.

His indisposition to the extent of Catholic liberty – nourished by the prejudice of the times – was diminished by the patriotism of the people; – the Catholics of 1780 preferred their country to their claims, as those of 1800 preferred their claims to their country – and amongst that sect he gained by his honesty, what he lost by his intolerance, and lived just long enough to experience and to mourn the fallibility of his predictions.

Around this Nobleman the Irish Volunteers flocked as around a fortress; – the standard of liberty was supported by his character – the unity of the Empire was protected by his loyalty; and as if Providence had attached him to the destinies of Ireland, he arose – he flourished – and he sunk with his country.

[60] A judgement on Lord Charlemont by Edmund Burke; from Francis Hardy's *Memoirs of the Earl of Charlemont*.

Every foreigner, of taste congenial to his own, and every Englishman of rank and talents, visited Lord Charlemont during their occasional residence in Dublin. . . . Mr Burke once said to me of this accomplished nobleman: 'Lord Charlemont is a man of such polished manners, of a mind so truly adorned, and disposed to the adoption of whatever is excellent and praiseworthy, that, to see and converse with him, would alone induce me, or might induce anyone who relished such qualities, to pay a visit to Dublin.'

Belvedere House

[61] After the hell-fire sermon at Belvedere College; from *Portrait of the Artist as a Young Man* by James Joyce.

(Belvedere College in Great Denmark Street was originally the town house of the Earls of Belvedere and one of the last great houses to be built north of the Liffey. By 1841 it had already become a Jesuit College. James Joyce attended the school briefly in the 1890s, and later used the terrifying hell-fire sermon given during a religious retreat as the climax of his autobiographical novel.)

He came down the aisle of the chapel, his legs shaking and the scalp of his head trembling as though it had been touched by ghostly fingers. He passed up the staircase and into the corridor along the walls of which the overcoats and waterproofs hung like gibbeted malefactors, headless and dripping and shapeless. And at every step he feared that he had already died, that his soul had been wrenched forth of the sheath of his body, that he was plunging headlong through space.

He could not grip the floor with his feet and sat heavily at his desk, opening one of his books at random and poring over it. Every word for him! It was true, God was almighty. God could call him now, call him as he sat at his desk, before he had time to be conscious of the summons. God had called him. Yes? What? Yes? His flesh shrank together as it felt the approach of the ravenous tongues of flames, dried up as it felt about it the swirl of stifling air. He had died. Yes. He was judged. A wave of fire swept through his body: the first. Again a wave. His brain began to glow. Another. His brain was simmering and bubbling within the cracking tenement of the skull. Flames burst forth from his skull like a corolla, shrieking like voices:

— Hell! Hell! Hell! Hell! Hell! —
— Voices spokes near him: —
— On hell. —
— I suppose he rubbed it into you well. —
— You bet he did. He put us all into a blue funk. —

— That's what you fellows want: and plenty of it to make you work. —

He leaned back weakly in his desk. He had not died. God had spared him still. He was still in the familiar world of the school. Mr Tate and Vincent Heron stood at the window, talking, jesting, gazing out at the bleak rain, moving their heads.

— I wish it would clear up. I had arranged to go for a spin on the bike with some fellows out by Malahide. But the roads must be kneedeep. —

— It might clear up, sir. —

The voices that he knew so well; the common words, the quiet of the classroom when the voices paused and the silence was filled by the sound of softly browsing cattle as the other boys munched their lunches tranquilly lulled his aching soul.

O'Connell Street
(called Sackville Street until 1922)

[62] Shelley preaches the revolution in Sackville Street in 1812; from *Letters to Elizabeth Hitchener* by Percy Bysshe Shelley.

(Shelley came to Dublin aged nineteen with his young wife Harriet and took rooms in Sackville (now O'Connell) Street which had become the main Dublin thoroughfare after the building of Carlisle (O'Connell) Bridge in the 1790s. His attempt to awaken Dubliners to their wrongs by his 'Address to the Irish people' ('printed at the lowest possible cost of 5d') met with little success, despite his hopes.)

I have already sent 400 of my Irish pamphlets into the world, and they have excited a sensation of wonder in Dublin. Eleven hundred yet remain for distribution. Copies have been sent to sixty public-houses. No prosecution is yet attempted. I do not see how it can be. Congratulate me, my friend, for everything proceeds well. I could not expect more rapid success. The persons with whom I have got acquainted approve of my principles. . . .
 Expectation is on the tip-toe. I send a man out every day to distribute copies, with instructions how and where to give them. His account corresponds with the multitudes of people who possess them. I stand at the balcony of our window and watch till I see a man *who looks likely*. I throw a book to him.

[63] George IV makes a royal progress down Sackville (O'Connell) Street in 1821; from the journal of Colonel William Blacker, in Constantia Maxwell's *History of Trinity College*.

(William Blacker was a landowner from Co. Armagh who served as Vice-treasurer of Ireland from 1817 to 1829. His account shows Dubliners still far from revolutionary nine years after Shelley's visit.)

Dublin now presented a singularly animated scene . . . preparations were busily carried on for His Majesty's grand entry into the city. At the head of Sackville St. was erected an edifice in wood intended to represent a triumphal arch. This was the Temple Bar of Dublin where the Lord Mayor and civic authorities were to receive the sovereign and go through the antiquated farce of handing him a bunch of keys and getting them back again. This erection, which I saw nearly blown topsy-turvey the evening before, was covered with evergreens in the midst of which roosted a trumpeter of the Enniskillen Dragoons who was to give the signal on his instrument when His Majesty turned into Rutland Square. Scaffolding was erected in front of many of the houses especially in Sackville St. and being generally filled with 'elegantly draped females' as the newspapers say . . . The neighbouring counties sent forth their peasantry in their Sunday clothes and the entire of Sackville St (except what was clear) – was a mass of [frieze?] and jolly faces. We were fortunate enough to get a window in the drawing room of Mr Geoghan [?] our apothecary, half-a-dozen doors from the head of the street and consequently commanding a full view of the overgrown wig of evergreen before mentioned. A magnificent regiment of Highlanders, the 78th, lined a portion of the street, their right resting on the arch. The whole scene was most amusing. 'Arrah, then Paddy dear will he have a crown of gold upon his head?' 'To be sure he will, Judy.' 'Will you take your elbow out of me ribs. Stan' quiet can't ye and not be rouling about in that fashion.' 'Take care of ye pockets,' etc.

[Blacker explains that this last advice was very necessary, for a number of London pickpockets had come over for the occasion, and his father was robbed of a pocket-book containing bank notes which he had in his breast pocket. His coat had been cut open without his noticing it.]

And now the Enniskillener has 'his loud uplifted trumpet blew' and all eyes are bent in the direction of Cavendish Row and the evergreen arch. A mighty shout came rolling on heralding his Majesty's approach and after a pause of a few minutes while the Lord Mayor was going through the aforesaid farce of the keys, the royal barouche penetrated the mass of laurels.

I have his Majesty's bloated person at this moment in my eye as he stood up in the barouche dressed in scarlet and holding in his hand his hat decorated with an immense bunch of Shamrock which he took care should not escape the notice of the nobility as he repeatedly pointed to it with his finger . . . At length the royal barouche rolled slowly on followed by Lord Talbot and the civic authorities – the Lord Mayor and the 'Lord knows who,' and in due time the King found himself in the Castle with a good luncheon before him which he did full justice to and returned to the Lodge in a closed carriage with a small escort.

[64] The magnificent new Dublin Post Office and the postal services of the time; described by William Curry in his *New Picture of Dublin, 1820.*

The first stone of this magnificent edifice was laid by his Excellency Earl Whitworth, on the 12th of August, 1815. With the exception of the Board-room, which is rather an elegant apartment, and in which there is a white marble bust of Earl Whitworth, there is no object worthy the notice of the Tourist in the interior. The departure of the coaches from the office, would by some be deemed rather an interesting exhibition. Ten or twelve mail-coaches leave Dublin every evening for different parts of Ireland. They are provided with a double guard well armed; the cattle and accommodations are excellent, and the drivers, in general, sober, correct, and intelligent. They all assemble at the General Post Office every evening, a little before seven o'clock, and having received the bags, each in their turn, set out for their different destinations. This nightly exhibition always attracts a crowd of spectators, when the sound of the horns, the prancing of the horses, and the last adieus of friends, form altogether a very interesting and animated picture.

As a public convenience of the highest utility, the Post-Office, in its present improved state, must be considered as one of the most useful and important establishments in any country. . . .

The introduction of Mail Coaches has been attended with the greatest advantage to the general interests of Ireland and has greatly improved the system of the Post-office. Previous to their introduction, the state of the roads was such, that it commonly took five or six days to perform a journey from Dublin to Cork; and it is said that persons, in those days, deemed it a matter of more serious importance to undertake a long journey through Ireland, than many do at present to undertake a voyage to

America. The first mail-coaches commenced running from Dublin to Cork and Belfast on the 5th of July, 1790. A regular improvement in the state of the Irish roads has continued from that time to the present, and they are now allowed to be amongst the best in Europe.

The most admirable regularity and despatch are apparent in all the proceedings of this office. Houses are appointed for receiving letters in various parts of the city, where boxes are open till four o'clock in the evening, after which the letter-carriers, (of whom there are sixty-five for the Irish and twenty for the English departments,) go about for another hour, with a bell, to collect letters, with which a penny each are paid. At the General Post Office, inland letters are received until six o'clock, but a small sum must be paid with any put in after that hour. English letters are received at any hour. A Penny Post is the medium of conveyance from the several parts of the city with each other. From sixty receiving-houses the letters are delivered four times a day with such celerity and exactness that two persons living at opposite extremities of the city may write four letters and receive three answers every day, for the trifling expense of three pence.

[*See also the section,* 'Dublin in revolution']

The Custom House

[65] Building the new Custom House in 1781 – political problems; from *The Life of James Gandon* by T.J. Mulvaney.

(As this letter from John Beresford to Gandon, the architect, makes clear, the plan for a new customs house east of Sackville Street aroused ferocious opposition. John Beresford (1750–1805), Commissioner of Revenue, was one of the most powerful men in Ireland, and had already pioneered many Dublin improvements as head of the Wide Streets Commission.

James Gandon (1743–1825), his choice for architect of the Custom House, was a brilliant pupil of Sir William Chambers. He turned down an invitation to become the official architect in St Petersburg to come to Dublin, and settled permanently in Ireland.)

> *Dublin, 15th January,* 1781

SIR, – I have the pleasure to inform you, that I have at length obtained an order from Government for the building of a new Custom House, with all possible expedition, and I have proceeded so far as to send to take possession of a large lot in the lower situation. I expect to accomplish this in the course of this week, and the sooner afterwards we can settle our plans the better. This business must be kept a profound secret, as long as we can, to prevent clamour, until we have everything secured.

Our first step will be, to wall in the ground as soon as we shall get possession of it. This will discover us, and the clamour will then be made that there will not be sufficient room for shipping: to answer which, it will be right to have our plans for the new docks ready, to shew the people how well they will be accommodated.

I therefore request you will turn your thoughts immediately to that subject, and, as I hope we may hereafter claim you as our own, that you attend to us in the first instance, as the business is of a delicate nature, and must be managed still with dexterity, having the city [*Corporation*] of Dublin, and a great number of the merchants, together with what is considered as the most desperate of the mob, to contend with, on this side of the water; and also some persons of high interest and weight on your side, who will make use of every exertion to prevent us.

However, a Custom House must now be built, so we shall now expect you; and I must beg to know when you think you can come over? . . .

I am, Sir,

Your humble Servant,
JOHN BERESFORD.

[66] Building the Custom House – constructional problems; Gandon's account from *The Life of James Gandon* by T.J. Mulvaney.

The labourers had scarce got down two feet below the surface when they came to water, which four men emptied with scoops as they continued to extend the line of trenches, which were carried on in short lengths, and, for convenience, of different depths. It became necessary to make dams across parts of them with sods, and to empty the water from the lower to the higher dam, until it was at last sent off in a drain prepared for that purpose, our pumps not being then ready. The ground was opened first at the north and continued round to the east front; then to the south end, where a boiling spring with sand appeared at about four-feet below the surface, which filled up as fast as it was cast out. It extended for a considerable distance. Inch and half sheeting piles, about seven feet long, were driven down with a maul, to keep up the bank, and sods were fitted in layers between it and the piles, which prevented the sand from being washed out, thereby enabling the men to clear out the trenches to the depth required. The general texture of the ground was gravel, mixed in some places with a layer of blue clay and sand, under which was a hard strong gravel. When the trenches were thus prepared and cleared out, the rough masons then proceeded to carry on the first bench or course with all possible expedition with the black stone, and immediately filling in with earth, in order to give less water to the pumps. In the meantime another length, and of the same depth, was got ready, and an additional number of masons set to work. In this manner the

James Gandon's magnificent Custom House, which was built on reclaimed marsh; aquatint by James Malton, 1797

whole was continued until all was brought up to the level of the ground.

The sort of pumps required could not be obtained; those now procured were only for temporary service. They were one foot square and vertical, worked by two or more men day and night. . . .

[Having drained and levelled his site with enormous difficulties, Gandon directed his builders to lay a foundation of a huge timber grating covered with 'four inch fir planks'. Here is his humorous account of some unwanted Dublin advice:]

The novelty of this operation drew many visiters to the works, and a very whimsical opinion, delivered with suitable gravity, was very near giving some interruption to the progress of the works. Amongst the visiters were several of the 'faculty,' and one of these gentlemen, who had increased his fortune more by speculating in building than in gallipots, assumed vast knowledge and consequence on the occasion, and, of course, was by many much attended to. He gave his opinions freely and without a fee! He surveyed the grating, and inquired of the master bricklayer for what purpose such large balks of timber were laying down? On being informed, he observed with great sagacity, 'that it would answer no durable purpose, as fir was an improper timber to lay in salt water, an immediate decay being brought on by its destruction of the turpentine!' This he averred, from his own knowledge, to be the fact. . . .

The Quays

[67] Edmund Burke goes for a sail in the cellar; from *The Early Life and Correspondence of Edmund Burke* by Arthur Samuels.

(The family home of Edmund Burke (see p. 170) was on Arran Quay – built in the early 1700s, but still subject to flooding in the 1740s, as this letter to Burke's schoolfriend, Dick Shackleton, shows.)

I have not seen such a flood in the Liffey as is now for some years; and our cellars as well as all on the quay, are full of water; and I, like a good child, spent most of the morning sailing on it in a tub; and I believe I should be at it till now, had not the water grown too deep, and an accident befallen me, which was this. After having made two or three pretty successful voyages into the Ocean of our street kitchen, I had a mind to try my fortune in the Back Sea; but to be short, as soon as I entered it, I perceived at a distance two bottles in a terrible condition; who making signals of distress I made what sail I could to their relief. But lo! my ballast leaning starboard sunk me to the bottom, so I was thrown ashore at a great distance from where I foundered, and having changed clothes (my courage, as you may guess, being pretty well cooled) I sat down to write to my dear Dick.

[68] An English tourist admires the nearly completed Four Courts, 1799; from *Letters on the Irish Nation* by George Cooper.

(The Four Courts – James Gandon's second great masterpiece on the Dublin Quays – was, like his Custom House, a subject of furious political debate and took twenty years to complete.)

I next walked to the *Four Courts*, and surveyed the building from the opposite bank of the Liffey, . . . I was astonished at the elegance of its exterior, exhibiting all the embellishments which architectural and sculptural science can bestow. In order to take a view of the interior of the building I then crossed the narrow stream of the Liffey, over a bridge which the prototype of was at Westminster. As if making my approach to an Athenian Temple I ascended a lofty range of stone steps. I was soon ushered by an Irish Cicerone into a splendid circular hall, nearly seventy feet in diameter, from which the four courts of justice radiate at equal distances. My eye dwelt with pride and admiration on fluted shafts and Corinthian Capitals. I enumerated the emblematical devices which adorn this hall; the signing of the great Charter of our common liberties by King John at Runnymede, and those of the city of Dublin by King James, with crowds of feudal knights and barons bold, armed at all points. I looked higher towards the roof of the building and numbered eight statues as if supporting the dome. There was Liberty and Eloquence, Prudence and Justice, Wisdom and Law, with Punishment and lastly Mercy bringing up the rear. Roving thus from ornament to ornament from the intersecting black and white marble squares of the hall . . . up to the cupola where the emulous plaisterer had exerted all his skill; I began to fancy myself in one of these Fairy palaces which some ingenious romance-writers have described. But by some accident in coming out; the talisman was broke . . . the visionary fabric melted into air. I found myself as much surprised as many other simple knights-errant have been when they awakened from a similar trance. My olfactory nozzle (vulgarly called the nose) was assailed by the horrid stench which arises from the Liffey, (the cloaca maxima of Dublin;) my auditory nerves were assaulted with the clamorous importunities of a crowd of beggars; and my organs of sight turned away with disgust from every edifice and object within the horizon.

[69] A soup kitchen on the Quays, 1847; from 'An open letter to Lord John Russell' by John Mitchel, quoted in M.J. McManus's *Irish Cavalcade*.

(Dublin escaped the worst horrors of the Great Famine, but not the ruin of many of its small tradesmen and an influx of refugees. John Mitchel (1815–1875), a Protestant lawyer, was originally a supporter of Daniel O'Connell (see p. 194), but had left him eventually to found and edit the Republican newspaper, *The United Irishman*, which declared 'holy war' on the English government. He was arrested in 1848, and transported for 'treason felony' to Tasmania. He escaped to America in 1853, and his *Jail Journal* (published in 1854) became a classic.)

On the Easter Monday of last year Dublin saw one of the most ignominious Easter festivals – one of the ghastliest galas ever exhibited under the sun – the solemn inauguration of the Irish nation in its new career of national pauperism.

There, in the esplanade before the Royal Barracks, was erected the national model soup-kitchen, gaily bedizened, laurelled and bannered, and fair to see; and, in and out, and all around, sauntered parties of our supercilious second-hand 'better classes' of the Castle offices, fed on superior rations at the people's expense, and bevies of fair dames, and military officers, braided with public braid, and padded with public padding.

And there, too, were the pale and piteous ranks of model-paupers, broken tradesmen, ruined farmers, destitute sempstresses, ranged at a respectful distance till the genteel persons had duly inspected the arrangements – and then marched by policemen to the place allotted them, where they were to feed on the meagre diet with chained spoons – to show the 'gentry' how pauper spirit can be broken, and pauper appetite can gulp down its bitter bread and bitterer shame and wrath together; and all this time the genteel persons chatted and simpered as pleasantly as if the clothes they wore, and the carriages they drove in, were their own – as if Royal Barracks, Castle and soup-kitchen were to last for ever.

St Mary's Pro-Cathedral

[70] Death of the Liberator: Daniel O'Connell's body is brought home to Dublin for burial, May 1847; from *The Illustrated London News*.

(Daniel O'Connell (see p. 194) died in Geneva aged seventy-one, on his way to Rome. Here the funeral rites are performed over his body in the Marlborough Street Chapel – the future Pro-Cathedral, Dublin's main Catholic church.)

As the steamer neared the Custom House, opposite to which it was arranged that the debarkation of the Remains should take place, the quays presented from end to end one vast mass of human beings; yet, save occasionally a low wail which broke from the multitude, not a sound issued from amongst them. It was all sad and respectful silence. The arrangements for the reception of the Remains were very complete. An open bier, without canopy, drawn by six black horses, was in attendance, with mutes and wand-bearers, under the superintendence of the undertaker, Mr Lawlor, of Henry-street. The Members of the Associated Trades were drawn up in procession order, each Member bearing a wand tied with love ribbon.

Preparations were now made for the debarkation. The side curtains of the Chapel were thrown up, exposing to public view the coffin within, surrounded by its lighted tapers. And then, of that vast crowd not one remained standing where room was left to kneel. The scene was solemn and impressive beyond description; many on board the vessel, as well as on the quays, were moved to tears. . . .

The coffin was next placed on the bier, and the procession having formed, the Remains, preceded by the Trades, headed by Thomas Reynolds, Esq, the City Marshal, and followed by sons, relatives, and friends, moved through the dense crowd along the quay, and up Marlborough-street, to the chapel. The great gate was opened, and displayed a partial view of the interior, with its numerous lights and dark drapery. . . . The coffin was then borne into the chapel, and surrounded by the acolytes bearing torches, whilst a Sub-Decon in a white surplice and soutan, held the lofty crucifix at the foot . . .

At the conclusion of the ceremonial, the officiating Clergy and the choir retired to the vestry, leaving the Remains lying in state. The tapers round the catafalque were lit, and the anxious people were allowed to enter the church, and view its splendid arrangement, until eleven o'clock, when the doors were closed.

THE OBSEQUIES IN THE CHAPEL

On Wednesday, the funeral rites of the Catholic Church were solemnized over the Remains . . . The rain fell in torrents; but, for more than two hours before the commencement of the solemnities, every approach to the Chapel was crowded with Priests, and gentry, to be admitted by tickets.

THE INTERIOR OF THE CHAPEL

was fitted up for the occasion, very appropriately, by Mr Crooke, of Sackville-street. The nave was clothed from floor to ceiling with sable drapery. The pillars surrounding the nave were covered with black cloth – the arches between the columns were festooned with the same – the windows partially darkened by a lighter description of black drapery. The entire of the interior was clad in mourning, except the white marble altar, which was left uncovered. The catafalque, on which rested the coffin, consisted of a dais, elevated on four steps, covered with fine black cloth; from which sprung four pillars, supporting a canopy surmounted by a ball and cross. Upon the dais, and between the pillars, was placed the platform, shaped after the model of a Grecian altar. The canopy supported a magnificent drapery, looped with rich black cordage and tassels. To each pillar was attached a splendid ormolu chandelier. . . .

The front gallery was set apart for the immediate friends and relatives of the illustrious deceased. In it were seated the four sons of the Liberator – Maurice, John, Morgan, and Daniel – with many other relatives, and several of the ladies of the family. . . . In front of it was suspended the O'Connell arms, with the supporters, motto, and crest, beautifully executed in the form of a hatchment. On the sides and ends of the upper dais of the catafalque, the arms of the family were emblazoned. Over the front door they were also on stained glass, on a white ground, diapered with shamrocks, and surrounded with a border of the same national emblem. In the corners of this stained glass were the Irish Harp, and the initials D.O.C. in ornamental letters of

Daniel O'Connell's body lies in state in Marlborough Street Chapel
(later the Pro-Cathedral); from *The Illustrated London News*, 1847

golden hue. In front of the organ-loft, and round the catafalque, were suspended scrolls, on which were written in Latin the inscriptions adopted at the Obsequies in Rome. . . .

The Office commenced a little after eleven. The nine lessons of the Nocturns were read by nine of the prelates present. Peculiarly mournful was the low deep chant of the solemn office for the dead. The joyous notes of the organ were hushed. Nothing was heard but the saddest tones of the human voice, and ever and anon the tolling of the death-bell. The Grand High Mass, at which Dr Whelan acted as celebrant, and the Venerable Metropolitan presided, commenced as soon as the Office had terminated.

The Funeral Oration was preached by Dr Miley. It will be found reported entire, in the *Weekly Freeman's Journal* for Saturday last.

The Absolution, a ceremony but rarely celebrated, and which raised O'Connell to the dignity of a Prince in the Catholic church of his native land, was then performed. The five senior Bishops left the sacristy in black copes, followed the Master of the Ceremonies to the catafalque, and took their positions at the respective corners, the celebrant remaining at the head. Each in turn then gave the usual absolution prescribed in the Roman pontifical. And thus ended the Obsequies.

❧ Dublin moves south ❧

Trinity College

[71] The founding of Trinity College in 1591 – Queen Elizabeth I's letter to the Lord Deputy, the Lord Chancellor and the Council of Ireland; from Constantia Maxwell's *Irish History from Contemporary Sources*.

(The original recommendation for the founding of a university in Dublin had been made in a papal bull in the fourteenth century, but the need only became acute in English eyes after the Reformation, to provide Protestant ministers for Ireland. The site chosen was that of a ruined monastery built originally by the King of Leinster, Dermot Mac Murchadha and by then the property of the Dublin mayor and corporation. The first Provost of Trinity was the Lord Chancellor of Ireland, Adam Loftus.)

Whereas by your letters and the rest of our Council, joined with you, directed to our Council here, we perceive that the Mayor and the citizens of Dublin are very well disposed to grant the site of the Abbey of All Hallows, belonging to the city ... to serve for a college for learning, whereby knowledge and utility might be increased by the instruction of our people there, whereof many have usually heretofore used to travel into France, Italy, and Spain, to get learning in such foreign universities, where they have been infected with popery and other ill qualities, and so become evil subjects. ... We do by these our letters, warrant and authorise you our Deputy and our Chancellor, in our name, to erect and make a foundation and corporation of a college for learning in the place aforementioned, taking order that the college may be erected and established in such manner, and with such good orders and statutes, as some other of our colleges here in England in our universities are. ...

[72] Catholic fears at the founding of Trinity – a petition to the Pope from Irish Catholics in exile, 1595; from Constantia Maxwell's *Irish History from Contemporary Sources*.

Though Ireland was once such a school of religion and learning that many came from neighbouring nations to learn, and from it went out many to spread special knowledge and faith abroad, this glory had gradually decayed, whether by frequent and fierce invasions of foreign nations (i.e. Northmen) or because of the constant civil wars among the chiefs, or by other concurrent causes. At all events the English (who) became masters of Ireland, though they corrected there some things inconsistent with the Christian religion, yet afterwards deliberately contrived to keep the natives in the gloom of barbaric ignorance, so as thus to retain them like slaves in abject obedience. Whence it happened that the Irish, though full of genuine love of the Catholic faith, were not educated enough to detect and repel that corruption of religion which for some decades of years the English have sought by fraud and force to introduce into Ireland. This policy of keeping the Irish in ignorance dates from the days when the Catholic faith flourished both in England and Ireland, but now, a year or two since, a new policy has been adopted, whereby England, devoted to heresy, may draw Ireland into the same snare, and bind it closer to itself. This is the building of a certain ample and splendid college beside Dublin, in which the Irish youth shall be taught heresy by English teachers. From this college a great danger threatens the Irish.

[73] Seventeenth-century student offences listed in the Book of Censures; from *Trinity College, Dublin* by W. MacNeile Dixon.

Aug. 4, 1617. – Gower and Tolles punished with the rod for going into the country and lodging in the town all night. Gower censured for his negligence in his studies, which was by the Examiners of the Midsummer Term discovered and complained of. Patrick Smith removed from the College for non-proficiency and incapacity of learning.

Nov. 21, 1617. – Mr Taylor, Senior Fellow and Dean, severely censured and punished for a wound committed upon the person of Gower, a Scholar of the House.

June 2, 1619. – Thomas Cuff and Jos. Travers for abusing M. Middop's servant, and for their irreverent and savage carriage in the presence of Sir John King, to make three public acknowledgments of their faults at three several times in the Hall; to forbear going out into town for six months except to hear sermons; and for six months not to keep company with each other. Cuff for wounding with a knife the scullion of the kitchen to lose his privilege of adult age, and to rest subject to the rod until he graduates.

Sept. 15, 1619. – Rowland Eustace, for his drunkenness and other misdemeanours, was punished with a public acknowledgment of his fault in the Hall at dinner, to be performed for three days together on his knees, from the beginning of dinner to the end; . . . Beere, Temple (son of the Provost), and Paget were sharply corrected for departing from the Sermon (at Christ Church) to go a-walking, and for consenting to the plucking of cherries from a tree of dean Wheeler's garden hanging on the wall.

From Bedell's Register:

1628, July 29. – Six natives, Dominus Kerdiffe, Ds Conway, Ds Baker, Ds Davis, Ds Kerdiffe, jun, and Burton, admonished for being often absent from Irish prayers.

1629, Aug. 19. – The natives to lose their weekly allowance if they are absent from prayers on the Lord's Day.

1629, Aug. 29. – Sir Springham said to keep a hawk. Rowley for drunkenness and knocking Strank's head against the seat of the Chapel, to have no further maintenance from the house.

Booth, for taking a pig of Sir Samuel Smith's, and that openly in the day time before many, and causing it to be dressed in town, inviting Mr Rollon and Sir Conway (who knew not of it), was condemned to be whipped openly in the Hall, and to pay for the pig.

[74] The fate of the College under James II – extracts from Trinity College Register; from *Trinity College, Dublin* by W. MacNeile Dixon.

(James II, the Catholic King, made a triumphal entry into Dublin on Palm Sunday, March 1689. Although he originally declared religious tolerance, the Trinity dons' fears were soon justified. The College became a barracks and prison, and by October, Mass was being said in the College chapel. But the College was largely saved from destruction by its new Catholic Provost, Dr Michael Moore.)

Feb. 19, 1688/9 – It was agreed on by the Vice-Provost and Senior Fellows that two hundred pounds of the College money should be sent into England for the support of those Fellows that should be forc't to fly thither. At the same time the dangers of staying in the College seemed so great that it was judged reasonable that all those who thought fit to withdraw themselves from the College for their better security might have free liberty to do so.

Feb. 25, 1688/9 – All the Horse, Foot and Dragoons were drawn out and posted at several places in the town, from whence they sent parties, who searcht the Protestant houses for arms, whilst others were employed in breaking open stables and taking away all their horses. Two Companies of Foot, commanded by Talbot, one of the Captains in the Royal Regiment of Foot Guards, came into the College, searcht all places, and took away those few fusils, swords, and pistols that they found. At the same time a party of Dragoons broke upon the College stables, and took away all the horses. The Foot continued in the College all night; the next day they were drawn off. . . .

March 1, 1688/9 – Dr Browne, Mr Downes, Mr Barton, Mr Ashe, and Mr Smyth, embark't for England; soon after followed Mr Scroggs, Mr Leader, Mr Lloyd, Mr Sayers, and Mr Hasset. Mr Patrickson soon after died; and (of ye Fellows) only Dr Acton, Mr Thewles, Mr Hall, and Mr Allen, continued in the College.

March 12, 1688/9 – King James landed in Ireland; and upon the 24th of the same month, being Palm Sunday, he came to Dublin. The College, with the Vice-Chancellor, waited upon him, and Mr Thewles made a speech, which he seemed to receive kindly, and promis'd 'em his favour and protection . . .

Sept. 6. – The College was seized on for a Garrison by the King's order, and Sir John Fitzgerald took possession of it. Upon Wednesday the 11th, it was made a prison for Protestants of the City, of whom a great number were confined to the upper part of the Hall. Upon the 16th the Scholars were all turned out by souldiers, and ordered to carry nothing with 'em but their books. But Mr Thewles and some others were not permitted to take their books with 'em. Lenan, one of the Scholars of the House, was sick of the small-pox, and died, as it was supposed, by removing. At the same time the King sent an order to apprehend six of the Fellows and Masters, and commit 'em to the main guard, and all this without any provocation or crime as much as pretended; but the Bishop of Meath, our Vice-Chancellor, interceded with the King, and procured the last order to be stopt.

Sept. 28. – The Chappel-plate and the Mace were seized on and taken away. The plate was sent to the Custom-house by Colonel Lutterel's order; but it was preserved by Mr Collins, one of the Commissioners of the Revenue.

Oct. 21. – Several persons, by order of the Government, seized upon the Chappel and broke open the Library. The Chappel was sprinkled and new consecrated, and Mass was said in it; but afterwards being turned into a storehouse for powder, it escaped all further damage. The Library and Gardens and the Provost's lodgings were committed to the care of one Macarty, a Priest and Chaplain to ye King, who preserved 'em from the violence of the souldiers, but the Chambers and all other things belonging to ye College were miserably defaced and ruined.

[75] Inventory of a Collegian's chamber; from *The Poems of John Winstanley*.

(John Winstanley (1676–1750), Dublin poet and satirist, attended Trinity College briefly at the turn of the century.)

Imprimis, there's a *table* blotted;
A tattered *Hanging* all bespotted;
A *Bed* of Flocks as one may rank it
Reduc'd to Rag and half a Blanket;
A Tinder-box as People tell us;
A Broken-winded pair of Bellows.
A pair of *Tongs*, bought from a Broker
A Fender, and a rusty Poker.
A *Penny-pot* and *basin*, this
Design'd for Water, that for Piss
A *Trencher*, and a *College-bottle*
Riding on *Locke* or *Aristotle*
A smutty *Ballad*, musty *Libel*
A *Burger's dissius*, and a *Bible*;
A *Prayer-book*, he seldom handles;
Item a Pound of *Farthing-candles*;

A rusty Fork, a blunted *Whittle*
To cut his *table*, and his *Vittle*
There is likewise a pair of *Breeches*
But patch'd, and fallen in the stitches.
Item, a *Surplice*, not unmeeting
Either for *chappel*, or for *sheeting*,
Hung up in study very little,
Plastered with Cobwebs, Ink and Spittle
With lofty *Prospect*, all so pleasing
And Sky-Light window without Glazing
Item, if I'm not mistaken
A *mousetrap*, with a Bit of Bacon
A *Candlestick*, without a Snuffer
Whereby his Fingers often suffer;
And *Chairs* a couple (I forgot 'em)
But each of them without a *Bottom*
A *Battle Standish*, *Pen* unmended,
His inventory thus is ended.

[76] Edmund Burke is admitted to Trinity, 1744; from *The Early Life and Correspondence of Edmund Burke* by Arthur Samuels.

(Edmund Burke (1729–1797), the famous philosopher and statesman, entered Trinity aged just fifteen, and proved a precocious scholar. He later helped to found the College Debating Society, ancestor of the 'Hist'. His statue stands outside Trinity, beside that of his less successful fellow-student, Oliver Goldsmith. Here he is writing to his friend, Dick Shackleton, whose father's school in Ballitore he had attended as a boy.)

Without further prologue I shall acquaint you with my adventures since I left you, which though perhaps not so entertaining nor so full of surprising events as those of Don Quixote, Josey etc. may serve to let you know that Dick Chidley and I arrived pretty safe at this City rather of the latest, for the ρασκελλει watchman had the impudence to inform the town how bad travellers we were by saying, 'Past twelve o'clock'! I was however let in, went to bed, slept, and was sent in company with Jack Baily immediately after breakfast next morning (i.e.

Monday morning) to Dr Pellasier, Fellow of Trinity College, near Dublin, a gentlemen (since it falls my way to give his conjectural character) accounted one of the most learned in the University, an exceedingly good humoured, cleanly, civil fellow (NB I judge by outward appearances). We were admitted into his rooms, and he has three very grand ones. He and Jack Baily had a good deal of chat and a couple of men were setting up a barometer in his room – so he could not for a while examine me. At last he brought out Francis's Horace, Dauphine's Virgil and Homer, with I don't know whose notes; he made me construe *Scriberis Vario* &c. *Eheu fugaces, Postume* &c. and in Virgil I began the 103rd line of the Sixth Aeneid, and in Homer with the 227th line of the Third Iliad, and the 406th of the Sixth and he was pleased to say (what I would not say after him unless to a particular friend) that I was a good Scholar, understood the Authors very well, and seemed to take pleasure in them (yet by the bye, I don't know how he could tell that) and that I was more fit for the College than three parts of my class; but he told me I must be examined again by the Senior Lecturer. He was sent for but was not at home, therefore Dr Pellasier told me I must have the trouble of calling again. He was going out and introduced me (according to custom I believe) to the Provost, who is an old sickly looking man. To be short, this morning I was examined very strictly with another young lad by Mr Aubins or Robbins (I don't know which) the Senior Lecturer, in the Odes, Sermons and Epistles of Horace, and am admitted. . . .

Tell Master Pearce for his comfort that I was examined in *As in praes* and give my service to all the girls, and inform Nanny Morris that I have thought of her once or twice, and that if she has a mind for a coach and six let her tell what coloured horses she will have, and it shall be sent her by the first opportunity, but in the mean time give her a box, and place it to account, and this shall be sufficient warrant for so doing, and it is almost night, and I must write to the Master, so I must conclude without more ado, all-a-one-now.

NED BURKE.

The interior of Trinity College Library;
aquatint by James Malton from *Picturesque Views of Dublin, 1794*

[77] A visit to the Trinity College cellars; from the *Recollections* of John O'Keeffe.

It was a custom with the students to lend their cellar-books to a friend. These books, consisting of seven leaves, were passports to the college cellar. One of them being lent to me, I brought with me two companions, and, on hearing the bell ring at nine o'clock, the notice that the cellar is open, we went. It was on the left hand of the first court, and stretched under the great dining-hall, in low arches, extending very far, and containing large butts of ale regularly arranged. Close by the entrance, on the left hand, was a little box, like a kind of pulpit, and there sat the college butler, as he was termed. I delivered to him the little book; he with few words, quiet and proper in his manner, gave his orders to his attendants, and we were led to a large table, of which there were many in the cellar. On our table was a great iron candlestick with three legs, and in it a wax candle, as thick as my wrist, which spread a brilliant light through the vaulted gloom. A silver cup or vase, with two handles, was placed before us; this was full of the college ale, called Lemon October: the cup held about three quarts. A wicker basket was brought full of small loaves, called by them Manchets; but such ale or such bread, I never tasted before or since, except in this college cellar. The tinkling bell continued ringing until half-past nine, the signal when the cellar doors are closed. While we were enjoying this, indeed, delicious regale, we observed numbers of the servants of the collegians giving the little books to the butler up in his box, for them to receive ale, and take it to their masters in their several apartments: the butler's business was to put down in those books the quantity delivered out or drunk in the cellar. I once went to the entrance of the college kitchen, and saw five or six spits, one over another, and of great length, full of legs of mutton roasting: the notice for dinner was, a man bawling under the cupola, 'The Dean's in the hall!'

I thought it whimsical to see the students, some sixteen years of age or so, thrust their heads through windows, and cry 'Boy!' when a little old man would get up from a bench in the court or hall, and shuffle up to him, answering, 'Yes, Sir.' These old men, constantly in waiting, are called Boys.

[78] A visit to the Anatomy House in the 1770s; from *A Philosophical Survey of the South of Ireland* by the Revd Thomas Campbell.

The gentlemen of Ireland are full as tall as those of England; the difference then, between them and the commonality can only proceed from the difference of food. The following case may, perhaps, tend to illustrate this matter, which, however, I only give upon uncertain authority. In the Anatomy-house of Trinity College, Dublin, is a human skeleton, of between seven and eight feet high. They told me, it belonged to one Magrath, an orphan, in this county, somewhere near Cloyne. The child fell into the hands of the famous Berkeley, then bishop of that see. This subtile doctor, who denied the existence of matter, was as inquisitive in his physical researches, as he was whimsical in his metaphysical speculations. When I tell you, that he had well nigh put an end to his own existence, by experimenting what are the sensations of a person dying on the gallows, you will be more ready to forgive him for his treatment to the poor foundling, whose story I am now to finish.

The bishop had a strange fancy to know whether it was not in the power of art to increase the human stature. And this unhappy orphan appeared to him a fit subject for trial. He made his essay according to his preconceived theory, whatever it might be, and the consequence was, that he became seven feet high in his sixteenth year. He was carried through various parts of Europe for the last years of his life, and exhibited as the prodigious *Irish giant*. But so disproportioned were his organs, that he contracted an universal imbecility both of body and mind, and died of old age at twenty. His under-jaw was monstrous, yet the skull did not exceed the common size.

In the same place, I saw the skeleton of one Clark, a native of this city, whom they call the *ossified man*. Early in life his joints stiffened, his locomotive powers were lost, and his very jaws grew together. They were obliged, for his sustenance, to pour liquids into his mouth by a hole perforated through his teeth. He lived in this state for several years, leaning against a wall, till at length the very organs of life were converted into bone. Account for this, Doctor, if you can.

[79] The Trinity students lose their Parliamentary privileges in the 1790s; from *Ireland Sixty Years Ago* by J.E. Walsh.

The Irish House of Commons was a rotunda, the most ill-contrived in point of convenience that ever was built. Round it was a narrow circular gallery for spectators. . . . Admission to this place was obtained by a member's order only, except by students of the University, who were always admitted.

The student's passport was his gown. He rapped at the wicket, and the porter looked through a grating; the applicant held up his gown, and the door was opened, admitted him, and again closed. This was a privilege often abused. The students' gowns were lent out indiscriminately to friends and acquaintances, and the gallery appeared sometimes half full of gownsmen, not half of whom were members of the University. When I first entered College, I was very fond of using this privilege. It was a proud thing for a 'gib' [*Trinity term for a freshman*] to present himself to a crowd round the door, hear many a cry, 'Make way for the gentleman of the College!' pass the avenue made for him, find the door expand to the 'open sesame' of his gown, and himself admitted alone to the great council of the nation, while the suppliant crowd were excluded. . . .

After the fire the business of the house was adjourned to the Speaker's chamber, and the students of Trinity College were particularly favoured. At the end of the apartment, behind the Speaker's chair, there was a deep and convenient gallery, which was exclusively devoted to the gownsmen. They were instantly admitted here on presenting themselves, and listened to the debate at their ease, while the public in general now found it difficult to obtain passes, and when they got admission were confined to a narrow strip of a gallery, from some parts of which they could neither see nor hear.

This proud distinction the gownsmen, however, soon forfeited. Lord Fitzwilliam had been sent over as a popular Viceroy, and on his sudden recall a strong feeling of disappointment prevailed. On a night when the subject was brought before the House, our gallery was full, and I remember well the inexpressible excitement that seemed to actuate us all. At length it broke out. Grattan rose to deprecate the measure as one calculated to cause the greatest disturbance in Ireland, by what was considered the perfidy of the Government, first exciting the high hopes of the people by promised measures of liberal policy, and then dashing them by the sudden removal of the man who had been sent over expressly to accomplish them. At the conclusion of Grattan's inflammatory speech, the enthusiasm in the gallery was no longer capable of restraint. We rose as one man, shouting and cheering with the boisterous tumult of a popular meeting. When this subsided Foster's peculiar voice was heard through his nose, ordering the students' gallery to be cleared, and a serjeant-at-arms with a posse of messengers entered among us. We were pushed out in a heap, without the slightest ceremony, and were never again suffered to enter as privileged persons.

The Speaker had counted on the loyalty and propriety of the students of the University, and this display of what he considered riot and sedition at once changed his estimate of their character. Many a penitent memorial was presented, and solemn promises were made of better manners in future, but Foster was inexorable. No student ever after found his gown a passport to the House, till the Union removed the Parliament, and extinguished the hope of recovering the lost privilege for ever. Groups of us were constantly seen in the passages, waiting to intercept the Speaker, or entreating, with uplifted hands, a passage to the gallery; but stern Charon passed in at the door, leaving us, like ghosts on the banks of the Styx, casting wistful and unavailing looks on the Elysium on the opposite side of the house.

[80] Student japes in the early 1820s – and an eccentric Vice-Provost; from *Charles O'Malley* by Charles Lever.

(*Charles O'Malley* is the most autobiographical of Lever's novels – he went to Trinity in 1822 and lived very much the wild life recorded here. Dr Jacky Barrett (1753–1821) was Professor of Oriental languages, famous for his scholarship and his eccentricity. He lived in a garret in Library Square.)

They voted morning chapels a bore, Greek lectures a humbug, examinations a farce, and pronounced the Statute Book with its attendant train of fines and punishment an 'unclean thing' . . . We rose about eleven and breakfasted, after which succeeded fencing, sparring, billiards or tennis in the Park; about three, got on horseback and cantered in the Phoenix or about the squares

A Trinity student reels back to college after a night's dissipation; engraving from Walker's *Hibernian Magazine*, 1774

till visiting time; after which made our calls, and then dressed for dinner, which we never thought of taking at Commons, but had it from Morrison's, we both being reported sick in the Dean's list, and thereby exempt from the routine fare of the Fellows' table. In the evening our occupations became still more pressing; there were balls, suppers, whist parties, rows at the theatre, shindies in the street, devilled drum-sticks at Hayes', select oyster parties at the Carlingford; in fact every kind of method of remaining up all night, and appearing both pale and penitent the following morning. . . .

Dr Barrett was, at the time I speak of, close upon seventy years of age, scarcely five feet in height, and even that diminutive stature lessened by a stoop. His face was thin, pointed, and russet-coloured; his nose so aquiline as nearly to meet his projecting chin, and his small grey eyes, red and bleary, peered beneath his well-worn cap with a glance of mingled fear, and suspicion. His dress was a suit of the rustiest black, threadbare, and patched in several places, while a pair of large brown leather slippers, far too big for his feet, imparted a sliding motion to his walk, that added an air of indescribable meanness to his appearance; a gown that had been worn for twenty years . . . covered his rusty habiliments, and completed the equipments of a figure that it was somewhat difficult for the young student to recognize as the Vice-Provost of the University. Such was he in externals. Within, a greater or more profound scholar never graced the walls of the college; a distinguished Grecian, learned in all the refinements of a hundred dialects; a deep Orientalist, cunning in all the varieties of Eastern languages, and able to reason with a moonshee, or chat with a Persian ambassador. With a mind that never ceased acquiring, he possessed a memory ridiculous for its retentiveness even of trifles; no character in history, no event in chronology, was unknown to him, and he was referred to by his contemporaries for information in doubtful and disputed cases, as men consult a lexicon or dictionary. With an intellect thus stored with deep and far-sought knowledge, in the affairs of the world he was a child. Without the walls of the college, for above forty years, he had not ventured half as many times, and knew absolutely nothing of the busy, active world that fussed and fumed so near him, his farthest excursion was the Bank of Ireland, to which he made occasional visits to fund the ample income of his office, and add to the wealth which already had acquired for him a well-merited repute of being the richest man in College.

[81] A tall story about Dr Barrett; from *The Dublin Penny Journal*, 1840.

SIMPLICITY OF CHARACTER

Dr Barrett having on a certain occasion detected a student walking in the Fellows' Garden, Trinity College, Dublin, asked him how he had obtained admission. 'I jumped over the library, sir,' said the student. 'D'ye see me now, sir? – you are telling me an infernal lie, sir!' exclaimed the Vice-Provost. 'Lie, sir!' echoed the student; 'I'll do it again!' and forthwith proceeded to button his coat, in apparent preparation for the feat; when the worthy doctor, seizing his arm, prevented him, exclaiming with horror, 'Stop, stop – you'll break your bones if you attempt it!'

[82] Provost Mahaffy remembered; from *It isn't This Time of Year at all* by Oliver St John Gogarty.

(Sir John Pentland Mahaffy (1839–1918) was Professor of Ancient History at Trinity for more than thirty years, and a legendary scholar and conversationalist. Passed over for the Provostship of Trinity in 1904, for political reasons, he finally became Provost on the eve of the First World War. His books ranged from a study of Kant's philosophy to Greek antiquities, Egyptian papyri and Irish history. As founder of the first Irish Georgian Society, he also helped carry out a massive survey of Dublin's historic buildings between 1908 and 1914.)

Mahaffy was the greatest don I ever met. The examination for fellowship, which leaves its successful candidates text-drunk and good for nothing but to draw the salary that goes with what is a lifelong appointment, and take a few pupils, had not the least effect on him. He had taken it in his stride as a matter of course. He had taken much more in his stride: long before Egyptology had become a subject for research workers, Mahaffy had written a book on the subject which after all these years has not been found wanting. He had a perfect musical ear, and that, they tell me, is a thing that appears only once in a century . . .

He was as omniscient as the scholarship and science of his day permitted. Now people grow tired of omniscience.

It is related how one night the dons of the college conspired to get the great man on some subject on which he was not an authority and so could not talk. After a consultation they selected Chinese music as the subject that they would bring up, as it were, accidentally at dinner. They discoursed on Chinese music, traced its origin and its effect, and expounded the difference in the Chinese conception of music and the European attitude. Mahaffy said not a word. The dons, inwardly delighted, kicked each other under the table. When they had exhausted the subject, Mahaffy said, 'Gentlemen, you have fallen into two errors that I myself nearly fell into, and you know how I hate to do anything foolish, when I wrote the article which you have been discussing; for the *Encyclopaedia Britannica* twenty years ago.'

Parliament House, College Green

[83] The first Parliament on College Green; from *The History of the Parliament House* by Sir John Gilbert.

(Chichester House was purchased as the first Parliament House on College Green to replace the old Assembly Hall at the Castle. It was demolished and replaced by Edward Lovett Pearce's splendid Parliament House – now the Bank of Ireland – in 1728.)

The first Parliament held in Ireland after the Restoration was opened at Chichester House, on the 8th of May, 1661. In the House of Peers, the Lords having taken their places, John Bramhall, the Protestant Primate of Ireland, seated on the woolsack, delivered the King's commission constituting him Speaker; the Lords Justices, Sir Maurice Eustace, Roger Boyle, Earl of Orrery, and Charles Coote, Earl of Mountrath, took their seats in chairs set on an elevation under the cloth of state, – Lord Baltinglas bearing the sword, Viscount Montgomery carrying the cap of maintenance, and the Earl of Kildare holding the robe. The House of Commons was composed almost exclusively of settlers and officials. The Speaker, Sir Audley Mervyn, in his official address to the Lords Justices, observed: – 'I may warrantably say, since Ireland was happy under an English Government, there was never so choice a collection of Protestant fruit that ever grew within the walls of the Commons' House. Your Lordships have piped in your summons to this Parliament, and the Irish have danced. How many have voted for and signed to the returns of Protestant elections? So that we may hope for, as we pray, that Japhet may be persuaded to dwell in the tent of Shem.' Among the members of the House of Commons were Sir William Temple, Sir James Ware, Sir William Petty, and Dr Dudley Loftus.

This Parliament continued, with various prorogations, to sit till the 8th of August, 1666, when it was dissolved. In the previous year it had passed the Acts of Settlement and Explanation, placing the Cromwellian adventurers in the possession of the lands of the Irish adherents of the Stuarts, to the extent of seven millions eight hundred thousand acres. 'A measure of such sweeping and appalling oppression,' observed an English writer, 'is, perhaps, without parallel in the history of civilized nations: its injustice could not be denied; and the only apology offered in its behalf was the stern necessity of quieting the fears and jealousies of the Cromwellian settlers, and of establishing on a permanent basis the Protestant ascendancy in Ireland.'

[84] A diatribe against Parliamentary corruption in the 1730s; anonymous, from Sir John Gilbert's *History of the Parliament House.*

Ye paltry underlings of state;
Ye senators who love to prate;
Ye rascals of inferior note,
Who, for a dinner, sell a vote;
Ye pack of pensionary peers,
Whose fingers itch for poets' ears;
Yet bishops, far removed from saints,
Why all this rage? why these complaints?
Why against printers all this noise?
This summoning of blackguard boys?
Why so sagacious in your guesses?
Your F's, and T's, and R's and S's!
Take my advice; to make you safe,
I know a shorter way by half.
The point is plain: – remove the cause;
Defend your liberties and laws;
Be sometimes to your country true;
Have once the public good in view;
Bravely despise champagne at court,
And choose to dine at home with port;
Let prelates, by their good behaviour,
Convince us they believe a Saviour;
Nor sell what they so dearly bought –
This country – now their own – for nought.

[85] Benjamin Franklin admires the Irish Parliament; from a letter to Thomas Cushing, in Sir John Gilbert's *The History of the Parliament House*.

(Benjamin Franklin (1706–1790) visited Dublin in 1771 when he was based in London trying to negotiate political and trading rights for the American Colonies, and took a close interest in the Irish Parliament which had already extracted concessions from the English administration.)

Their Parliament makes a most respectable figure, with a number of very good speakers in both parties and able men of business.... I supposed I must have gone to the gallery, when the Speaker [Pery] having been spoken to by some of the members, stood up and acquainted the members that there was in town an American gentleman of character, a member or delegate of some of the Parliaments of that country, who was desirous of being present at the debates of this House; that there was a standing rule of the House for admitting members of the English Parliament; that he did suppose the House would consider the American Assemblies as English Parliaments, but this being the first instance, he had chosen not to give any order without receiving their directions. On the question, the whole House gave a loud unanimous Aye, when two members came to me without the bar where I was standing, led me in and placed me very honorably. This, I am the more particular in to you, as I esteemed it a mark of respect for our country and a piece of politeness, in which I hope our Parliament will not fall behind theirs whenever an occasion shall offer. Ireland is itself a poor country, and Dublin a magnificent city; but the appearances of general extreme poverty among the lower people are amazing. They live in wretched hovels of mud and straw, are clothed in rags, and subsist chiefly on potatoes. Our New England farmers, of the poorest sort, in regard to the enjoyment of all the comforts of life are princes when compared to them.

The Speaker enters the Irish House of Commons, 1780s;
from a painting by Francis Wheatley

[86] The Irish Parliament debates the Budget over dinner;
from *Personal Sketches of His Own Times* by Sir Jonah
Barrington.

. . . On the day whereon the routine business of the Budget was to
be opened, for the purpose of voting supplies, the Speaker invited
the whole of the members to the dinner in the House, in his own
and the adjoining chambers. Several Peers were accustomed to
mix in the company, and I believe an equally happy, joyous, and
convivial assemblage of legislators never were seen together. All
distinctions as to Government or Opposition parties were totally

laid aside; harmony, wit, wine, and good humour reigning triumphant. The Speaker, Clerk, Chancellor of the Exchequer, and a very few veteran financiers, remained in the House till the necessary routine was gone through, and then joined their happy comrades, the party seldom breaking up till midnight. On the ensuing day the same festivities were repeated; but on the third day, when the report was to be brought in, and the business discussed in detail, the scene totally changed: the convivialists were now metamorphosed into downright public declamatory enemies, and, ranged on opposite sides of the House, assailed each other without mercy. Every questionable item was debated – every proposition deliberately discussed – and more zealous or assiduous senators could nowhere be found than in the very members who, during two days, had appeared to commit the whole funds of the nation to the management of half-a-dozen arithmeticians.

[87] Henry Grattan hails the new Irish 'nation' in 1782; from Sir Jonah Barrington's *Rise and Fall of the Irish Nation.*

(Henry Grattan (1746–1820), statesman and orator, gave his name to the Irish Parliament which wrested an apparent measure of independence from England in the wake of the American Revolution. This famous speech was the high point of his career, and he was voted £50,000 by a grateful Parliament. But he retired ill and disillusioned with Irish Ascendancy politics in 1797.)

It is not unworthy of remark, that in describing the events of that important evening, the structure of the Irish House of Commons at the period of these debates was particularly adapted to convey to the people an impression of dignity and of splendour in their legislative assembly. The interior of the Commons' House was a rotunda of great architectural magnificence; an immense gallery, supported by Tuscan pillars, surrounded the inner base of a grand and lofty dome. In that gallery, on every important debate, nearly 700 auditors heard the sentiments and learned the characters of their Irish representatives; the gallery was never cleared on a division; the rising generation acquired a love

Henry Grattan, dressed in the uniform
of the Irish Volunteers, addresses the
Irish House of Commons, 1782; a
contemporary painting

of eloquence and of liberty; the principles of a just and proud ambition; the details of public business; and the rudiments of constitutional legislation. The front rows of this gallery were generally occupied by females of the highest rank and fashion, whose presence gave an animating and brilliant splendour to the entire scene; and, in a nation such as Ireland then was, from which the gallant principles of chivalry had not been altogether banished, contributed not a little to the preservation of that decorum so indispensable to the dignity and weight of deliberative assemblies. This entire gallery had been crowded at an early hour by personages of the first respectability of both sexes – it would be difficult to describe the interesting appearance of the whole assemblage at this awful moment.

After the speech of Mr Hutchinson, which, in fact, decided nothing, a low confidential whisper ran through the House, and every member seemed to court the sentiments of his neighbour, without venturing to express his own; the anxious spectators, inquisitively leaning forward, awaited with palpitating expectation the development of some measure likely to decide the fate of their country, themselves, and their posterity; no middle course could be possibly adopted; immediate conciliation or tranquillity, or revolt and revolution, was the dilemma which floated on every thinking mind – a solemn pause ensued – at length Mr Grattan, slowly rising from his seat, commenced the most luminous, brilliant, and effective oration ever delivered in the Irish Parliament.

'I am now,' said he, 'to address a free people: ages have passed away, and this is the first moment in which you could be distinguished by that appellation. – I found Ireland on her knees, I watched over her with an eternal solicitude; I have traced her progress from injuries to arms, and from arms to liberty. Spirit of Swift! spirit of Molyneux! your genius has prevailed! Ireland is now a nation! in that new character I hail her! and, bowing to her august presence, I say, "Esto perpetua!" She is no longer a wretched colony, returning thanks to her Governor for his rapine, and to her King for his oppression; nor is she now a squabbling, fretful sectary, perplexing her little wits, and firing her furious statutes with bigotry, sophistry, disabilities, and death, to transmit to posterity insignificance and war.'

[88] Grattan returns to Parliament to vote against the Union; from *The Life and Times of Henry Grattan by his son*.

(In the wake of the Rebellion of 1798, William Pitt, the English Prime Minister, resolved to abolish Ireland's legislative independence and transfer Irish representation to Westminster. The Act of Union was finally pushed through the Irish Parliament after a massive handout of bribes and patronage. This dramatic episode in the struggle is related first by Grattan's wife, then by his son. Grattan's statue still stands, with mute appeal, outside the old Parliament House.)

At the close of 1799 he returned from the Isle of Wight, and retired to Tinnehinch, almost broken-hearted – not only hopeless, but helpless; enfeebled in body and depressed in spirits, but in mind still unsubdued. Immediately on his arrival, a deputation from his friends waited on him to request that he would re-enter Parliament; but he was obliged to decline the offer in consequence of the state of his health. Soon after they informed him that a seat was vacant, Mr Gahan, one of the members for the town of Wicklow having died, and Mr William Tighe, the patron of the borough, would not be averse that he should be returned for it. Mr Arthur Moore, a most zealous and sincere friend of Mr Grattan, was very zealous on the occasion, and pressed him strongly to comply. . . . Mr Moore at length succeeded, and arranged that Mr Grattan should be put in nomination.

The Sheriff being friendly, he allowed the election to be held after 12 o'clock on the night of the 15th. Mr Tighe got the officer to sign the return, and set off immediately on horseback with it. He arrived in Dublin about five in the morning, when we heard a loud knocking at the door. Mr Grattan had been very ill, and was then in bed, and turning round, he exclaimed, 'Oh, here they come, why will they not let me die in peace?' The question of Union had become dreadful to him; he could not bear the idea or listen to the subject, or speak of it with any degree of patience; he grew quite wild, and it almost drove him frantic.

I shall never forget the scene that followed. I told him he must get up immediately, and go down to the House: so we got him out of bed, and dressed him. I helped him down stairs; then he went into the parlour and loaded his pistols, and I saw him put them in his pocket, for he apprehended he might be attacked by the Union party, and assassinated. We wrapped a blanket round him, and put him in a sedan chair, and when he left the door I stood there, uncertain whether I should ever see him again. Afterwards, Mr M'Can came to see me and said that I need not be alarmed, as Mr Grattan's friends had determined to come forward in case he was attacked, and if necessary take his place in the event of any personal quarrel. When I heard that, I thanked him for his kindness, but told him, 'My husband cannot die better than in defence of his country' . . .

At seven o'clock in the morning Mr Egan had risen to speak, when Mr Grattan entered the House. He was so debilitated that he was scarcely able to walk, and was supported by Mr W.B. Ponsonby and Mr Arthur Moore. The scene that took place was interesting in the extreme, and highly characteristic of the individual; novel to the House, and quite unexpected by the Ministers, who were not aware that the election had taken place, or that the writ could be returned so soon. They were much surprised at his entrance and more so at his appearance. The House and the galleries were seized with breathless emotion; and a thrilling sensation, a low murmur, pervaded the whole assembly, when they beheld a thin, weak and emaciated figure, worn down by sickness of mind and body, scarcely able to sustain himself; the man who had been the founder of Ireland's independence in 1782 was now coming forward, feeble, helpless, and apparently in his last moments, to defend or to fall with his country.

His friends crowded round him, anxious to assist him, – Bowes Daly, in particular, seeing that Mr Grattan had on his hat, he told him it was contrary to the rules of the House. Mr Grattan calmly replied, 'Do not mind me, I know what to do.' He was dressed in the Volunteer uniform, blue, with red cuffs and collar. He had placed his cocked hat square to the front, and kept it on till he advanced half way up the floor; he then stopped and looked round the House with a steady and fearless eye, as if he wished to let them know that, though exhausted, he was yet prepared to give battle . . .

Grattan concluded his speech against the Act of Union in the following words:

'The constitution may be *for a time* so lost; the character of the country cannot be so lost; the Ministers of the Crown will, or may perhaps at length, find that it is not so easy to put down forever an ancient and respectable nation, by abilities, however great, and by power and by corruption, however irresistible. . . . Identification is a solid and imperial maxim, necessary for the preservation of freedom – necessary for that of empire; but without union of hearts identification is extinction, is dishonour, is conquest.

'Yet I do not give up the country; I see her in a swoon, but she is not dead. Though in her tomb she lies helpless and motionless, still there is on her lips a spirit of life, and on her cheek a glow of beauty.

> Thou art not conquered; beauty's ensign yet
> Is crimson on thy lips and in thy cheeks,
> And death's pale flag is not advanced there.'

[89] The last hours of the Irish House of Commons; from *The Rise and Fall of the Irish Nation* by Sir Jonah Barrington.

The Speaker rose slowly from that chair which had been the proud source of his honours and of his high character; for a moment he resumed his seat, but the strength of his mind sustained him in his duty, though his struggle was apparent. With that dignity which never failed to signalize his official actions, he held up the Bill for a moment in silence; he looked steadily around him on the last agony of the expiring Parliament. He at length repeated, in an emphatic tone, 'as many as are of opinion that THIS BILL do pass say aye.' The affirmative was languid but indisputable, another momentary pause ensued, again his lips seemed to decline their office: at length, with an eye averted from the object which he hated, he proclaimed with a subdued voice, '*the AYES have it.*' The fatal sentence was now pronounced, for an instant he stood statue-like; then indignantly, and with disgust, flung the Bill upon the table, and sunk into his chair with an exhausted spirit. An independent country was thus degraded into a province, Ireland as a nation, WAS EXTINGUISHED.

[90] The last hours of the Irish House of Lords in 1799; from Thomas de Quincey's *Autobiographic Sketches*.

(Thomas de Quincey (1785–1859) poet, essayist and author of the famous *Confessions of an Opium Eater*, was a schoolboy of fifteen, and staying with his friend, Lord Altamont, the young heir of the Marquis of Sligo, when he witnessed this scene.)

It was about the middle of the day, and a great mob filled the whole space about the two Houses. As Lord Altamont's coach drew up to the steps of that splendid edifice, we heard a prodigious hissing and hooting; and I was really agitated to think that Lord Altamont, whom I loved and respected, would probably have to make his way through a tempest of public wrath – a situation more terrific to him than to others from his embarrassed walking. I found, however, that I might have spared my anxiety; the subject of commotion was, simply, that Major Sirr, or Major Swan, I forget which (both being so celebrated in those days for their energy as leaders of the police), had detected a person in the act of mistaking some other man's pocket-handkerchief for his own – a most natural mistake, I should fancy, where people stood crowded together so thickly. . . .

We entered; and, by way of seeing everything, we went even to the robing-room. The man who presented his robes to Lord Altamont seemed to me, of all whom I saw on that day, the one who wore the face of the deepest depression. But, whether this indicated the loss of a lucrative situation, or was really disinterested sorrow, growing out of a patriotic trouble at the knowledge that he was now officiating for the last time, I could not guess. The House of Lords, decorated (if I remember) with hangings representing the battle of the Boyne, was nearly empty when we entered. . . .

Gradually the House filled: beautiful women sat intermingled amongst the peers. . . . Next came a stir within the House, and an uproar resounding from without, which announced the arrival of His Excellency. Entering the House, he also, like the other peers, wheeled round to the throne, and made to that mysterious seat a profound homage. Then commenced the public business, in which, if I recollect, the Chancellor played the most conspicuous part – that Chancellor (Lord Clare) of whom it was affirmed in those days, by a political opponent, that he might swim in the innocent blood which he had caused to be shed. . . .

At which point in the order of succession came the royal assent to the Union Bill, I cannot distinctly recollect. But one thing I *do* recollect – that no audible expression, no buzz, nor murmur, nor *susurrus* even, testified the feelings which, doubtless, lay rankling in many bosoms. Setting apart all public or patriotic considerations, even then I said to myself, as I surveyed the whole assemblage of ermined peers, 'How is it, and by what unaccountable magic, that William Pitt can have prevailed on all these hereditary legislators and heads of patrician houses to renounce so easily, with nothing worth the name of a struggle, and no reward worth the name of an indemnification, the very brightest jewel in their coronets? This morning they all rose from their couches Peers of Parliament, individual pillars of the realm, indispensable parties to every law that could pass. To-morrow they will be nobody – men of straw – *terrae filii*. What madness has persuaded them to part with their birthright, and to cashier themselves and their children for ever into mere titular Lords?'

Perhaps there might be a little pause – a silence like that which follows an earthquake; . . . All was or looked courtly, and free from vulgar emotion. One person only I remarked whose features were suddenly illuminated by a smile, a sarcastic smile, as I read it; which, however, might be all a fancy. It was Lord Castlereagh; who, at the moment when the irrevocable words were pronounced, looked with a penetrating glance amongst a party of ladies. . . . After this I had no leisure to be interested in anything which followed. 'You are all,' thought I to myself, 'a pack of vagabonds henceforward, and interlopers, with actually no more right to be here than myself. I am an intruder, so are you.' Apparently they thought so themselves; for, soon after this solemn *fiat* of Jove had gone forth, their lordships, having no farther title to their robes (for which I could not help wishing that a party of Jewish old-clothesmen would at this moment have appeared, and made a loud bidding), made what haste they could to lay them aside for ever. The House dispersed much more rapidly than it had assembled. Major Sirr was found outside, just where we left him, laying down the law (as before) about pocket-handkerchiefs to old and young practitioners, and all parties adjourned to find what consolation they might get in the great evening event of dinner.

[91] An epitaph for the Parliament House; from *The Story of Dublin* by D.A. Chart.

> Here, where old Freedom was wont to wait
> Her darling Grattan nightly at the gate,
> Now little clerks in hall and colonnade
> Tot the poor items of provincial trade;
> Lo! round the walls that Bushe and Plunket shook,
> The teller's desk, the runner's pocket-book.

[92] Daniel O'Connell salutes the Parliament House, 1844; from *The Life of Daniel O'Connell* by Michael MacDonagh.

(Daniel O'Connell, the Liberator, who dominated the Irish political scene in the early nineteenth century, has already won Catholic emancipation, and here he is freed after his arrest for his campaign to repeal the Union – in a triumphal procession through Dublin, he salutes the symbol of Ireland's eighteenth-century Parliament.)

The electric telegraph was not yet at work. William Ford, one of the solicitors for the traversers, hurried to Dublin with the news. At Crewe he put his head out of the carriage window, and shouted: 'O'Connell is out!' 'Was it here the gentleman got out?' asked a stolid Saxon railway porter. On the evening of the 5th September thousands thronged the pier at Kingstown, Dublin, awaiting the arrival of the Mail steamer *Medusa* from Holyhead, which was expected to convey the issue of the proceedings before the House of Lords. Ford was on board, and as the vessel approached the pier, he shouted in a loud voice: 'O'Connell is free.' The news was received with wild uproar. The engine of the train which brought Ford from Kingstown to Dublin bore flags, on which were inscribed: 'Triumph of law and justice – the judgment reversed,' and 'O'Connell is free,' telling the glad tidings to thousands along the route. Clamorous shouts of joy were again raised as the train steamed into the terminus at Westland Row. In the crowd outside were several horsemen, who immediately spurred to Richmond Prison to be first with the intelligence. A messenger of the Repeal Association, named

Edmond O'Hagarty, won in the race. He dashed, panting, up the corridor leading to O'Connell's apartments, exclaiming, 'I'm first! I'm first!' 'What is it all about?' said Barrett, who was walking in the corridor. 'Only that you are free!' said the man. 'Hurrah! I'm first! Where's the Liberator? I'm first!' He rushed wildly into the drawing-room, where O'Connell, wearing his green Mullaghmast cap, was sitting between his daughter and daughter-in-law, with, as was his wont, their hands clasped in his. 'I'm first!' roared O'Hagarty. 'You're free, Liberator. Thanks be to God for that same! I'm first!' 'Bah! it isn't true – it can't be true,' said O'Connell. All doubt was set at rest by the appearance of Ford, pale, with tears in his eyes, and blowing from his exertions. 'On the merits,' were the first words used by the aged attorney, as he flung his arms round O'Connell's neck. 'On the merits,' he repeated. 'No technicalities at all – nothing but the merits.' Then, as the news spread among the prisoners and their friends, there was much shaking hands, embracing, and weeping. Even the governor of the prison, Mr Purdon, was so excited by the news that he fainted; and the deputy governor, an Englishman, rushed out of the room to hide his emotion. O'Connell was deeply impressed. 'The hand of man is not in this,' said he reverently to FitzPatrick. 'It is the response given by Providence to the prayers of the faithful, steadfast people of Ireland.' But the trials had cost the treasury of the Repeal Association the enormous sum of £50,000.

The next day the order for the release of the prisoners arrived from London. The jail doors were flung open, and the citizens poured in to congratulate O'Connell. For hours he stood in the garden, while thousands of men, women, and children filed past and shook him by the hand. . . .

Then came the triumphant departure of the 'martyrs' from the penitentiary. Outside were assembled the trades of Dublin, with bands and banners; the equipages of the Lord Mayor and Corporation, the committee of the Repeal Association, and thousands of well-to-do citizens. At the gate stood a triumphal chariot, consisting of three platforms, rising one above the other, gorgeous in purple velvet and gold fringe, and drawn by six splendid dapple greys. This cumbrous fantastical vehicle had been made specially for the occasion. At two o'clock the prison was thrown open. Out came O'Connell, led by the hand of William Smith O'Brien, MP, and followed by his fellow-prisoners. O'Connell mounted the very topmost stage of the chariot, accompanied by his son Daniel and his chaplain, the Rev Dr Miley, and, standing to his full height in his ample cloak, took off his green velvet Mullaghmast cap, and waved it again and again around his head, amid a prolonged roar of applause. At his feet, on the second platform, sat an old harper in ancient Irish garb, playing patriotic airs. On the third platform of the car were O'Connell's young grandchildren in green velvet tunics and caps with white feathers. The other liberated prisoners drove in open carriages, the eccentric Tom Steel, 'Head Pacificator of Ireland,' being distinguished by an immense green bough – the emblem of peace – which he bore in his hands. In a vehicle by themselves were the attornies of the traversers, carrying a copy of the indictment made up in a huge volume, like the file of a newspaper. The procession was six miles long, and in it marched 200,000 men. It proceeded slowly into the city, winding its way through the principal streets, packed with people, to the residence of O'Connell in Merrion Square. Opposite the Parliament House in College Green the chariot stopped. O'Connell, removing his cap, pointed with his finger to the noble edifice, which he hoped to re-animate with the soul of national life; and, turning slowly round, gazed silently into the faces of the people. It was a dramatic episode – that silent gesture, eloquent of the national hopes and aspirations – and thunderous cheers greeted it.

Daniel O'Connell in his triumphal car salutes the Parliament House after his release from Richmond Jail; from *The Illustrated London News*, 1844

St Stephen's Green

[93] The early history of Stephen's Green; from *Picturesque Dublin* by Francis Gerard.

The history of Stephen's Green goes back to the time of the Crusaders, who, it was said, brought the fell disease of leprosy from the East. On the site of the Green a lazar hospital and church were erected, and placed under the care of monks, who ministered to the souls and bodies of those afflicted. In the Reformation days hospital, church, and monks were swept away, and the Green remained a public common, the haunt of wild birds, especially snipe, which were attracted by the marshy nature of the land, and multiplied exceedingly.

In 1663 we find the burgesses of the City beginning to awake to the fact that such a large area as sixty acres might be turned to better advantage than feeding snipe. The Green was therefore parcelled out in lots, and seven years later (1670) the further step was taken of enclosing a certain portion by a thick hedge, outside which ran the deep ditch alluded to. Inside the hedge a wide walk was made between two rows of lime trees. Later on a high wall was added, when we must suppose the hedge was removed. The wall does not appear in Malton's engraving here reproduced [*pages 200–201*]; but we have the ditch. Malton visited Dublin in 1775, quite a hundred years after the first steps were taken to make the Green habitable. It was then, as we can see by the print, a fashionable promenade, especially on Sundays after church, when a gay company could be seen walking in the Beaux' Walk on the north side, which was more 'the mode' than the French Walk on the west side, or Leeson Walk on the south.

[94] Bishop Clayton's wife receives on Stephen's Green, 1731; from *The Autobiography and Correspondence of Mrs Delany*.

(Robert Clayton, Bishop of Cork, and his rich wife were among the most fashionable people in the Dublin of Mrs Delany's day (their portrait hangs in the Irish National Gallery). Their house on the west side of St Stephen's Green was designed by Richard Cassells, and now, much altered, forms part of Iveagh House, the Irish Foreign Office, still a venue for grand receptions.)

You must know, madam, yesterday being Wednesday, Mrs Clayton opened her apartment and admitted all her acquaintance. I will describe to you how they are disposed and furnished. First there is a very good hall well filled with servants, then a room of eighteen foot square, wainscoated with oak, the panels all carved, and the doors and chimney finished with very fine high carving, the ceiling stucco, the window-curtains and chairs yellow Genoa damask, portraits and landscapes, very well done, round the room, marble tables between the windows, and looking-glasses with gilt frames. The next room is twenty-eight foot long and twenty-two broad, and is as finely adorned as damask, pictures, and busts can make it, besides the floor being entirely covered with the finest Persian carpet that ever was seen. The bedchamber is large and handsome, all furnished with the same damask. There was abundance of good and agreeable company; they went away about half an hour after ten, and so delighted with their reception, that Mrs Clayton has promised to admit her friends every Wednesday. I preside at the commerce table. I must leave off, my letter wanted to go to the post.

[95] Lord Orrery writes to congratulate Bishop Clayton on his new house and retails the Dublin gossip; from *The Orrery Papers*, edited by the Countess of Cork and Orrery.

(Lord Orrery (1707–1762) was a great grandson of the great Earl of Cork (see p. 87). A dilettante of art and letters, he moved in the same circles as Swift, Pope and Dr Johnson, and wrote a life of Swift. His enormous correspondence is a mine of eighteenth-century Dublin gossip.)

Dublin, December 11th, 1736.

MY LORD, – This comes to congratulate your Lord^p upon your new House in Stevens-Green. *Felices quorum iam maria surgunt!* Mr Percival was so Kind as to go with me there yesterday. and Signor Cassells honoured us with his Company; but as your Lord^{ps} Commands did not extend so far as to order me to break

Dublin's most fashionable promenade – The Beaux Walk – on the north side of St Stephen's Green; aquatint by James Malton, 1797

my Neck or my Limbs, I ventur'd no further than the Hall Door, from whence my Prospect was much confin'd, except when I look'd upwards to the Sky. Your Palace, my Lord, appears finely upon Paper, and to shew You that the whole pleases me, I even admire your Coal Cellars. Your great Room will probably bring the Earl of Burlington over to this Kingdom, and do not wonder, my Lord, if Marcellus quits his Nitch and flings himself at Miss Donallan's Feet as soon as ever '*Verdi prati*' reach his ears, but however your Hearing or Sight may be delighted, I am in some Fear that your Smell will not be regal'd from your Stables unless you stock your Garden as soon as possible with Roses, Lilies, and All the Flowers that are celebrated in Song. This inconvenience might be prevented if your Lord^P can purchase a little more Ground behind your House: but so that the Stable has a beautiful Cornish, Signor Cassells does not seem to care where it stands.

Our Town, which is now quite tir'd of curing and killing and killing and curing Doctor Vanleuen, has the dreadfull Topic of a Fire to employ its discourse. Nero had not more Pleasure in the Flame of Rome than we have in talking of a Sugar House that was burnt some Nights ago. I was last Night in Company with ten Ladies who each of Them had a different Story on the Occasion. As I was oblig'd to put in my Mite I sent the Sugar Baker into the Flames for a Box, and brought him safe out again. This Tale may probably last two Days, but unless the six Packetts due from England come in to-morrow, I fear we must go back again to the Devil and the Game of Pickett . . .

Mrs Rochfort has gathered new Beauties by her Marriage. She charms more as a Wife than she did as a Maid: . . . Nelly Grove's Eyes shine like Diamonds sett in Jett, and the Chetwoods are as charming, tho' not as brisk as in a Parliament Winter. Lady Ross defies the circling Years, and as Antaeus gather'd Strength from the Ground, She gathers Charms from Age, so does likewise her Grandmother the gay Lady Dunn. This, my Lord, is the State of Beauty in this Metropolis, and yet in this fortunate Situation do I languish for Corke, which your Lordship's Family made me so happy in, that I can relish no other Place:

[96] The poet Gerard Manley Hopkins arrives at New-man College on Stephen's Green; from *Letters of Gerard Manley Hopkins to Robert Bridges.*

(Newman College was housed in another of the great eight-eenth-century houses on the west side of Stephen's Green, built by Richard 'Burn-Chapel' Whaley, a notorious priest-baiter, in 1765. It was acquired by Cardinal Newman for his new Jesuit University College in the 1850s. Newman also helped design the beautiful Romanesque chapel next door.

The gentle English poet-priest, Gerard Manley Hopkins (1844–1889), was sent there to teach classics in 1884. He never felt at home in Dublin, and died, aged forty-five, a few years later.)

University College, 85 & 86, Stephens Green, Dublin.

March 7, 1884

My dearest Bridges, – Remark the above address: it is a new departure or a new arrival and at all events a new abode. I dare say you know nothing of it, but the fact is that, though unworthy of and unfit for the post, I have been elected Fellow of the Royal University of Ireland in the department of classics. I have a salary of £400 a year, but when I first contemplated the six examinations I have yearly to conduct, five of them running, and to the Matriculation there came up last year 750 candidates, I thought that Stephen's Green (the biggest square in Europe) paved with gold would not pay for it. . . .

The house we are in, the College, is a sort of ruin and for purposes of study very nearly naked. And I have more money to buy books than room to put them in.

I have been warmly welcomed and most kindly treated. But Dublin itself is a joyless place and I think in my heart as smoky as London is: I had fancied it quite different. The Phoenix Park is fine, but inconveniently far off. There are a few fine buildings. . . .

My examinations are over till the next attack of the plague. My lectures, to call them by that grand name, are begun: vae unum abiit et vae alterum venit. I was I cannot tell when in such health and spirits as on my return from Cadwalader and all his goats but 331 accounts of the First Punic War with trimmings, have sweated me down to nearer my lees and usual alluvial low water mudflats, groans, despair, and yearnings.

[97] Stephen Dedalus calls on the Dean of Studies at the Jesuit University College; from *Portrait of the Artist as a Young Man* by James Joyce.

(James Joyce (1882–1941) attended the Jesuit University College from 1899 to 1902, specializing in languages but sharpening his wits with discussions of Thomas Aquinas' aesthetics, as in this extract. A bust of Joyce opposite Newman House in Stephen's Green commemorates his student days.)

But the trees in Stephen's Green were fragrant of rain and the rainsodden earth gave forth its mortal odour, a faint incense rising upward through the mould from many hearts. The soul of the gallant venal city which his elders had told him of had shrunk with time to a faint mortal odour rising from the earth and he knew that in a moment when he entered the sombre college he would be conscious of a corruption other than that of Buck Egan and Burnchapel Whaley.

It was too late to go upstairs to the French class. He crossed the hall and took the corridor to the left which led to the physics theatre. The corridor was dark and silent but not unwatchful. Why did he feel that it was not unwatchful? Was it because he had heard that in Buck Whaley's time there was a secret staircase there? Or was the jesuit house extra-territorial and was he walking among aliens? The Ireland of Tone and of Parnell seemed to have receded in space.

He opened the door of the theatre and halted in the chilly grey light that struggled through the dusty windows. A figure was crouching before the large grate and by its leanness and greyness he knew that it was the dean of studies lighting the fire. Stephen closed the door quietly and approached the fireplace.

– Good morning, sir! Can I help you? –

The priest looked up quickly and said:

– One moment now, Mr Dedalus, and you will see. There is an art in lighting a fire. We have the liberal arts and we have the useful arts. This is one of the useful arts. –

– I will try to learn it – said Stephen.

– Not too much coal – said the dean – working briskly at his task – that is one of the secrets. –

He produced four candle butts from the side pockets of his soutane and placed them deftly among the coals and twisted

papers. Stephen watched him in silence. Kneeling thus on the
flagstone to kindle the fire and busied with the disposition of his
wisps of paper and candle butts he seemed more than ever a
humble server making ready the place of sacrifice in an empty
temple, a levite of the Lord. . . .

The dean rested back on his hunkers and watched the sticks
catch. Stephen, to fill the silence, said:

– I am sure I could not light a fire. –

– You are an artist, are you not, Mr Dedalus? – said the dean,
glancing up and blinking his pale eyes. – The object of the artist is
the creation of the beautiful. What the beautiful is is another
question. –

He rubbed his hands slowly and drily over the difficulty.

– Can you solve that question now? – he asked.

– Aquinas – answered Stephen – says *pulcra sunt quae visa
placent.–*

– This fire before us – said the dean – will be pleasing to the eye.
Will it therefore be beautiful? –

– In so far as it is apprehended by the sight, which I suppose
means here esthetic intellection, it will be beautiful. But Aquinas
also says *Bonum est in quod tendit appetitus.* In so far as it satisfies the
animal craving for warmth fire is a good. In hell, however, it is an
evil. –

– Quite so – said the dean – you have certainly hit the nail on
the head –

[98] W.M. Thackeray takes a grilled herring at the
Shelbourne Hotel and explores the Green; from his *Irish
Sketchbook*, 1843.

(The Shelbourne Hotel – most enduring of Dublin institutions –
was originally housed in three modest brick houses on the east
side of Stephen's Green. By the 1830s it had already become
Dublin's most fashionable hotel.)

This then is the chief city of the aliens. – The hotel to which I had
been directed is a respectable old edifice, much frequented by
families from the country, and where the solitary traveller may
likewise find society: for he may either use the 'Shelburne' as an
hotel or a boarding-house, in which latter case he is comfortably

accommodated at the very moderate daily charge of six-and-eightpence. For this charge a copious breakfast is provided for him in the coffee-room, a perpetual luncheon is likewise there spread, a plentiful dinner is ready at six o'clock: after which there is a drawing-room and a rubber of whist, with *tay* and coffee and cakes in plenty to satisfy the largest appetite. The hotel is majestically conducted by clerks and other officers; the landlord himself does not appear, after the honest, comfortable English fashion, but lives in a private mansion hard by, where his name may be read inscribed on a brass-plate, like that of any other private gentleman.

A woman melodiously crying 'Dublin Bay herrings' passed just as we came up to the door, and as that fish is famous throughout Europe, I seized the earliest opportunity and ordered a broiled one for breakfast. It merits all its reputation: and in this respect I should think the Bay of Dublin is far superior to its rival of Naples. Are there any herrings in Naples Bay? Dolphins there may be: and Mount Vesuvius, to be sure, is bigger than even the Hill of Howth; but a dolphin is better in a sonnet than at a breakfast, and what poet is there that, at certain periods of the day, would hesitate in his choice between the two? . . .

The papers being read, it became my duty to discover the town; and a handsomer town, with fewer people in it, it is impossible to see on a summer's day. In the whole wide square of Stephen's Green, I think there were not more than two nursery-maids to keep company with the statue of George I., who rides on horseback in the middle of the garden, the horse having his foot up to trot, as if he wanted to go out of town too. Small troops of dirty children (too poor and dirty to have lodgings at Kingstown) were squatting here and there upon the sunshiny steps, the only clients at the thresholds of the professional gentlemen whose names figure on brass-plates on the doors. A stand of lazy carmen, a policeman or two with clinking boot-heels, a couple of moaning beggars leaning against the rails and calling upon the Lord, and a fellow with a toy and book stall, where the lives of St Patrick, Robert Emmett, and Lord Edward Fitzgerald may be bought for double their value, were all the population of the Green.

Having a couple of letters of introduction to leave, I had the pleasure to find the blinds down at one house, and the window in papers at another; and at each place the knock was answered in that leisurely way, by one of those dingy female lieutenants who have no need to tell you that families are out of town. So the solitude became very painful, and I thought I would go back and talk to the waiter at the 'Shelburne,' the only man in the whole kingdom that I knew. I had been accommodated with a queer little room, and dressing-room on the ground floor, looking towards the Green: a black-faced, good-humoured chamber-maid had promised to perform a deal of scouring which was evidently necessary, (a fact she might have observed for six months back, only she is no doubt of an absent turn,) and when I came back from the walk, I saw the little room was evidently enjoying itself in the sunshine, for it had opened its window, and was taking a breath of fresh air, as it looked out upon the Green.

[99] George Moore stays at the Shelbourne and salutes the spring in Stephen's Green; from *Ave*, Volume I of his trilogy, *Hail and Farewell*.

(George Moore (1852–1933), novelist, returned to Ireland in 1900 to play (he believed) the leading role in the Irish Literary Renaissance with W.B. Yeats – a vision whose failure he used later with brilliant comic effect against himself and his friends in *Hail and Farewell*. His lyrical celebration of the Green in this extract contrasts with his biting view of Dublin in two earlier books, *Parnell and his Island* (see p. 219) and *A Drama in Muslin*. The 'neighbour in Mayo' he refers to rather grandly here is the first Lord Ardilaun, who in 1880 had had the Green landscaped at his own expense and presented to the people of Dublin.)

But it is difficult to be angry with Ireland on a May morning when the sun is shining, and through clouds slightly more broken than yesterday's, but full of the same gentle, encouraging light – dim, ashen clouds out of which a white edging rose slowly, calling attention to the bright blue, the robe that perhaps noon would wear. All about the square the old brick houses stood sunning themselves, and I could see a chimney stack steeped in rich shadow, touched with light, and beyond it, and under it, upon an illuminated wall, the direct outline of a gable; and at the end

'Mr W.B. Yeats presents Mr George Moore to the Queen of
the Fairies'; a cartoon by Max Beerbohm celebrates Moore's
recruitment to the Celtic Revival, early 1900s

of the streets the mountains appeared, veiled in haze, delicate and refined as *The Countess Cathleen*.

A town wandering between mountain and sea, I said as I stood before my glass shaving, forgetful of Edward [*Martyn, his cousin*], for below me was Stephen's Green, and it took me back to the beginning of my childhood, to one day when I stole away, and inspired by an uncontrollable desire to break the monotony of infancy, stripped myself of my clothes, and ran naked in front of my nurse or governess, screaming with delight at the embarrassment I was causing her. She could not take me home along the streets naked, and I had thrown my clothes out of reach into a hawthorn – cap and jacket, shirt and trousers. Since those days the Green had been turned into an ornamental park by a neighbour of mine in Mayo, and given to the public; and telling the hall-porter that if Mr Yeats called he would find me in the Green, I went out thinking how little the soul of man changes. It declares itself in the beginning, and remains with us to the end. Was this visit to Ireland any thing more than a desire to break the monotony of my life by stripping myself of my clothes and running ahead a naked Gael, screaming Brian Boru? . . .

The first thing I saw on entering the Green was a girl loosening her hair to the wind, and following her down a sunny alley, I found myself suddenly by a brimming lake curving like some wonderful caligraphy round a thickly planted headland, the shadows of some great elms reflected in the water, and the long, young leaves of the willow sweeping the surface. The span of a stone bridge hastened my steps, and leaning over the parapet I stood enchanted by the view of rough shores thickly wooded, and high rocks down which the water came foaming to linger in a quiet pool. I enjoyed standing on the bridge, feeling the breeze that came rustling by, flowing through me as if I were plant or cloud. The water-fowl beguiled me; many varieties of ducks, green-headed sheldrakes, beautiful, vivacious teal hurried for the bread that the children were throwing, and over them a tumult of gulls passed to and fro; the shapely little black-headed gull, the larger gull whose wings are mauve and whose breast is white, and a herring gull, I think, its dun-coloured porpoise-like body hanging out of great wings. Whither had they come? From their nests among the cliffs of Howth? Anyhow, they are here, being fed by children and admired by me. . . . A nurse-maid rushes forward, a boy is led away screaming; and wondering what the cause of his grief might be, I went in quest of new interests, finding one in an equestrian statue that ornamented the centre of the Green. There were parterres of flowers about it, and in the shadow people of all ages sat half asleep, half awake, enjoying the spring morning like myself; perhaps more than I did, they being less conscious of their enjoyment.

I wandered on, now enchanted by the going and coming of the sun, one moment implanting a delicious warmth between my shoulder-blades, and at the next leaving me cold, forgetful of Yeats until I saw him in his black cloak striding in a green alley...

[100] A nightly drama for Dubliners; from *The Shelbourne* by Elizabeth Bowen.

(Elizabeth Bowen (1899–1973), novelist and historian, spent much of her early childhood living in Dublin, where her father worked as a lawyer, and described it later in her fragment of autobiography, *Seven Winters* (see p. 324).)

Only a fool would glorify Dublin's climate: rain often slashed at finery, gales rocked carriages. Seldom, however, did the dirtiest night dislodge all onlookers from their vantage point across the road from the Shelbourne; and on more springlike evenings large crowds gathered. The departure in splendour, from the hotel, of guests bound for a ball or Drawing-room was one of the spectacles of Dublin, a drama played to an audience of old-timers, critical, but well mannered. Nor were the rights of this audience ever denied. Very early, people took up their places – some climbed the Stephen's Green railings, to see better. All eyes, expectant, were fixed on the Shelbourne's door – which, frequently opening, exposed to view the bright-lighted hall, ivory pillars, and crimson carpet. The actors in this drama were grouped ideally – tier upon tier up the steps of the noble staircase would be seated the ladies and gentlemen waiting for their carriages. They wore the impersonality of extreme grandeur – ladies' plumes nodded, satins gleamed, jewels shot out rays; the black-and-white of the gentlemen was immaculate. One after another, round rolled the carriages – each, as it stopped, for a moment, blocking the view. Each time, a name was called: a couple or a party rose from the stairs, advanced down the carpet, emerged from the porch, drove off. The crowd looking on had come to be connoisseurs: each equipage drew an inspecting glance; the profiles inside its windows were closely scanned.

That ceremony, satisfying to all, was repeated night after night for unnumbered winters – being briefly renewed each August, when Horse Show Week brought its own special round of festivities. The Eighties and the Nineties, the Edwardian decade, and the few years left to run out before the cataclysm of 1914, swim together into a rosy haze.

[101] George Moore dines at Ely House; from *As I was going down Sackville Street* by Oliver St John Gogarty.

(George Moore, during his decade in Dublin (1900–1911), lived at No. 4, Upper Ely Place, south of Stephen's Green, where his mannerisms and quarrels with his neighbours were mercilessly noted by Oliver Gogarty who lived opposite at No. 5. Sir Thornley Stoker, the owner of Ely House, was the brother of Bram Stoker, the creator of Dracula. Augustine Birrell was the Irish Secretary of State (see p. 295), and a noted conversationalist.

Gogarty (1878–1957), Dublin poet, wit and surgeon (later cruelly immortalized as 'Buck Mulligan' in Joyce's novel, *Ulysses*), published this first volume of memoirs in 1937. They were considered highly scandalous and brought him a libel action; he eventually left Dublin to live in America.)

Ely Place, Dublin. Like its namesake in London, it is a *cul-de-sac*. From St Stephen's Green, Hume Street runs into it at right angles, and Ely House, the residence of the long-dead Marquis, looks down Hume Street to the west. The prevailing wind, which is western, blows the dust of Hume Street against the great house, seven windows wide, and makes it unsafe to keep them open. Ely House is one of the few remaining palaces of the spacious Eighteenth Century which exist in Dublin without having fallen long ago into decay: old houses which were dedicated to mythological persons. Belvedere House to Venus, Ely House to Hercules. The Farnese Hercules stands like a pillar at the foot of the great stairs, which are balustraded by representations in gilt

bronze of the wild beasts such as the Nemean Lion which fell to
his club and whose hide he holds for ever on his left arm.

Sir Thornley Stoker, the famous surgeon, lives in Ely Place,
and in the Eighteenth Century, which he never really leaves;
hence the house is filled with period furniture, of which he is a
collector and connoisseur. Chippendale, Adams, and old silver
candelabra, match the silver jambs of the doors, and are
contemporary with the silver linings of the great fireplaces,
under their mantels of Siena and statuary marble.

A figure [*Moore*] with hair silver as a dandelion in summer,
pink porcelain face, sloping shoulders and peg-topped trousers
in a suit of navy blue, came strolling down Ely Place from its
garden end. He carried a Malacca cane with an ivory top shaped
like an egg; he strolled leisurely, as became a novelist, a
personage and a man of independent means. When he reached
the long railings of Ely House he drew his stick across them as he
went, causing a noise which he calculated would reach and
irritate the somewhat strange and irascible owner. He passed on.

'Be sure you come punctually,' said Sir Thornley to me, 'it's a
sign of bad manners to be late for dinner. Augustine Birrell is
dining with us; but it's not for that reason that I ask you to be
punctual, but for the general principle.'

The great dining-room was lit with candles, which of course
were waxen.

'Nobody ever heard of paraffin candles at the time that this
house was built; you see how much better the stucco designs
appear on the blank walls in this mellow light. This is Mr Birrell;
now I think we can all be seated. There is no use waiting any
longer, and one has to consider the soup more than a tardy guest.
Take your places, gentlemen.'

We had just finished the soup when the door of Domingo
mahogany swung silently, reflecting the light. The butler said,
'Mr George Moore.'

Sir Thornley Stoker only half rose and turned sideways,
holding his napkin like an apron in his lap.

'Sit down, Moore,' he said testily, 'sit down. We couldn't wait
for you any longer.'

Moore went over to his empty chair, balanced it on its hind
legs, admired what Sir Thornley would call 'the excellent skin' of
its glossy Chippendale wood, and turning from his scrutiny, with
a look of inquiry towards his host, asked: 'A cancer, Sir

Thornley, or a gallstone?' referring to Sir Thornley's habit of buying after a big operation 'a museum piece.'

Moore resented the presence of Birrell. He had decided for the evening not to have read *Obiter Dicta* or, at the worst, if anyone mentioned it, to be unaware of its relation to Mr Birrell, or of Mr Birrell's relation to it.

Sir Thornley asked: 'The shoulder or the belly of this salmon, Moore? I'm chining the salmon. I killed this fish in the Slaney – King Harmon's water – and I think we'll find it a palatable fish. Shall I help you to the shoulder?'

'No, I think the fin, Sir Thornley.'

'Now, Moore, don't be peevish. You are the last that should pretend to be careless about your food. I've just been reading your long letter in the *Irish Times* on the grey mullet. Nobody ever heard of a fin.'

'On the contrary, the Chineses – as my friend here insists on calling them – find sharks' fins delicious.'

These antics fail to draw Birrell, so Moore addresses his remarks to me. Then Birrell says, 'How is your brother Bram, Sir Thornley?'

'Haven't seen him for some time.'

'Is he living in Herbert Street, or is he in London at all these days?'

'He is engaged on scientific research somewhere,' said Sir Thornley.

'Not on the habits of Dracula?' said Birrell, with a laugh.

At this stage the mahogany door burst open, and a nude and elderly lady came in with a cry, 'I like a little intelligent conversation!' She ran round the table. We all stood up. She was followed by two female attendants, who seized whatever napery was available, and sheltering her with this and their own bodies, led her forth, screaming, from the room.

Our consternation held us in the positions we had suddenly taken. Birrell looked like a popular figure in Madame Tussaud's, Sir Thornley, with his knuckles on the table, inclined his head as if saying a silent grace. At last he broke silence with: 'Gentlemen, pray sit down.'

Nobody liked to begin a conversation, because the farther it was off the subject, the more purposefully self-conscious it would seem. Sir Thornley recovered himself and spoke:

'Gentlemen, under my mahogany, I hope you will keep this

incident, mortifying as it is to me, from any rumour of scandal in this most gossipy town. And now, Moore, I conjure you most particularly, as you are the only one who causes me grave misgivings.'

'But it was charming, Sir Thornley. I demand an encore.'

Sir Thornley rose, went over to Moore's chair, and pointing his beard into Moore's ear, hissed something. Then, taking the novelist by the shoulder, he pushed him to the door and into the hall, and out into the street. We heard the door banging and the yapping of her Ladyship's Pomeranian dog.

Sir Thornley insisted on his guests drinking more wine. The dinner dragged on, Sir Thornley asking questions without waiting for answers, from each of us in turn. I was counting the minutes towards the end of this melancholy feast. After some minutes the butler leant over and said something to Sir Thornley.

'Did you admit that scoundrel?' said Sir Thornley harshly.

'He says, sir, it's a matter of life and death.'

'Will you, pray, excuse me, gentlemen? I have to leave the room for a moment.'

We could hear the inarticulate sound of voices, and suddenly two loud screams. It transpired that George, on his way home, had been bitten by a mad dog and was in danger of hydrophobia. Sir Thornley had enlarged the two slight scratches on Moore's right calf and was screwing caustic into the wound. The yells increased, and through the door, which Sir Thornley had forgotten to close, we could hear him saying, 'I don't care whether you're in a dinner-jacket or not. You'll have to send to your house for my honorarium, which is five guineas, before you leave this hall.' Moore produced a wallet of flexible green leather and handed Sir Thornley a five-pound note, with 'I'll send the silver in the morning by my cook.' The butler opened the door, to let out George Moore, and to let in a little Pomeranian dog. . . .

[102] W.B. Yeats recites at Lady Ardilaun's tea-party; from *Bricks and Flowers* by Katherine Everett.

(Lady Ardilaun was the widow of the Lord Ardilaun, whose munificence had restored St Patrick's Cathedral and transformed Stephen's Green into a beautiful public garden, and was

herself a generous patron of the arts, especially of the Abbey
Theatre. Katherine Everett, who acted as her secretary and
companion during the First World War, published this delightful autobiography in 1949.)

The Ardilauns had owned three large houses: one in Carlton
House Terrace, one called Ashford near Galway, with extensive
shooting and, of course, St. Anne's, four miles from Dublin, but I
think no one of these places gave Olive as much pleasure as her
small house overlooking St Stephen's Green. She was touchingly
delighted when connoisseurs admired her rooms, for she had
never before enjoyed informed appreciation of her great posses-
sions. . . .

Sometimes to entertain our guests we had musical afternoons,
or actors from the Abbey, and very good they were. I remember
Sara Allgood's charming voice as she enacted funny scenes with
that perfect absence of self-consciousness characteristic of the
Irish players. Another time Olive thought it might result in a
wonderful experience if she ventured to ask W.B.Yeats to address
us and to recite some of his own poems; this he consented to do. A
very mixed gathering awaited him: soldiers from the Phoenix
Park, some Castle people and other Dublin friends, and an old
and deaf peer from the country. Talk was general when Yeats
arrived late, and when he was announced he remained standing
in the doorway, voices being hushed while everyone looked at his
sombre figure. Then, as he did not move, Olive came forward to
greet him with charming kindliness, asking if he would prefer to
have tea before we were to have the pleasure of hearing his verses.

'I'll speak now,' he answered.

There was some confusion getting everyone to sit down, but at
last Yeats stood alone in silence in the centre of an expectant
circle, his lock of black hair falling over his forehead and his eyes
on the floor. After a pause which made for discomfort, though I
suppose it lasted for less than two minutes, he looked past us all as
if seeing some distant vision and said, 'I speak of the moon.'

He spoke a lot about the moon in a slow, chanting voice,
sometimes as if she were a siren to allure and destroy, again as a
medium of strange magic, or as a cold menace, and nobody
understood any of it.

When he had stopped as abruptly as he began, Olive said,
'Perhaps, Mr Yeats, you would recite "The Lake Isle of

Innisfree" for us.' But he seemed not to have heard and announced, 'A verse to the moon.'

This verse had only four lines, which he half said, half sung, and then he bowed and backed towards the door, saying he wouldn't stay for tea.

When he was gone and chattering began again with varied comments, an officer was heard saying in a clear, clipped voice, 'Quite batty, I suppose, poor fellow,' and the deaf peer rumbled:

'Couldn't catch it all, but there's no moon to-night.'

[103] A glimpse of Yeats and Maud Gonne on Stephen's Green; from *My Ireland* by Kate O'Brien.

(Kate O'Brien (1897–1974), novelist and playwright, was a student at University College during the First World War. She later lived and worked mainly in London and Spain, but returned to Ireland in the 1950s. Her most famous novel, *That Lady*, was banned in Spain.)

[*Yeats*] lived then in Maud Gonne's house in Stephen's Green – she being in prison in England. We students saw him often as he strode about. I remember following him one cold night between the chains and the railings of the Green, along the East side and the North, past the Shelbourne lights and under the bare trees until he strode across the tramlines and into his club near Grafton Street. One followed and watched him with avid concern; as later, when she came back from jail, one followed Maud Gonne [*see p. 268*] over the same courses. And curiously, though both impressed, and solemnised the foolish young passion of intrusiveness – an inescapable passion, for both were myths to us, and he had made them – curiously each failed to illumine in their flesh the immortal two of the poet's creation. . . . Maud Gonne indeed strode through our common crowd as if on forgetful travel down from some absurd and glorious Valhalla; dark veils flying, rain beating foolishly against the prow-like face, and her two wolfhounds profiling as low as to the curve of her great draped knees. And after the first disappointment it hardly mattered that the figure was too much, too mythical – that the whiff of saga, of simplicity was a warning. That, after all, was a question of personal taste, of nerves. What mattered was that the poet could not be discovered in the proud and picturesque figure one pursued so cheekily from street lamp to street lamp. Yeats looked magnificent. He was tall and heavy and he strode head in air, and chanting or talking to himself. The head was heavy, the heavy hair fell back from it; the ribbon fluttered from the eye-glasses, the fur-collared coat flapped open; the wide-awake hat was sometimes on the back of his head, sometimes swinging in his hand; he always carried books and papers; he always walked as if through empty space.

[104] Brendan Behan's mother remembers Yeats; from *Brendan Behan's Island* by Brendan Behan.

(Kathleen Behan (1889–1984), mother of the great Dublin talker and writer, was a remarkable character in her own right. Brought up in a Dublin orphanage, she married twice, reared a family of six sons on republican principles, and ran messages to the GPO during the Rising of 1916. Her autobiography, *Mother of all the Behans*, dictated to her fifth son, Brian, was published when she was ninety-five.)

My mother was a maid in the house owned by Madame Maud Gonne MacBride, and she knew Yeats quite well. . . . He used to visit that house which was in St Stephen's Green, and he used to call her 'Kitty' which she disliked for her name is Kathleen. He arranged his entrances to the house so infallibly that he was there just as she'd be coming up the stairs with a tray of tea and cakes and sandwiches for the visitors, and he'd stop and talk to her for a couple of minutes. I think it was probably an inverted form of snobbery to show the guests that he'd as leave talk to the housemaid as to a lord. But this didn't excuse my mother from Maud Gonne's tongue when she scolded her for having the tea cold.

My mother also told me that at lunch, where she often served Yeats, he was absolutely impervious to what he ate, as he didn't know what he was eating half the time. He absent-mindedly would put sugar in the soup and salt in the coffee and all sorts of peculiar things like that. The one dislike that he had in the way of food was parsnips. Once he was served parsnips by some mistake and he remarked: 'This is a very peculiar pudding.'

I was in the 'Deux Magots' in Paris one time and an American that I was introduced to asked me if I had known James Joyce. I said that I hadn't had that honour, but I told him that my mother had often served a meal to W.B. Yeats in Maud Gonne's house on Stephen's Green and that the poet turned up his nose to the parsnips. 'He didn't like parsnips?' said the American reaching for his notebook, 'You're sure this is factual?'

'It is to be hoped,' I replied, 'that you are not calling my mother a liar?'

'No, no, of course not,' he said, 'but she might have been mistaken – it might have been carrots,' he added hastily.

'You must think I'm a right fool to have a mother that can't tell a carrot from a parsnip.' I said nastily.

'No, no, of course – I mean I'm sure she could but it is very important. . . .' He wrote in the book: *Parsnips – attitude of Yeats to.* 'And you say he didn't like Stephen's greens either – now, what kind of vegetables are they?'

Kildare Street

[105] The Kildare Street Club; from *Parnell and His Island* by George Moore.

(Moore wrote *Parnell and His Island*, a biting attack on all aspects of Irish life, in 1886, when the Irish Land war was at its height. The O'Shea brothers, who sculpted the stonework of the club's windows, evidently shared his view of the club members – witness the monkeys playing billiards around the base of one of the capitals in Kildare Street. The building is now divided between an insurance company and the National Library.)

The Kildare Street Club is one of the most important institutions in Dublin. It represents in the most complete acceptation of the word the rent party in Ireland; better still, it represents all that is respectable, that is to say, those who are gifted with an oyster-like capacity for understanding this one thing: that they should continue to get fat in the bed in which they were born. This club is a sort of oyster-bed into which all the eldest sons of the landed gentry fall as a matter of course. There they remain spending their days, drinking sherry and cursing Gladstone in a sort of dialect, a dead language which the larva-like stupidity of the club has preserved. The green banners of the League are passing, the cries of a new Ireland awaken the dormant air, the oysters rush to their window – they stand there open-mouthed, real pantomime oysters, and from the corner of Frederick Street a group of young girls watch them in silent admiration.

Leinster House

[106] A description of Leinster House; from *A Picturesque and Descriptive View of Dublin* by James Malton.

(James Malton, one of a famous family of artists, came to Dublin in the 1780s, probably to work as James Gandon's pupil. He published his famous aquatints of Dublin in 1797, 'desirous to make a display of its (beauty) to the world'; and they ran to a great number of editions.

The second Duke of Leinster (son of the builder of Leinster House) was a highly popular figure – he had been one of the leaders of the Volunteer movement in the 1780s (see p. 140) and was the brother of the unfortunate Lord Edward FitzGerald (page 104).)

Leinster House, the town residence of his Grace the Duke of Leinster, is the most stately private edifice in the city, pleasantly situated at the south-east extremity of the town, commanding prospects few places can exhibit, and possessing advantages few city fabrics can obtain, by extent of ground both in front and rear; in front, laid out in a spacious courtyard; the ground in the rear, made a beautiful lawn, with a handsome shrubbery on each side, screening the adjacent houses from view; enjoying, in the tumult of a noisy metropolis, all the retirement of the country. A dwarf wall, which divides the lawn from the street, extends almost the entire side of a handsome square, called Merrion-square. . . . The greater part of the building is of native stone [quarried at Ardbraccan, in the county of Meath], but the west front, and all the ornamental parts throughout, are of Portland. South of the building are commodious offices and stables. The inside of this mansion in every respect corresponds with the grandeur of its external appearance.

The hall is lofty, rising two stories, ornamented with three-quarter columns of the Doric order, and an enriched entablature; the ceiling is adorned with stucco ornaments, on coloured grounds; and the whole is embellished with many rich and tasty ornaments. To the right of the hall are the family

private apartments; the whole convenient, beautifully ornamented, and elegantly furnished: overlooking the lawn is the
great dining parlour, and adjoining it, at the north end, is an
elegant long room, the whole depth of the house, twenty-four feet
wide, called the supper room, adorned with sixteen fluted Ionic
columns, supporting a rich ceiling. Over the supper room is the
picture gallery, of the same dimensions, containing many fine
paintings by the first masters, with other ornaments, chosen and
displayed with great elegance; the ceiling is arched, and highly
enriched and painted, from designs by Mr Wyatt. The most
distinguished pictures are a Student, drawing from a bust, by
Rembrandt; the Rape of Europa, by Claude Lorraine; the
Triumph of Amphitrite, by Luca Giordano; two capital pictures
of Rubens and his two wives, by Van Dyck; dogs killing a stag; a
fine picture of St Catherine; a landscape, by Barret; with many
others. In a bow, in the middle of one side, is a fine marble statue,
an Adonis, executed by Poncet; a fine bust of Niobe, and of
Apollo, are placed one on each side. In the windows of the bow
are some specimens of modern stained glass, by Jervis. Several of
the apartments on this floor are enriched with superb gildings,
and elegantly furnished with white damask. From the windows
of the attic story, to the east, are most delightful prospects over
the Bay of Dublin, which, for three miles, is divided by that great
work, the South Wall, with a beautiful light-house at the
termination: the sea, for a considerable extent, bounds the
horizon, and every vessel coming in or going out of the bay must
pass in distinct view.

[107] A balloon ascent from Leinster House lawn, 1785;
from Sir John Gilbert's *The History of the City of Dublin*.

(Richard Crosbie (1755 – 1800) was the first Irishman to make a
balloon ascent. A huge burly man from Co. Wicklow, he was
described by a contemporary as a mechanical genius, and had
worked out his own system of ballooning after reading of
Montgolfier's success. His ballooning dress is reported elsewhere
as being 'a robe of white silk, lined with white fur, his waistcoat
and breeches in one, of white satin quilted, . . . morocco boots
and a . . . cap of leopardskin'.)

At half-past two P.M. Mr Crosbie ascended with an elegant balloon from the Duke of Leinster's lawn, after being twice forced to descend; but, on throwing out more of his ballast, he surmounted all obstacles. The current of the wind, which carried him at first at due east, soon after seemed inclined to bear him north-east, and pointed his voyage towards Whitehaven. When the balloon was seventeen minutes in view, it immersed in a cloud, but in four minutes after, its appearance again was testified by the numerous plaudits of the multitude. It now continued in sight, by the aid of achromatic glasses, thirty-two minutes from its ascent, when it was entirely lost to the view; some rockets were then sent off, and the troops of Volunteers, who attended, discharged their last volleys. Mr Crosbie had about 300 lbs weight of ballast, but discharged half a hundred in his first rise of ascension. At upwards of fourteen leagues from the Irish shore, he found himself within clear sight of both lands of the sister kingdoms, at which time, he says, it is impossible to give the human imagination any adequate idea of the unspeakable beauties which the scenery of the sea, bounded by both lands, presented. 'It was such,' said he, 'as should make me risk a life to enjoy again.' He rose, at one time, so high that the mercury in the barometer sunk entirely into its globe, and he was constrained to put on his oil-cloth cloak, but unluckily found his bottle of cordial broke, and could obtain no refreshment. The upper current of air was different from the lower, and the cold so intense that his ink was frozen. . . . He now entered a black cloud, and encountered a prepulsion of wind, with lightning and thunder, which brought him rapidly towards the surface of the water. Here the balloon made a circuit, but, falling lower, the water entered his car, and he lost his notes of observation; but recollecting that his watch was at the bottom of the car, he groped for it, and put it into his pocket. All his endeavours to throw out ballast were of no avail; the intemperance of the weather plunged him into the ocean. He now thought of his cork waistcoat, and by much difficulty having put it on, . . . he went before the wind as regularly as a sailing vessel. In this situation, he found himself inclined to eat a morsel of fowl. When at the distance of another league, he discovered some vessels crowding after him; but as his progress outstripped all their endeavours, he lengthened the space of the balloon from the car, which gave a consequent check to the rapidity of his sailing, when the

Richard Crosbie and his balloon ascend from Leinster House lawn, 1785; a contemporary engraving

Dunleary barge came up, and fired a gun. One of the sailors jumped into his car, and made it fast to the barge, on which the aëronaut came out with the same composure and fortitude of mind which marked the whole complexion of his adventure. . . .

The barge now steered for Dunleary, and towed the balloon after it. About ten o'clock they landed. On the morning of the 20th Mr Crosbie had the honour of receiving the congratulations and breakfasting with their Graces the Duke and Duchess of Rutland, at Mr Lee's elegant lodge at Dunleary. He was afterwards conducted to town. . . .

[108] A spy reports on Lord Edward FitzGerald in 1798; from Sir John Gilbert's *History of the City of Dublin*.

(The informer in this government report is the brother-in-law of Wolfe Tone, Thomas Reynolds, who had infiltrated the directory of the United Irishmen. The day after this letter, almost all the other leaders of the 1798 Rebellion were arrested, on his information, at Oliver Bond's house on the Quays.)

About 4 o'clock on Sunday, the 11th of March, I called at Leinster House upon Lord Edward Fitzgerald. I had a printed paper in my hand, which I had picked up somewhere, purporting to be directions or orders, signed by Counsellor Saurin, to the Lawyers' corps. These required them, in case of riot or alarm, to repair to Smithfield, and such as had not ball-cartridge were to get them at his house, and such as were going out of town, and did not think their arms safe, were to deposit them with him; and there was a little paper inside, which mentioned that their orders were to be kept secret. Lord Edward Fitzgerald, upon reading this paper, seemed greatly agitated: he said he thought Government intended to arrest him, and he wished he could get to France, to hasten the invasion, which he could do by his intimacy with Talleyrand Perigord, one of the French Ministers. He said he would not approve of a general invasion at first, but that the French had some very fine fast-sailing frigates, and that he would put on board them as many English and Irish officers as he could procure to come over from France, and as many men as were capable of drilling, and stores and ammunitions of different kinds, and run them into some port in this country; he said he thought Wexford might do: that it would be unsuspected, and if they succeeded they could establish a rallying point until other helps should come. Lord Edward, after this conversation, walked up and down the room in a very agitated manner: 'No,' said he, 'it is impossible; Government cannot be informed of it; they never have been able to know where the Provincial meet.' Shortly after this the servant came, and asked was he ready for dinner. I went away; – he wanted me to stay [to] dinner, but I would not.

[109] Lady Sarah Napier describes Lord Edward FitzGerald's escape from Leinster House, March 1798, from Sir John Gilbert's *The History of the City of Dublin.*

(Lady Sarah Napier was the sister of the dowager Duchess of Leinster, and mother of three (later) famous sons, Charles, George and Henry Napier.)

The separate warrant went by a messenger, attended by Sheriff Carlton, and a party of soldiers, commanded by a Major O'Kelly, into Leinster House. The servants ran up to Lady Edward, who was ill with the gathering in her breast, and told her; she said directly, 'there is no help, send them up:' they asked very civilly for her papers and Edward's, and she gave them all. Her apparent distress moved Major O'Kelly to tears; and their whole conduct was proper. They left her, and soon returned (Major Boyle having been with two dragoons to Frescati, and taken such papers as were in their sitting-room, and not found Edward) to search Leinster House for him, and came up with great good nature, to say, 'Madam, we wish to tell you our search is in vain, Lord Edward has escaped.'
(*Lord Edward was captured eleven weeks later in Thomas Street – see p. 104.*)

[110] The 'greening' of Leinster House (Dáil Eireann), 1930; from *In Search of Ireland* by H.V. Morton.

(The Free State Parliament rejected Daniel O'Connell's dream of restoring an Irish Parliament to the old Parliament House on

College Green (see p. 182), in favour of Leinster House, partly for reasons of security – a decision which might have gratified Lord Edward FitzGerald!)

The Poet came on the following day to say that he would show me the most interesting sight in Dublin:

'We are,' he explained, 'going to see Dáil Eireann which, as you may know, is the Parliament of the Free State.'

The Dáil meets in a large eighteenth-century house, formerly the residence of the Dukes of Leinster. In front of it is a statue of Queen Victoria, which, while not complimentary, is not so bad as the one that sits so heavily on Manchester.

'That,' explained the Poet, pointing to the statue, 'is known with justice as "Ireland's Revenge".'

The entrance to the Dáil is like that to any big London club. Members enter smoking pipes and cigarettes, collect their letters from a porter's box on the right, and go on through Grosvenor Square galleries and up wide ducal stairways to the 'House'.

The Free State Parliament meets in the old lecture theatre of the Royal Dublin Society, which was founded in 1731 for the purpose of promoting useful arts and sciences. The gallery has recently been altered and fitted wih protective railings to prevent the accidental fall of spectators or other objects on the deputies' heads, but the floor of the theatre has been fitted with shining mahogany seats, which rise in tiers in a horseshoe round the Speaker's chair. The House is dignified. Beneath the gallery are old prints of Dublin in Hogarth frames.

One's first impression is that immense pains have been taken to introduce as much green into the landscape as possible. Members hold green question papers. When they turn them in unison it is as if a breeze has blown through a forest! The files are green. The note-books are bound in green. Now and then messengers tiptoe down through the seats to deliver emerald green telegrams. At the top of the steps and at the doors stand the most competent-looking chuckers-out seen in public since the heyday of the old music-hall. I would give a man of average physique two seconds to maintain a real row in the Dáil!

Merrion Square

[111] Daniel O'Connell at home in Merrion Square; from *Sketches of the Irish Bar* by W.H. Curran.

(Daniel O'Connell bought No. 58 (formerly No. 30) on the south side of Merrion Square in 1809 – much to his frugal wife Mary's dismay – 'Where on earth will you be able to get a thousand guineas...?' – and lived there on and off until his death in 1847.)

If any one of you, my English readers, being a stranger in Dublin, should chance as you return upon a winter's morning from one of the 'small and early' parties of that raking metropolis – that is to say, between the hours of five and six o'clock – to pass along the south side of Merrion Square, you will not fail to observe that among those splendid mansions there is one evidently tenanted by a person whose habits differ materially from those of his fashionable neighbours. The half-open parlour shutters and the light within, announce that some one dwells there whose time is too precious to permit him to regulate his rising with the sun. Should your curiosity tempt you to ascend the steps, and, under cover of the dark, to reconnoitre the interior, you will see a tall, able-bodied man standing at a desk, and immersed in solitary occupation. Upon the wall in front of him hangs a crucifix. From this and from the calm attitude of the person within, and from a certain monastic rotundity about the neck and shoulders, your first impression will be that he must be some pious dignitary of the Church of Rome, absorbed in his matin devotions. But... no sooner can the eye take in the other furniture of the apartment, the bookcases clogged with tomes in plain calf-skin bindings, the blue-covered octavos that lie on the table and the floor, the reams of manuscript in oblong folds and begirt with crimson tape, than it becomes evident that the party meditating amidst such objects must be thinking far more of the law than the prophets. He is unquestionably a barrister, but, apparently, of that homely, chamber-keeping, plodding cast, who labour hard to make up by assiduity what they want in wit. . . . Should you happen in the course of the same day to stroll down to the hall of the Four Courts, you will not be a little surprised to find the

Daniel O'Connell at home in Merrion Square;
from *The Illustrated London News*, 1843

object of your pity miraculously transformed from the severe recluse of the morning into one of the most bustling, important, and joyous personages in that busy scene.

[112] Dr William Wilde stands trial; from *The Life of Oscar Wilde* by Frank Harris.

(Oscar Wilde's father, Dr William Wilde, was a well-known surgeon and antiquary who lived at No. 1 Merrion Square. In 1864 he became the central figure in a *cause célèbre* – one of his patients, a Miss Mary Travers, accused him of rape in the course of a trial for libel, Isaac Butt appearing as her lawyer.

Frank Harris (1856–1931) writer and journalist, and himself a compulsive philanderer, makes the most of the scene.)

The excitement in the court was becoming breathless. It was felt that the details were cumulative; the doctor was besieging the fortress in proper form. The story of embracings, reconciliations and loans all prepared the public for the great scene.

The girl went on, now answering questions, now telling bits of the story in her own way, Mr Butt, the great advocate, taking care that it should all be consecutive and clear with a due crescendo of interest. In October, 1862, it appeared Lady Wilde was not in the house at Merrion Square, but was away at Bray, as one of the children had not been well, and she thought the sea air would benefit him. Dr Wilde was alone in the house. Miss Travers called and was admitted into Dr Wilde's study. He put her on her knees before him and bared her neck, pretending to examine the burn; he fondled her too much and pressed her to him: she took offence and tried to draw away. Somehow or other his hand got entangled in a chain at her neck. She called out to him 'You are suffocating me,' and tried to rise: but he cried out like a madman: 'I will, I want to,' and pressed what seemed to be a handkerchief over her face. She declared that she lost consciousness.

When she came to herself she found Dr Wilde frantically imploring her to come to her senses, while dabbing water on her face, and offering her wine to drink.

'If you don't drink,' he cried, 'I'll pour it over you.'

For some time, she said, she scarcely realized where she was or what had occurred, though she heard him talking. But gradually consciousness came back to her, and though she would not open her eyes she understood what he was saying. He talked frantically:

'Do be reasonable, and all will be right. . . . I am in your power. . . . spare me, oh, spare me . . . strike me if you like. I wish to God I could hate you, but I can't. I swore I would never touch your hand again. Attend to me and do what I tell you. Have faith and confidence in me and you may remedy the past and go to Australia. Think of the talk this may give rise to. Keep up appearances for your own sake. . . .'

He then took her upstairs to a bedroom and made her drink some wine and lie down for some time. She afterwards left the house; she hardly knew how; he accompanied her to the door, she thought; but could not be certain; she was half dazed.

The judge here interposed with the crucial question:

'Did you know that you had been violated?'

The audience waited breathlessly; after a short pause Miss Travers replied:

'Yes.'

Then it was true, the worst was true. The audience, excited to the highest pitch, caught breath with malevolent delight. But the thrills were not exhausted. Miss Travers next told how in Dr Wilde's study one evening she had been vexed at some slight, and at once took four pennyworth of laudanum which she had bought. Dr Wilde hurried her round to the house of Dr Walsh, a physician in the neighbourhood, who gave her an antidote. Dr Wilde was dreadfully frightened lest something should get out. . .

[113] Dancing parties in Merrion and Fitzwilliam Squares; by Eilis Dillon, from *Victorian Dublin*, edited by Tom Kennedy.

(Eilis Dillon, novelist, playwright and children's author, was born in Galway in 1920. Here she describes her grandparents' household and life in Dublin before the First World War.)

Every winter, the families living in and around Fitzwilliam and Merrion Squares entertained each other to dances. Each family decided on a date well in advance and the Plunketts always booked a pianist named Miss Gasparro, and her violinist, to make music. It was always the same violinist but his name has not survived. It was noticed that she kicked him on the ankle if he displeased her while they played.

Between them and some cousins in Palmerston Road, they owned enough unbleached, figured damask linen to cover the floors of the double drawing-room for dancing. The linen was tacked on to the carpets, which were too heavy to be moved out. The guests usually numbered one hundred and fifty and even then the rooms were not overfilled. Supper was laid in the study and dining-room, and the pine rafters sprang up and down visibly without cracking the ornamental plaster-work of the ceiling below when everyone leaped together during the Lancers. . . .

The entertainment began with a children's party in the afternoon and after the children had gone, dancing took over for the rest of the evening. There was no singing, no performances of any kind except from the professional musicians, unless a guest had a particularly good voice. Dances where guests of indifferent talent rendered songs at the piano or played their pieces were frowned upon. While the little dance-band had supper, an older man who was a friend of the family played the piano very willingly so long as he had a glass of whiskey beside him. The young people found it difficult to impress upon my grandmother that the whiskey was essential to his performance. The rest of the company had wine with supper, which was by intention kept rather simple. It was served at midnight and consisted of cold dishes, chicken and ham and galantines, with home-made fruit salad, cream and ice-cream. All of this was prepared in the house by the cook and the maids, helped out by the family, and served by the parlourmaid, the housemaids and the nurses.

Dancing finished at six in the morning and then the remains of supper were eaten. If too much was left over, my mother said calmly, a small dance was held the next day. Almost all of those energetic young men went off to the war in 1914 and were very soon killed.

❧ Dublin Theatre ❧

[114] Handel describes the rapturous reception of his *Messiah* at its first performance in 1742; from *Autograph Letters of Handel and Jennens*, edited by Edward, sixth Earl of Howe.

(G.F. Handel (1685–1759) had left London for Dublin in 1741 in search of a more appreciative audience for his music. The *Messiah*, probably composed in the early spring of 1742, was put on as a surprise extra at a charity concert on 8 April, given in Neal's Music-hall (now demolished) in Fishamble Street, near Christ Church Cathedral. The letter is to his friend, Charles Jennens, who had written the words for the oratorio.)

Sir, it was with the greatest Pleasure I saw the Continuation of Your Kindness by the Lines You was pleased to send me, in Order to be prefix'd to Your Oratorio Messiah, which I set to Musick before I left England. I am emboldned, Sir, by the generous Concern You please to take in relation to my affairs, to give You an Account of the Success I have met here. The Nobility did me the Honour to make amongst themselves a Subscription for 6 Nights, which did fill a Room of 600 Persons, so that I needed not sell one single Ticket at the door, and without Vanity the Performance was received with a general Approbation. Sig^ra Avolio, which I brought with me from London pleases extraordinary, I have form'd an other Tenor Voice which gives great satisfaction, the Basses and Counter Tenors are very good, and the rest of the Chorus Singers (by my Direction) do exceeding well, as for the Instruments they are really excellent, Mr Dubourgh being at the Head of them and the Musick sounds delightfully in this charming Room, which puts me in such spirits (and my Health being so good) that I exert my self on my Organ whit more then usual success. I opened with the Allegro, Penseroso, & Moderato, and I assure you that the Words of the Moderato are vastly admired. The Audience being composed (besides the Flower of Ladies of Distinction and other People of the greatest quality) of so many Bishops, Deans, Heads of the Colledge, the most eminents People in the Law as the Chancellor, Auditor general & tc. all which are very much taken with the Poëtry. So that I am desired to perform it again the next time. I cannot sufficiently express the kind treatment I receive here, but the Politeness of this generous Nation cannot be unknown to You, so I let you judge of the satisfaction I enjoy, passing my time with Honnour, profit, and pleasure.

[115] The young Edmund Burke describes a fierce battle at Smock Alley Theatre in 1747, between two factions of Trinity students; from *The Early Life and Correspondence of Edmund Burke* by Arthur Samuels.

(Thomas Sheridan (see p. 93) had taken over Smock Alley in 1747 with the avowed intention of making Dublin theatre respectable, and staged a brilliant season of Shakespeare and Restoration comedies.

Smock Alley Theatre was pulled down in 1815, but the stone stairs of the old pit can still be seen in the vaults of the Catholic church of St Michael and St John in West Essex Street.)

I shall now give you some news, but not as news, for I fancy you heard it before. I mean the grand theatre squabble between Mr Kelly, Gentleman, and Sheridan the Player, which has divided the town into two parties as violent as Whig and Tory; and because the scholars of our University have engaged themselves on Sheridan's side, possibly some reports may have been spread as far as you, to our disadvantage. To prevent them from having any influence on you, I shall relate the affair as impartially as I can, and with the utmost regard to truth. First then you must know that sometime ago there was a play performed here which greatly pleased the town called 'Aesop'. During the performance Mr Kelly comes in flushed with liquor, and going into the Green room where the players dress – and began to entertain the actresses in the most nauseous bawdry and ill language calling them bitches and whores, put his hands under their petticoats and would have forced some of them if ability answered his inclinations. This was represented to Sheridan, who is Manager of the Theatre, upon which he ordered Kelly out of the house, who enraged at this, goes into the pit, and as soon as Sheridan came on the stage, pelted him with oranges &c. and called him a thousand ill names, bidding him go off the stage and quite interrupting the performance. At length Sheridan advances to the front of the stage, and tells him that unless some gentleman takes care of him, he would be obliged to turn him out of the house. Ten times more enraged at this, he goes after the act to Sheridan's room and insults him again. Sheridan represented calmly to him his abuse of the female players and of himself; and he, persisting in his ill language, Sheridan gave him a flogging, which he bore with Christian patience, not, however, without vowing vengeance, which he effected the next night by bringing such a party as hindered Sheridan from playing, broke open all the doors, and would very probably have killed him had he not escaped by the usage they gave the playhouse taylor. These doings made him shut up the playhouse and indict Kelly, who also indicted him. During this time thousands of 'States of Cases,' answers, replies, &c. flew about from both parties, and a great deal of dispute concerning the word 'gentleman,' for it seems Sheridan had said he was as good a gentleman as Kelly, or (as others will have it) as any in the house. This gained Kelly a great party, who called their cause the Gentleman's quarrel, taking it extremely ill that a gentleman should be struck by a player, and insisted that Sheridan should never play till he had publicly asked Kelly's pardon. The scholars, who had till now stood neuter, seeing how ill one who was of their body was treated, and the town deprived of their diversion by private pique, took the affair on themselves, and encouraged Sheridan to open the theatre again, which he did, and acted 'Richard the Third,' where a numerous body of the scholars appeared to keep the peace. At the beginning the party began to be riotous, but by menaces they were kept quiet, and one or two of the principal turned out. Thus the play went on regularly, to the satisfaction of the audience.

[116] Mrs Siddons drowns a Dublin audience in tears, 1783; from *The Kemble Era* by Linda Kelly.

(The celebrated actress, Sarah Siddons, was the sister of Smock Alley's leading actor of the period, John Philip Kemble, and joined him in Dublin for the summer season of 1783. Here she is ironically described by an anonymous critic in her most famous role, Isabella in Southerne's tragedy *The Fatal Marriage*.)

On Saturday Mrs S –, about whom all the world has been talking, exposed her beautiful, adamantine, soft and lovely person, for the first time, at Smock-Alley theatre . . . She was nature itself! She was the most exquisite work of art! . . . Several fainted, even before the curtain drew up . . . The very fiddlers in the orchestra, 'albeit unused to the melting mood', blubbered like hungry children crying for their bread and butter . . . One hundred and nine ladies fainted! forty six went into fits! and ninety seven had strong hysterics! the world will scarcely credit the truth when they are told, that fourteen children, five old women, one hundred taylors and six common councilmen, were actually drowned in the inundation of tears that flowed from the galleries, lattices and boxes, to increase the briny pond in the pit.

[117] William Macready recalls the liveliness of a Dublin theatre audience in the early nineteenth century; from his *Reminiscences*, edited by Sir F. Pollock.

(William Charles Macready (1793–1873) was the son of a Dublin actor-manager who had moved to England in the late 1780s. Originally intended for the bar, he took up professional acting aged sixteen to save his father from bankruptcy, and became one of the most brilliant actors of his age, a protégé of Mrs Siddons and later, rival to Edmund Kean. His memories of Dublin date from his two seasons in Ireland in 1815 and 1816.)

The value of the principle that I had lain down as a primary duty in my art, namely *always be in earnest*, was enforced upon me still more strongly by my experience before a Dublin audience. Their attention arrested, and their feelings once excited, the actor enjoyed in their glowing sympathy the full triumph of his art. The national character might be read with tolerable correctness in their theatre. Keenly sensitive to the commanding truth of the poet's or player's passion, they would as often find recourse in their own humour from their dullness or inefficiency. It would not infrequently happen that the humour of the gallery would prove the ruler of the hour, disturbing the more sedate of the spectators and utterly discomposing the player; until, checked by perhaps some energetic declamation, or sobered by some touch of nature, they would surrender themselves to the potent influence of the scene, and beneath its charm no assembly could watch more intently, with more discriminating taste, or more lavish applause, the dream of passion passing before them.

I remember on one occasion acting the character of Pierre in *Venice Preserved*. My friend Jaffier displayed a rotundity of person that might have agreed with the simile to which he likened himself of 'a full ear of corn', but certainly showed no appearance of being 'withered in the ripening'. As if in accordance with this obesity, his delivery was drawling, and his deportment heavy. In the scene prepared for the execution of Pierre, after he had struck me and himself with his dagger, (and gasping out the few spirited words of the defiant conspirator, I had closed my part with the cordial plaudits of the audience), a long and rather drowsy dying speech of my poor friend Jaffier was 'dragging its slow length along', when one of the gallery, in a tone of great impatience, called out very loudly: '*Ah now, die at once!*': to which another from the other side immediately replied: 'Be quiet, you black-guard,' – then turned with a patronizing tone to the lingering Jaffier – '*Take your time!*'

[118] The Dublin theatre in the doldrums in 1842; from W.M. Thackeray's *An Irish Sketchbook*.

How do the Irish amuse themselves in the capital? The love for theatrical exhibitions is evidently not very great. Theatre Royal – Miss Kemble and the Sonnambula, an Anglo-Italian importa-tion. Theatre Royal, Abbey Street – The Temple of Magic and the Wizard, last week. Adelphi Theatre, Great Brunswick Street – The Original Seven Lancashire Bell-ringers: a delicious excitement indeed! Portobello Gardens – 'THE LAST ERUPTION BUT SIX,' says the advertisement in capitals. And, finally, 'Miss Hayes will give her first and farewell concert at the Rotunda, previous to leaving her native country.' Only one instance of Irish talent do we read of, and that, in a desponding tone, announces its intention of quitting its native country. All the rest of the pleasures of the evening are importations from cockney-land. The Sonnambula from Covent Garden, the Wizard from the Strand, the Seven Lancashire Bell-ringers from Islington, or the City Road, no doubt; and as for 'The last Eruption but Six,' it has *erumped* near the 'Elephant and Castle' anytime these two years, until the cockneys would wonder at it no longer. . . .

I was at a fine concert, at which Lablache and others performed, where there were not a hundred people in the pit of the pretty theatre, and where the only encore given was to a young woman in ringlets and yellow satin, who stepped forward and sang 'Coming through the rye,' or some other scientific composition, in an exceedingly small voice. On the nights when the regular drama was enacted, the audience was still smaller. The theatre of Fishamble Street was given up to the performances of the Rev Mr Gregg and his Protestant company, whose soirées I did not attend; and, at the Abbey Street Theatre, whither I went in order to see, if possible, some specimens of the national humour, I heard a company of English people ranting through a melodrama, the tragedy whereof was the only laughable thing to be witnessed.

The Abbey Theatre

[119] Reviving the Irish Theatre – George Moore is taken by W.B. Yeats to see 'the ghost of a theatre down by the Quays': the future Abbey Theatre; from George Moore's *Hail and Farewell*.

The quays were delightful that day, and I wished Yeats to agree with me that there is nothing in the world more delightful than to dawdle among seagulls floating to and fro through a pleasant dawdling light.

'But how is it, Yeats, you can only talk in the evening by the fire, that yellow hand dropping over the chair as if seeking a harp of apple-wood?'

Yeats cawed; he could only caw that morning, but he cawed softly, and my thoughts sang so deliciously in my head that I soon began to feel his ideas to be unnecessary to my happiness, and that it did not matter how long the clerk kept us waiting. When he appeared he and Yeats walked on together, and I followed them up an alley discretely remaining in the rear, fearing that they might be muttering some great revolutionary scheme. I followed them up a staircase full of dust, and found myself to my great surprise in an old library.

'Very like a drawing by Phiz,' I said to myself, bowing, for Yeats and the clerk were bowing apologies for our intrusion to twenty or more shabby genteel scholars who sat reading ancient books under immemorial spider webs. At the end of the library there was another staircase, and we ascended, leaving footprints in the dust. We went along a passage, which opened upon a gallery overlooking a theatre, one that I had no difficulty in recognizing as part of the work done in Dublin by the architects that were brought over in the eighteenth century from Italy. The garlands on the ceiling were of Italian workmanship, the reliefs that remained on the walls. Once the pit was furnished with Chippendale chairs, carved mahogany chairs, perhaps gilded chairs in which ladies in high-bosomed dresses and slippered feet had sat listening to some comedy or tragedy when their lovers were not talking to them; and in those times the two boxes on either side of the stage let out at a guinea or two guineas for the evening.

Once supper-parties were served in them, for Abbey Street is only a few yards from the old Houses of Parliament, and even Grattan may have come to this theatre to meet a lady, whom he kissed after giving her an account of his speech. It amused me to imagine the love-scene, the lady's beauty and Grattan's passion for her, and I wondered what her end might have been, if she had died poor, without money to buy paint for her cheeks or dye for her hair, old, decrepit, and alone . . . I looked on the plank benches that were all the furniture of this theatre, I thought of the stevedores, the carters, the bullies and their trulls, eating their suppers, listening the while to some farce or tragedy written nobody knows by whom. Grattan's mistress may have sat among such, eating her bread and onions about eighty years ago . . .

Yeats and the clerk were talking about the rebuilding of the theatre, saying that the outer walls seemed sound enough, but all the rest would have to be rebuilt, and I wandered round the gallery wondering what were Yeats' dreams while looking into the broken decorations and the faded paint. Plays were still acted in this bygone theatre. But what plays? And who were the mummers that came to play them?

As if in answer, a man and two women came on the stage. I heard their voices, happily not the words they were speaking, for at the bottom of my heart a suspicion lingered that it might be *The Colleen Bawn* they were rehearsing, and not to hear that this was so I moved up the gallery and joined Yeats, saying that we had been among dust and gloom long enough, that I detected drains, and would like to get back into the open air.

We moved out of the theatre, Yeats still talking to the clerk about the price of the building, telling him that the proprietor must never know from whom the offer came; for if he were to hear that there was a project on foot for the establishment of an Irish Literary Theatre his price would go up fifty per cent. The clerk muttered something about a hundred per cent. 'And if he were to hear that Mr Edward Martyn was at the back of it —' Yeats muttered. The clerk interjected that if he were to hear that it would be hard to say what price he would not be putting upon his old walls.

A dried-up, dusty fellow was the clerk, a man about fifty, and I wondered what manner of revolution it might be that he was supposed to be stirring, and how deep was his belief that Maud Gonne would prove herself to be an Irish Joan of Arc; not very much deeper than Yeats' belief that he would one day become possessed of a theatre in Dublin and produce literary plays in it for a people unendowed with any literary sense whatever. Yet they continued shepherding their dreams up the quays, just as if *The Countess Cathleen* had not been hissed the night before, as if Cardinal Logue were not about to publish an interdiction, as if Edward [*Martyn*] were one that could be recovered from ecclesiasticism. . . .

[120] The battle for *The Playboy* – Lady Gregory's account; from *Our Irish Theatre* by Augusta Gregory.

(Augusta Gregory (1852–1932) was, with Yeats, the chief driving power behind the Irish dramatic movement. She and Yeats had discovered the brilliant Irish playwright John Millington Synge. Two of his early plays, *The Shadow of the Glen* and *Riders to the Sea*, had already aroused hostility in Dublin, but his great comedy, *The Playboy of the Western World*, staged in 1907, caused a riot.)

There was a battle of a week. Every night protestors with their trumpets came and raised a din. Every night the police carried some of them off to the police courts. Every afternoon the paper gave reports of the trial before a magistrate who had not heard or read the play and who insisted on being given details of its incidents by the accused and by the police. (Curiously like the old theatre-riots of mid-eighteenth century London – except for the part played by the police.) There was a very large audience on the first night a Saturday, January 26th. Synge was there, but Mr Yeats was giving a lecture in Scotland. The first act got its applause, and the second, though one felt the audience were a little puzzled, a little shocked at the wild language. Near the end of the third act there was some hissing. We had sent a telegram to Mr Yeats after the first act 'Play great success'; but at the end we sent another – 'Audience broke up in disorder at the word shift.'. . . On the Monday night . . . I noticed on one side of the pit a large group of men sitting together, not a woman among them. I told Synge I thought it a sign of some organized disturbance and he telephoned to have the police at hand. The first part of the first act went undisturbed. Then suddenly an uproar began. The group of men I had noticed booed, hooted, blew tin trumpets. . . . It was impossible to hear a word of the play. The curtain came down for a minute, but I went round and told the actors to go on playing to the end, even if not a word could be heard. . . . The disturbance lasted to the end of the evening, not one word had been heard after the first ten minutes.

[121] The battle for *The Playboy* – an outraged citizen's account; from *Joseph Holloway's Abbey Theatre*, edited by Roger Hogan and Michael J. O'Neill.

(Joseph Holloway (1861–1944), an architect and famous Dublin 'character', attended every play in Dublin until his death, and recorded his impressions in journals which ran to 28,000,000 words.)

Saturday, January 26. The Abbey was thronged in the evening to witness the first performance of Synge's three-act comedy *The Playboy of the Western World*, which ended in fiasco owing to the coarseness of the dialogue. The audience bore with it for two and a half acts and even laughed with the dramatist at times, but an unusually brutally coarse remark put into the mouth of 'Christopher Mahon,' the playboy of the title, set the house off into hooting and hissing amid counter applause, and the din was kept up till the curtain closed in.

On coming out, Lady Gregory asked me, 'What was the cause of the disturbance?'

And my monosyllabic answer was, 'Blackguardism!'

To which she queried, 'On which side?'

'The stage!' came from me pat, and then I passed on, and the incident was closed. . . .

'This is not Irish life!' said one of the voices from the pit, and despite the fact that Synge in a note on the programme says, 'I have used one or two words only that I have not heard among the country people of Ireland, or spoken in my own nursery before I could read the newspapers,' I maintain that his play of *The Playboy* is not a truthful or just picture of the Irish peasants, but simply the outpouring of a morbid, unhealthy mind ever seeking on the dunghill of life for the nastiness that lies concealed there. . . . Synge is the evil genius of the Abbey and Yeats his able lieutenant. Both dabble in the unhealthy. Lady Gregory, though she backs them up when they transgress good taste and cast decency to the winds, keeps clean in her plays.

Monday, January 28. . . . Henderson and I went down to the Abbey . . . and on our way spoke of Synge's nasty mind – to store those crude, coarse sayings from childhood and now present them in a play. The influence of Gorki must be upon him. Henderson also told me that the new English manager had arrived, and he was thinking of retiring before being dismissed. The new man was to get £5 a week; he was only getting 30/-.

By this time we arrived at the Abbey. Two stalwart police at the vestibule suggested trouble, and we found plenty and to spare when we went in. The performance was just concluding amid a terrific uproar (the piece had not been listened to, we were told). The curtains were drawn aside, and W.G. Fay [*playing Christy Mahon, the Playboy*] stood forward amid the din. After some minutes, in a lull, he said, 'You who have hissed to-night will go away saying you have heard the play, but you haven't.'

'We heard it on Saturday!' came from the back of the pit, and the hissing and hooting were renewed.

The scene which followed was indescribable. Those in the pit howled for the author, and he with Lady Gregory and others held animated conversation in the stalls. Denis O'Sullivan made himself very conspicuous railing against the noise producers, and Signor Esposito gesticulated abundantly. Small knots of people argued the situation out anything but calmly, and after about a quarter of an hour's clamour, the audience dispersed hoarse. 'Heblon,' in a half-tight state, blackguarded the Irish people and upheld the dramatist, and George Roberts said, 'The play is the finest ever written if you had only the wit to see it!' I wished him joy of the dungheap of a mind he must possess to arrive at that conclusion, and Lawrence and I departed.

[122] The battle for *The Playboy* – a schoolboy's memory; from Walter Starkie's autobiography, *Scholars and Gypsies*.

(Walter Starkie (1894–1976) was brought up in Dublin, studied at Trinity just before the First World War, and was a lecturer and professor there in the 1920s and '30s. He spent much of his later life in Spain, where he became an expert on gipsy folklore, and finally worked at the University of California.)

The most exciting theatrical experience of my youth took place in my thirteenth year when J.M. Synge's play *The Playboy of the Western World* was produced for the first time at the Abbey Theatre in January 1907. It was my first visit to the Abbey Theatre, and Paddy Tobin, whom at school we all considered an expert in theatrical matters as he had acted with his three cousins, the Wogan Brown girls (all of them excellent actresses, and one of them, Dorothy, so vivacious that she appealed to Bernard Shaw as the ideal embodiment of Dolly in *You Never Can Tell*), promised to bring me round to the Green Room to introduce me to Lady Gregory.

'Tonight,' he said, when I met him at Nelson's Pillar, 'my father says there will be the hell of a row as the newspapers have been publishing attacks on the play, saying that it is an insult to Ireland.' When we reached Abbey Street we found a great crowd assembled in the streets adjoining the theatre. Inside, the atmosphere was electric and there was suspense in the air, as though everyone in the auditorium expected a political revolution to break out. Instead of waiting quietly in their seats for the play to begin, many gathered together in groups talking excitedly, and I was struck, too, by the varying types I saw in the audience. In addition to the usual middle-class theatre-goers, there were numbers of workers, and here and there gentlemen and ladies in evening dress, and young men whose tousled hair and beards proclaimed them initiates of the Dublin Latin quarter. A wizened old man sitting next to me pointed out the literary and political celebrities as they took their places. 'See that long thin rake of a fellow, that's Best the Librarian arguing with Dr R.M. Henry, one of the Belfast Home-Rules. Next but two to him is a fine upstanding man with a beard: that's AE, our Irish Buddha! Over there by himself is the victim of the evening, John Millington Synge. Every one of the Irish intellectuals are present, but it's not the play they've come to see, but to spy on one another.' I longed to ask the old man for an explanation for his cryptic words, but just then the lights dimmed and I heard a dismal gong sounding the knell as it seemed to me, and the curtain rose.

Although I tried very hard to concentrate upon the play it was impossible to hear the actors after the first few minutes because of the interruptions and disturbances which took place all over the auditorium. When these reached a climax, one of the company advanced to the footlights and tried to appeal for silence. He said, as far as I could make out, that anyone in the audience who did not like the play was at liberty to get up and leave, but nobody left. Instead, pandemonium broke loose, and my wizened neighbour, whom I had considered an inoffensive old man, jumped to his feet shouting: 'Clear the decks! Down with Willie Fay!' And his shouts were taken up in chorus by the gallery. Then came shouts from the pit below and many started to sing the revolutionary song, *The West's asleep*.

While all this rumpus was going on the actors and actresses on the stage continued valiantly to act their parts, but they were puppets; I could see their lips move but hardly a word reached me. Paddy Tobin and I recognized some friends who were from Trinity College. They had come at the request of Lady Gregory's nephew with other students to support the play. Seeing that the disturbances increased in the second act they thought the best way in which they could show their support of the play would be by singing *God Save the King* in chorus. Even today, when I look back at that fateful night in the history of the Irish National Theatre, I cannot imagine how such a crazy notion as singing the British National Anthem could have entered their heads. Instead of pouring oil on troubled waters they enraged the Irish patriots in the pit by singing what the latter considered a political song.

Paddy Tobin and I enjoyed ourselves immensely in the hullabaloo. Through the tempest of shouting and hissing we heard cries '*Sinn Fein Amhain*' and 'kill the author', and from our seats at the side of the gallery we had a wonderful view of the milling mob in the pit and gallery. Then suddenly the doors of the auditorium opened and a posse of Dublin Metropolitan police entered, and many of the rowdy elements were cast out. We expected the burly giants to draw their batons and made ready to join the wild stampede, but there was a momentary lull as another figure advanced to the footlights to speak to the mob; but he was no more successful than his predecessor had been in the first act, and his voice was drowned by catcalls and the strident tones of toy trumpets. Those who thought the display of force by the police would calm the rioters were mistaken, for Act

III of the play began amidst scenes of even greater chaos. As we were unable to hear a single word of the play, and knowing that the fight was spreading to the street outside, we left our seats and mingled with the crowd in the vestibule. Following Paddy during the interval I managed to reach the back of the stage through a side door leading into the lane, and we joined the actors and their supporters gathered round Lady Gregory and J.M. Synge. While to me it seemed that all the players were wringing their hands, tearing their hair and running hither and thither, Lady Gregory stood at the door of the Green Room as calm and collected as Queen Victoria about to open a charity bazaar. Seeing Paddy Tobin and myself, she beckoned us over and handed each of us a piece of the huge barmbrack which she had baked at Coole and brought up to Dublin for the Abbey cast. While we were munching our cake we observed the author, J.M. Synge, mooning about among the actors like a lost soul. I had seen him on various occasions in Kingstown, and when I passed him striding along the Dalkey road swinging his stick I used to wonder whether he was French or Austrian, for he had moustaches and a little goatee or 'imperial'. When I saw him on the night of the Abbey riot his face was pale and sunken, and he looked like a ghost of the sun-tanned wanderer I had seen walking by the sea. I watched him closely as he sat motionless through the dumb-show of his play, amidst the rioting and insults of the mob, but not a trace of emotion could I discern in his pale mask-like face that gazed unseeing at the raging auditorium.

[123] Backstage at the Abbey – Lady Gregory's journal, 1908; from *Seventy Years* by Augusta Gregory.

Oh, this theatre! 1.00 o'clock now, and I have been writing on its affairs ever since breakfast time.

I came round before matinee. M. wanted to speak to me 'to tender his resignation' in consequence of Miss N. having insulted him during *Cross Roads* last night, before the stagehands, asked him what the devil he meant because he had missed his cue . . . Also he was knocked down in *Cross Roads* by O. instead of being choked sitting in a chair, and this he seems to think was revenge, because he had at some previous time hit O. with the pipe he

throws at him in *Workhouse Ward*. I spoke to Miss N. who accuses
him of a variety of small offences connected with cues . . . P. has
been up a few minutes ago asking for a rise of wages. On my way
back to the auditorium I met Miss Q. and asked her about the
quarrel. She says M. is desperately in love with N. He has been
much worse since Mr Yeats did her horoscope saying she was to
marry a fair man. He walked up and down saying, 'I am that fair
man'. She went to him the other day and told him he was foolish
and ought to put N. out of his head, but at the end he said, 'I
know very well that you are in love with me yourself!'

[124] Downstage at the Abbey – a memory of Yeats; from
Austin Clarke's autobiography, *A Penny in the Clouds*.

(Austin Clarke (1896–1974) poet, dramatist and novelist was
brought up in Dublin and educated at Belvedere and University
College, Dublin (where he was probably a student at the period
he recalls here). He left Ireland during the Civil War but
returned from 'exile' in 1931 and founded the Dublin Verse
Speaking Society which produced verse plays for the Peacock
and Abbey Theatres in the same tradition as Yeats's plays. From
1942 to 1955, he broadcast a weekly programme of poetry on
Radio Eireann and died in Dublin, loaded with literary
honours.)

The plays of Yeats were a deeply imaginative experience, and, as
the poet put on his own plays as often as possible, the experience
was a constant one. On such occasions the theatre was almost
empty. There were a few people in the stalls, including Lady
Gregory, and just after the last gong had sounded, Yeats would
dramatically appear at the top of the steps leading down into the
auditorium. Perhaps the actors spoke the lyric lines in tones that
had become hollow-sounding with time, borrowing the archaic
voice which is normally reserved for religious services. It seemed
right that the poetic mysteries should be celebrated reverently
and with decorum. Moreover, the presence of the poet himself in
the theatre was a clear proof that all was well.

Scarcely had the desultory clapping ceased, when Yeats
would appear outside the stage curtain, a dim figure against the
footlights. He swayed and waved rhythmically, telling humbly

W.B. Yeats lectures the audience at the Abbey Theatre, early 1900s

of his 'little play', how he had rewritten it, and what he had meant to convey in its lines. As the twenty or thirty people in the pit were more or less scattered, I was isolated usually in one of the back seats. On such occasions, I felt like Ludwig of Bavaria, that eccentric monarch, who sat alone in his own theatre. I enjoyed the poet's curtain-lecture, almost as if it were a special benefit performance for myself.

One night, however, my youthful and romantic illusions were suddenly shattered, and in a trice the Celtic Twilight was gone. As the poet appeared punctually outside the curtain, a dazzling light shone around him. It might have been the light of his later fame! I glanced up and saw that the brilliant shaft of illumination came from the balcony. A spotlight must have been clamped to the rail and switched on as the poet appeared. But my conclusions may have been unjust, for in youth we do not understand the complexities of human motives. I did not realize at the time that poetic drama was slowly vanishing from the Abbey Theatre. It seems to me now that, consciously or not, the poet might have been making a last despairing gesture to call attention, not to his own picturesque person, but to the struggling cause of poetry on the stage.

❧ The approaches to the city: Dublin on Sea

Ringsend

[125] John Dunton arrives at Ringsend in 1698; from Edward MacLysaght's *Irish Life in the Seventeenth Century*.

(Until the completion of the North and South Walls of Dublin harbour in the late eighteenth century, Ringsend provided the main embarkation point for Dublin, cut off by treacherous sands from the main city. Many early travellers complained of the discomfort of the Ringsend cars.)

After some refreshment here I looked towards Dublin but how to come at it I no more knew than the fox at the grapes, for though I saw a large strand yet twas not to be walked over because of a pretty rapid stream which must be crossed. I enquired for a coach, but found no such thing was to be had here unless by accident; but was informed that I might have a Ring's End car, which upon my desire was [got] and I got upon it, not into it. It is a perfect car with two wheels and towards the back of it a seat is raised cross-ways, long enough to hold three people, the cushion mine had was made of patchwork but of such coarse kind of stuff that I fancied they had stolen some poor beggar's coat for a covering, between me and the horse upon the cross bars of the car stood my charioteer who presently set his horse into a gallop which so jolted our sides though upon a smooth strand that I was in purgatory until I got at Lazy-hill, where I paid three halfpence for my fare of half a mile's riding, and almost as pleased as the young gentleman that drove the chariot of the sun would have been, to be rid of my seat. However they are a great convenience and you may go to Ring's End from Dublin, or from hence thither with a load of goods for three pence or a groat, and I was told there are one hundred more plying hereabouts that you can hardly be disappointed.

Dublin Bay

[126] Dublin harbour in 1810; from *An Englishman's Descriptive Account of Dublin* by Nathaniel Jeffreys.

A wonderful improvement has been made in Dublin harbour by a work truly magnificent, both for its appearance and utility . . . which is called the South Wall. It was begun in 1748 and finished in seven years. It extends in a straight line into the sea the surprising length of four English miles; it is formed of large blocks of mountain granite, strongly cemented and strengthened with iron cramps.

As far as the Pigeon house, which is three miles from Dublin, there is upon this wall a noble coach road of forty feet in breadth; the passengers upon which are securely protected from the violence of the sea in tempestuous weather by parapet walls; and at the extremity of this magnificent work is the LIGHTHOUSE which is built in an appropriate style of architecture perfectly corresponding to the bold dignity of the scene. It was begun in June 1762 when from the very great depth of the water and power of the winds in such an exposed position, together with the raging of a tempestuous sea, the most serious difficulties were to be encountered. But the perseverence and great professional skill of the architect (Mr Smith) bade defiance to the obstacles, the bare mention of which were enough to intimidate persons of less merit than himself.

The Pigeon House . . . about 3 miles from Dublin and 1 from the landing place, is the customary landing place of passengers from the packets . . . The breadth of the pier at this place is 250 feet, on which are erected a magazine, arsenal and custom-house. It is a place of great strength being surrounded with heavy cannon. . . . There are also in many parts of the Bay, the Martello Towers, which were so strongly recommended by Mr Windham when in power as Secretary of War, during the administration of Mr Pitt, which an Irish sailor in one of the packets being asked the use of by a passenger replied 'The devil a use can I think of, but to please Mr Windham and puzzle posterity.'

The mode of conveying the passengers to Dublin is the LONG COACH.

This carriage is upon the plan of those *elegant* vehicles upon low wheels which are used on the road between Hyde Park Corner and Hammersmith, and from the state of its repair and external appearance, as well as its internal decoration, it bears every mark of having retired on the superannuated list from that active duty . . .

This coach is generally very crowded from the anxiety of the passengers to proceed to Dublin; and from the manner in which some of the company may easily be supposed to have been passing their time on board . . ., from the effect of seasickness, the effluvia arising from 12 or 14 persons crammed together in a very small space, like the inmates of Noah's ark, *the clean and the unclean*, is not of that description which can entitle the long coach to be considered *a bed of roses*.

Three shillings for each passenger is the price of conveyance, and this is exacted beforehand – a mode of settling accounts which is frequently the cause of great dissatisfaction.

Dun Laoghaire

[127] W.M. Thackeray lands at Kingstown (Dun Laoghaire) in 1841; from his *Irish Sketchbook*.

A long pier, with a steamer or two at hand, and a few small vessels lying on either side of the jetty; a town irregularly built, with many handsome terraces, some churches, and showy-looking hotels; a few people straggling on the beach; two or three cars at the railroad station, which runs along the shore as far as Dublin; the sea stretching interminably eastward; to the north the Hill of Howth, lying grey behind the mist; and, directly under his feet, upon the wet, black, shining, slippery deck, an agreeable reflection of his own legs, disappearing seemingly in the direction of the cabin from which he issues: are the sights which a traveller may remark on coming on deck at Kingstown pier on a wet morning – Let us say on an *average* morning; for according to the statement of well-informed natives, the Irish day is more often rainy than otherwise. A hideous obelisk, stuck upon four fat balls, and surmounted with a crown on a cushion (the latter were no bad emblems perhaps of the monarch in whose honour they were raised), commemorates the sacred spot at which George IV *quitted* Ireland. You are landed here from the steamer; and a carman, who is dawdling in the neighbourhood, with a straw in his mouth, comes leisurely up to ask whether you will go to Dublin? Is it natural indolence, or the effect of despair because of the neighbouring railroad, which renders him so indifferent? – He does not even take the straw out of his mouth as he proposes the question – he seems quite careless as to the answer. . . .

Before that day, so memorable for joy and sorrow, for rapture at receiving its monarch and tearful grief at losing him, when George IV came and left the maritime resort of the citizens of Dublin, it bore a less genteel name than that which it owns at present, and was called Dunleary. After that glorious event Dunleary disdained to be Dunleary any longer, and became Kingstown henceforward and for ever. Numerous terraces and pleasure-houses have been built in the place – they stretch row after row along the banks of the sea, and rise one above another

Monument to George IV at Kingstown (Dun Laoghaire) 'a hideous obelisk, stuck upon four fat balls, and surmounted by a crown on a cushion' (Thackeray). An early nineteenth-century engraving on the hill. The rents of these houses are said to be very high; the Dublin citizens crowd into them in summer; and a great source of pleasure and comfort must it be to them to have the fresh sea-breezes and prospects so near to the metropolis.

The better sort of houses are handsome and spacious; but the fashionable quarter is yet in an unfinished state, for enterprising architects are always beginning new roads, rows and terraces: nor are those already built by any means complete. Beside the aristocratic part of the town is a commercial one, and nearer to Dublin stretch lines of low cottages which have not a Kingstown look at all, but are evidently of the Dunleary period. It is quite curious to see in the streets where the shops are, how often the painter of the sign-boards begins with big letters, and ends, for want of space, with small; and the Englishman accustomed to the thriving neatness and regularity which characterize towns great and small in his own country, can't fail to notice the difference here. The houses have a battered, rakish look, and seem going to ruin before their time. As seamen of all nations come hither who have made no vow of temperance, there are plenty of liquor-shops still, and shabby cigar-shops, and shabby milliners' and tailors' with fly-blown prints of old fashions. The bakers and apothecaries make a great brag of their calling, and you see MEDICAL HALL, or PUBLIC BAKERY, BALLYRAGGET FLOUR-STORE, (or whatever the name may be,) pompously inscribed over very humble tenements. Some comfortable grocers' and butchers' shops, and numbers of shabby sauntering people, the younger part of whom are barelegged and bareheaded, make up the rest of the picture which the stranger sees as his car goes jingling through the street.

After the town come the suburbs of pleasure-houses; low, one-storeyed cottages for the most part: some neat and fresh, some that have passed away from the genteel state altogether, and exhibit downright poverty; some in a state of transition, with broken windows and pretty romantic names upon tumble-down gates. Who lives in them? One fancies that the chairs and tables inside are broken, that the tea-pot on the breakfast-table has no spout, and the tablecloth is ragged and sloppy; that the lady of the house is in dubious curl-papers, and the gentleman, with an imperial to his chin, wears a flaring dressing-gown all ragged at the elbows.

Sandycove

[128] James Joyce at the Martello Tower in 1903; from *It isn't This Time of Year at all* by Oliver St John Gogarty.

(Joyce's famous opening scene in *Ulysses* between Stephen Dedalus and 'stately plump Buck Mulligan' is, like so much of his writing, autobiographical – and was much resented by Buck Mulligan/Oliver Gogarty. Here is Gogarty's version, written in the 1950s, which still retains some of the condescension which so galled Joyce.)

James Joyce said, 'Do you know that we can rent the Martello Tower at Sandycove? I'll pay the rent if you will furnish it.'

Sandycove is about seven miles from Dublin on the south side of its famous bay. It lies a little to the east of the harbor which takes the mail boat from England early in the morning and late at night. The water between Dun Laoghaire and Sandycove is called Scotsman's Bay and is bounded by the east pier of the harbor and the two-storied, thick-walled Martello Tower, with the Battery close by the Forty Foot, a resort for strong swimmers. . . .

The rent for the Tower at Sandycove was only eight pounds or about $32 per year, payable at Dublin Castle. We took it; and Joyce kept his word and stumped up the rent from a prize of twenty pounds that he had won in some examination. I did the furnishing from unmissed things from 5 Rutland Square. 'It's a poor house where there are not many things superfluous.' I learned that at school from the poet Horace. . . .

The Tower at Sandycove is built of clear granite. It is very clean. Its door, which is halfway up, is approached by a ladder fixed beneath the door, which is opened by a large copper key, for there was a powder magazine in the place and the copper was meant to guard against sparks which an iron key might strike out from the stone. There is a winding staircase in the thickness of the wall to the side that does not face the sea. On the roof, which is granite, is a gun emplacement, also of granite, which can be used for a table if you use the circular sentry walk for a seat. Over the door is a projection from which boiling oil or molten lead can be poured down upon an enemy. Beside this is a furnace for making cannon balls red hot. There were no shells in the days when it was built, but the red-hot cannon balls could burn a wooden ship if they hit it. Happily these towers were never used, though they were occupied by coast guards until quite recently.

We lived there for two years, greatly to the anxious relief of our parents. Joyce had a job at an adjoining school. I had some reading to do for my medical degree. When the weather was warm we sun-bathed on the roof, moving around the raised sentry platform with the sun and out of the wind. . . . One morning back in Sandycove I was shaving on the roof of the Tower, because of the better light – it is a good idea to shave before going into salt water – when up comes Joyce.

'Fine morning, Dante. Feeling transcendental this morning?' I asked.

'Would you be so merry and bright if you had to go out at this hour to teach a lot of scrawny-necked brats?'

Touché! He had me there: not a doubt about it. Why don't I think of other people's problems? I must develop a little sympathy: suffer with them; realize their difficulties. I am glad that he has a job, though it is only that of a teacher.

The golden down that would be a beard on a more robust man shone in the morning light. Joyce did not need a shave.

'Yes,' I said, 'that is enough to obscure the Divine Idea that underlies all life. But why be atrabilious about it?' He gave me a sour look. He turned and stooped under the low door.

'I suppose you will bear that in mind and attach it to me when you come to write your *Inferno?*' I said.

He turned and made a grave announcement: 'I will treat you with fairness.'

'Put a pint or two in the fairness and I won't complain.'

He was gone.

What would be the use of sympathy with a character like that? He would resent sympathy. He is planning some sort of novel that will show us all up and the country as well: all will be fatuous except James Joyce. . . . Presently I heard him climbing down the ladder. I went into the overhanging balcony, and called down, 'Don't stop at the Arch on your way back.' He never looked up but he raised his stick in a grave salute and loped off.

[129] Gogarty at the Martello Tower; from James Joyce's *Ulysses*.

Stately plump Buck Mulligan came from the stairhead, bearing a bowl of lather on which a mirror and a razor lay crossed. A yellow dressinggown, ungirdled, was sustained gently behind him by the mild morning air. He held the bowl aloft and intoned:

– *Introibo ad attare Dei.*

Halted, he peered down the dark winding stairs and called up coarsely:

– Come up, Kinch. Come up, you fearful jesuit.

Solemnly he came forward and mounted the round gunrest. He faced about and blessed gravely thrice the tower, the surrounding country and the awaking mountains. Then, catching sight of Stephen Dedalus, he bent towards him and made rapid crosses in the air, gurgling in his throat and shaking his head. Stephen Dedalus, displeased and sleepy, leaned his arms on the top of the staircase and looked coldly at the shaking gurgling face that blessed him, equine in its length, and at the light untonsured hair, grained and hued like pale oak.

Buck Mulligan peeped an instant under the mirror and then covered the bowl smartly.

– Back to barracks, he said sternly.

He added in a preacher's tone:

– For this, O dearly beloved, is the genuine Christine: body and soul and blood and ouns. Slow music, please. Shut your eyes, gents. One moment. A little trouble about those white corpuscles. Silence, all.

He peered sideways up and gave a long low whistle of call, then paused awhile in rapt attention, his even white teeth glistening here and there with gold points. Chrysostomos. Two strong shrill whistles answered through the calm.

– Thanks, old chap, he cried briskly. That will do nicely. Switch off the current, will you?

He skipped off the gunrest and looked gravely at his watcher, gathering about his legs the loose folds of his gown. The plump shadowed face and sullen oval jowl recalled a prelate, patron of arts in the middle ages. A pleasant smile broke quietly over his lips.

– The mockery of it, he said gaily. Your absurd name, an ancient Greek.

He pointed his finger in friendly jest and went over to the parapet, laughing to himself. Stephen Dedalus stepped up, followed him wearily halfway and sat down on the edge of the gunrest, watching him still as he propped his mirror on the parapet, dipped the brush in the bowl and lathered cheeks and neck.

Buck Mulligan's gay voice went on.

– My name is absurd too: Malachi Mulligan, two dactyls. But it has a Hellenic ring, hasn't it? Tripping and sunny like the buck himself. We must go to Athens. Will you come if I can get the aunt to fork out twenty quid?

He laid the brush aside and, laughing with delight, cried:

– Will he come? The jejune jesuit.

Ceasing, he began to shave with care.

– Tell me, Mulligan, Stephen said quietly.

– Yes, my love?

– How long is Haines going to stay in this tower?

Buck Mulligan showed a shaven cheek over his right shoulder.

– God, isn't he dreadful? he said frankly. A ponderous Saxon. He thinks you're not a gentleman. God, these bloody English. Bursting with money and indigestion. Because he comes from Oxford. You know, Dedalus, you have the real Oxford manner. He can't make you out. O, my name for you is the best: Kinch, the knifeblade.

He shaved warily over his chin.

– He was raving all night about a black panther, Stephen said. Where is his guncase?

– A woeful lunatic, Mulligan said. Were you in a funk?

– I was, Stephen said with energy and growing fear. Out here in the dark with a man I don't know raving and moaning to himself about shooting a black panther. You saved men from drowning. I'm not a hero, however. If he stays on here I am off.

Buck Mulligan frowned at the lather on his razorblade. He hopped down from his perch and began to search his trousers pockets hastily.

– Scutter, he cried thickly.

He came over to the gunrest and, thrusting a hand into Stephen's upper pocket, said:

– Lend us a loan of your noserag to wipe my razor.

Stephen suffered him to pull out and hold up on show by its corner a dirty crumpled handkerchief. Buck Mulligan wiped the razorblade neatly. Then, gazing over the handkerchief, he said:

– The bard's noserag. A new art colour for our Irish poets: snotgreen. You can almost taste it, can't you?

– He mounted to the parapet again and gazed out over Dublin bay, his fair oakpale hair stirring slightly.

– God, he said quietly. Isn't the sea what Algy calls it: a grey sweet mother? The snotgreen sea. The scrotumtightening sea. *Epi oinopa ponton.* Ah, Dedalus, the Greeks. I must teach you. You must read them in the original. *Thalatta! Thalatta!* She is our great sweet mother. Come and look.

Stephen stood up and went over to the parapet. Leaning on it he looked down on the water and on the mailboat clearing the harbour mouth of Kingstown.

– Our mighty mother, Buck Mulligan said.

He turned abruptly his great searching eyes from the sea to Stephen's face.

– The aunt thinks you killed your mother, he said. That's why she won't let me have anything to do with you.

– Someone killed her, Stephen said gloomily.

– You could have knelt down, damn it, Kinch, when your dying mother asked you, Buck Mulligan said. I'm hyperborean as much as you. But to think of your mother begging you with her last breath to kneel down and pray for her. And you refused. There is something sinister in you. . . .

He broke off and lathered again lightly his farther cheek. A tolerant smile curled his lips.

– But a lovely mummer, he murmured to himself. Kinch, the loveliest mummer of them all.

He shaved evenly and with care, in silence, seriously.

Stephen, an elbow rested on the jagged granite, leaned his palm against his brow and gazed at the fraying edge of his shiny black coatsleeve. Pain, that was not yet the pain of love, fretted his heart. Silently, in a dream she had come to him after her death, her wasted body within its loose brown graveclothes giving off an odour of wax and rosewood, her breath, that had bent upon him, mute, reproachful, a faint odour of wetted ashes. Across the threadbare cuffedge he saw the sea hailed as a great sweet mother by the wellfed voice beside him. The ring of bay and skyline held a dull green mass of liquid. A bowl of white china had stood beside her deathbed holding the green sluggish bile which she had torn up from her rotting liver by fits of loud groaning vomiting.

Buck Mulligan wiped his razorblade.

– Ah, poor dogsbody, he said in a kind voice. I must give you a shirt and a few noserags. How are the secondhand breeks?

– They fit well enough, Stephen answered.

Buck Mulligan attacked the hollow beneath his underlip.

– The mockery of it, he said contentedly, secondleg they should be. God knows what poxy bowsy left them off. I have a lovely pair with a hair stripe, grey. You'll look spiffing in them. I'm not joking, Kinch. You look damn well when you're dressed.

– Thanks, Stephen said. I can't wear them if they are grey.

– He can't wear them. Buck Mulligan told his face in the mirror. Etiquette is etiquette. He kills his mother but he can't wear grey trousers.

He folded his razor neatly and with stroking palps of fingers felt the smooth skin.

Stephen turned his gaze from the sea and to the plump face with its smokeblue mobile eyes.

– That fellow I was with in the Ship last night, said Buck Mulligan, says you have g. p. i. He's up in Dottyville with Conolly Norman. General paralysis of the insane.

He swept the mirror a half circle in the air to flash the tidings abroad in sunlight now radiant on the sea. His curling shaven lips laughed and the edges of his white glittering teeth. Laughter seized all his strong wellknit trunk.

– Look at yourself, he said, you dreadful bard.

Stephen bent forward and peered at the mirror held out to him, cleft by crooked crack, hair on end. As he and others see me. Who chose this face for me? This dogsbody to rid of vermin. It asks me too.

– I pinched it out of the skivvy's room, Buck Mulligan said. It does her all right. The aunt always keeps plainlooking servants for Malachi. Lead him not into temptation. And her name is Ursula.

Laughing again, he brought the mirror away from Stephen's peering eyes.

– The rage of Caliban at not seeing his face in a mirror, he said. If Wilde were only alive to see you.

Drawing back and pointing, Stephen said with bitterness:

– It is a symbol of Irish art. The cracked lookingglass of a servant.

Buck Mulligan suddenly linked his arm in Stephen's and walked with him round the tower, his razor and mirror clacking in the pocket where he had thrust them.

    – It's not fair to tease you like that, Kinch, is it? he said kindly. God knows you have more spirit than any of them.

    Parried again. He fears the lancet of my art as I fear that of his. The cold steelpen.

[130] James Joyce leaves the Martello Tower; from *Selected Letters of James Joyce* edited by Richard Ellmann.

15 September 1904   *7 S. Peter's Terrace, Cabra, Dublin*
Dear Starkey [*Seamus O'Sullivan, the Dublin poet*] My trunk will be called for at the Tower tomorrow (Saturday) between 9 and 12. Kindly put into it – a pair of black boots, a pair of brown boots, a blue peaked cap, a black cloth cap, a black felt hat, a raincoat and the MS of my verses which are in a roll on the shelf to the right as you enter. Also see that your host has not abstracted the twelfth chapter of my novel from my trunk. May I ask you to see that any letters coming to the Tower for me are redirected to my address at once? Please rope the trunk as it has no lock. Faithfully Yours

JAS A JOYCE

Howth

[131] A childhood in Howth, in the 1880s; from Maud Gonne MacBride's autobiography, *A Servant of the Queen*.

(Maud Gonne (1866–1953) was the daughter of a wealthy British army officer (the 'Tommy' in this extract). After her mother's early death from tuberculosis, she and her sister were sent to live in the healthy sea-air at Howth. She grew up to extraordinary beauty, and became the love of Yeats' life; but she refused to marry him, and spent her life in almost ceaseless revolutionary activity for the Irish cause. She married (unhappily) in 1903 John MacBride, who was to be one of the leaders of the 1916 rising.)

Howth was different then from what it is to-day. There was no tram, and very few houses. The ugly little house we rented had been built by the enterprising man who drove the one outside car in the district to and from the station at Sutton. He and his large family lived in a little cabin near by and his mother lived in another, even smaller and smokier, cabin farther up in the heather.

Tommy used to come for week-ends and Kathleen and I used to be strapped securely on to one side of the car, with our feet in a big sack of hay for the horse and a rug to keep us all compact, tucked in at each side of the cushions if the day was cold or windy; our landlord sat on the other side till we arrived at Sutton where Tommy, coming off the train, would take his place and he the driver's seat in the middle, while Tommy's bags and exciting parcels of cakes and toys filled the well of the car and the drive home seemed very long till we could get opening them.

No place has ever seemed to me quite so lovely as Howth was then. Sometimes the sea was as blue as Mama's turquoises, more strikingly blue even than the Mediterranean because so often grey mists made it invisible and mysterious. The little rock pools at the bottom of the high cliffs were very clear and full of wonder-life; sea-anemones which open look like gorgeous flowers with blue and orange spots and, if touched, close up into ugly brown humps, tiny crabs, pink star-fish, endless varieties of sea-snails, white, green, striped and bright buttercup-yellow. Nurse must have been a wonderful climber, for she often took us down to bathe in those ready-made bathing pools where Kathleen and I boastfully declared that we were swimming, with our feet and hands firmly touching the bottom. The waves used to come splashing into them and made us feel very brave. It must have been a fairly perilous enterprise for her to convey safely two young children up and down those zig-zag narrow cliff paths among the wheeling crying sea-gulls. We were never allowed to go near the cliffs alone, but on the other side of the house far up the heather-covered hill to Granny's cabin, we were free to wander and play as we pleased. The heather grew so high and strong there that we could make cubby houses and be entirely hidden and entirely warm and sheltered from the strong wind that blows over the Head of Howth. After I was grown up I have often slept all night in that friendly heather. It is as springy as the finest spring mattress and, if one chooses the place well, so cosy and sheltered and quiet. From deep down in it one looks up at the stars in a wonderful security and falls asleep to wake up only with the call of the sea birds looking for their breakfasts.

Nurse was a sociable soul. Very soon she knew all the people who lived in the little cabins along the road to the Post Office and away in the heather, and while, over a friendly cup of tea, she chatted, Kathleen and I played with the barefooted children and shared their slices of hot griddle cake baked at the turf fire, or their potatoes out of big iron pots hung in the chimneys. No potatoes and no bread ever tasted as good. All the hospitality was on their side for nurse would never let us bring them to share our meals, carefully set out by Annie the housemaid in the little sitting-room, and woe to Annie if our silver christening mugs and spoons were not brilliantly polished. Those elaborately set-out meals and the steel hoops of her own crinoline were nurse's way of keeping up respectability.

Our feelings towards the ragged children were mixed; they were better climbers than we were and better riders of donkeys, but we could boast of our exploits in swimming pools. If we had better clothes, they had more learning, for every day they trudged off to the far-away school-house, while we played all day with the kids and donkeys in the heather. On the whole honours were fairly equal. . . .

Nurse was a knowledgeable woman and gained great reputation for having saved a sick baby's life. She had a store of nursery remedies and came to be consulted whenever there was a sick child or a minor accident in Howth. She was very proud of this reputation; it gained her forgiveness for her crinoline and English accent, of which also she was proud, but which, if it had not been for her reputation as a doctor and her unfailing good nature, might have marred her popularity; all the cabins were hung with coloured pictures of Wolfe Tone, Emmet and Michael Dwyer and of Allen Larkin and O'Brien and the early Land-League heroes side by side with chromos of the Sacred Heart and of the Blessed Virgin. If nurse knew who these men were, she never said anything; but when she was not there, the old people used to say they were great men, the Lord have mercy on them, but would not say more because after all we too, as well as nurse, belonged to the other side, – the English garrison; nevertheless they made us welcome to their glowing turf fires.

Dublin in revolution

The Larkin Strike

[132] A police baton charge in O'Connell Street, 1913; from Sean O'Casey's *Drums under the Windows*.

(James Larkin (1876–1947) born in Liverpool of impoverished Irish parents, came to Dublin in 1908 after successfully organizing a massive strike in the Belfast docks, to found the Irish Transport and General Workers Union. A superb orator and magnetic personality, he rapidly attracted thousands of Dublin's unskilled workers (who lived and worked in some of the worst conditions in Europe), including the young Sean O'Casey. The Dublin employers, led by William Martin Murphy (who owned Clery's store, the Dublin United Tramways Company and the *Irish Independent*) forbade their employees to join his Union; and when they refused, he organized a general lock-out. The bitter struggle that followed opened with the brutal baton charge on unarmed crowds in O'Connell Street described here by O'Casey. The Dublin workers were eventually starved back to work; Larkin left for America in search of support, and was eventually arrested there for 'criminal syndicalism'. Although Larkin's strike split the rising militant Nationalist movement, it also acted as catalyst, and while it lasted, wrote Desmond Ryan, 'the very air of Dublin was electric with revolution'.)

The meeting of the locked-out workers, arranged for the following Sunday, had been proclaimed by Dublin Castle. The night the proclamation had come to Liberty Hall, a vast crowd gathered to hear what was to be done. The meeting would be held; Jim Larkin would be there in O'Connell Street. The darkness was falling, a dim quietness was spreading over the troubled city. Even the gulls muted their complaining cries; and the great throng was silent; silent, listening to the dark voice speaking from the window. To Sean, the long arm seemed to move about in the sky, directing the courses of the stars over Dublin; then the moving hand held up the proclamation, the other sturdy hand held a lighted match to it; it suddenly flared up like a minor meteor; in a dead silence it flamed, to fall at last in flakes of dark and film ashes down upon the heads of the workers below, fluttering here and there, uncertainly, by the wind from the mighty cheer of agreed defiance that rose to the sky, and glided away to rattle the windows and shake the brazen nails and knobs on the thick doors of Dublin Castle. Resolute and firm, thought Sean; but they have no arms, they have no arms.

Oh! O'Connell Street was a sight of people on that Sunday morning! From under the clock swinging pedantically outside of the *Irish Times* offices, across the bridge over the river, to well away behind the Pillar, topped by Nelson, the wide street was black with them; all waiting for Jim to appear somewhere when the first tick of the clock tolled the hour of twelve. . . .

There he is! suddenly shouted a dozen voices near Sean. Goin' to speak from the window of the very hotel owned be Martin Murphy himself! and there right enough, framed in an upper window, was a tall man in clerical garb, and when he swept the beard from his chin, the crowd saw their own beloved leader, Jim Larkin.

A tremendous cheer shook its way through the wide street, and Sean raised his right arm, and opened his mouth to join it, but his mouth was snapped shut by a terrific surge back from the crowd in front, while another section of it, on the outskirts, surged forward to get a better view, though now the cheer had been silenced by a steady scream in the near distance, by the frantic scuffling of many feet, and loud curses from frightened men. Twelve rows or so ahead of him, Sean saw a distended face, with bulging eyes, while a gaping mouth kept shouting, The police – they're chargin'; get back, get back, there! Let me out, let me out; make a way there for a man has a bad heart! They're batonin' everyone to death – make a way out for a poor, sick man, can't yous!

Sean made a desperate try to turn, but the jam became so close that he was penned tight to his struggling neighbour. He felt himself rising, but fought savagely to keep his feet on the ground; and try as he might, he couldn't get his lifted arm down to fend off the pressure on his chest that was choking him. He could neither get his right arm down nor his left arm up to loosen the collar of his shirt, to get more air, a little more air; he could only sway back and forward as the crowd moved. The breathing of the suffocating crowd sounded like the thick, steamy breathing of a herd of frightened cattle in a cattle-boat tossed about in a storm; and over all, as he tried to struggle, he heard the voices of the police shouting, Give it to the bastards! Drive the rats home to their holes! Let them have it, the Larkin bousys!

James Larkin, the great trade-union leader, at Liberty Hall
during the Dublin workers' strike, 1913; pen and ink sketch
by William Orpen

The Easter Rising

[133] Easter Monday, 1916 in St Stephen's Green; from *The Insurrection in Dublin* by James Stephens.

(James Stephens, (1880–1950) poet and story-teller, was brought up in a Dublin orphanage and worked as a solicitor's clerk until his novel *The Crock of Gold* won him recognition as a writer of genius. At the time of the Rising, he was working in the Dublin National Gallery. His eye-witness account, published May 1916, conveys the bewilderment with which the Rising was greeted by most Dubliners, and carried a plea for recognition of the idealistic motives of its leaders.)

This has taken everyone by surprise. It is possible, that, with the exception of their staff, it has taken the Volunteers themselves by surprise; but, today, our peaceful city is no longer peaceful; guns are sounding or rolling and cracking from different directions, and, although rarely, the rattle of machine guns can be heard also.

Two days ago war seemed very far away – so far, that I have covenanted with myself to learn the alphabet of music. . . . On Monday (a Bank Holiday) I went to my office at the usual hour, and after transacting what business was necessary I bent myself to the notes above and below the stave, and marvelled anew at the ingenuity of man. Peace was in the building, and if any of the attendants had knowledge or rumour of war they did not mention it to me.

At one o'clock I went to lunch. Passing the corner of Merrion Row I saw two small groups of people. These people were regarding steadfastly in the direction of St Stephen's Green Park, and they spoke occasionally to one another with that detached confidence which proved they were mutually unknown. I also, but without approaching them, stared in the direction of the Green. I saw nothing but the narrow street which widened to the Park. Some few people were standing in tentative attitudes, and all looking in one direction. As I turned from them homewards I received an impression of silence and expectation and excitement.

On the way home I noticed that many silent people were standing in their doorways – an unusual thing in Dublin outside the back streets. The glance of a Dublin man or woman conveys generally a criticism of one's personal appearance, and is a little hostile to the passer. The look of each person as I passed was steadfast, and contained an enquiry instead of a criticism. I felt faintly uneasy, but withdrew my mind to a meditation which I had covenanted with myself to perform daily, and passed to my house.

There I was told that there had been a great deal of rifle firing all the morning, and we concluded that the military recruits or Volunteer detachments were practising that arm. My return to business was by the way I had already come. At the corner of Merrion Row I found the same silent groups, who were still looking in the direction of the Green, and addressing each other occasionally with the detached confidence of strangers. Suddenly, and on the spur of the moment, I addressed one of these silent gazers.

'Has there been an accident?' said I.

I indicated the people standing about.

'What's all this for?'

He was a sleepy, rough-looking man about forty years of age, with a blunt red moustache, and the distant eyes which one sees in sailors. He looked at me, stared at me as at a person from a different country. He grew wakeful and vivid.

'Don't you know?' said he.

And then he saw that I did not know.

'The Sinn Feiners have seized the city this morning'.

'Oh!' said I.

He continued with the savage earnestness of one who has amazement in his mouth:

'They seized the city at eleven o'clock this morning. The Green there is full of them. They have captured the Castle. They have taken the Post Office.'

'My God!' said I, staring at him, and instantly I turned and went running towards the Green.

In a few seconds I banished astonishment and began to walk. As I drew near the Green rifle fire began like sharply-cracking whips. It was from the further side. I saw that the gates were closed and men were standing inside with guns on their shoulders. I passed a house, the windows of which were smashed in. As I went by a man in civilian clothes slipped through the Park gates, which instantly closed behind him. He ran towards me, and I halted. He was carrying two small packets in his hand. He passed me hurriedly, and, placing his leg inside the broken window of the house behind me, he disappeared. Almost immediately another man in civilian clothes appeared from the broken window of another house. He also had something (I don't know what) in his hand. He ran urgently towards the gates, which opened, admitted him, and closed again.

In the centre of this side of the Park a rough barricade of carts and motor cars had been stretched. It was still full of gaps. Behind it was a halted tram, and along the vistas of the Green one saw other trams derelict, untenanted.

I came to the barricade. As I reached it and stood by the Shelbourne Hotel, which it faced, a loud cry came from the Park. The gates opened and three men ran out. Two of them held rifles with fixed bayonets. The third gripped a heavy revolver in his fist. They ran towards a motor car which had just turned the corner, and halted it. The men with bayonets took position instantly on either side of the car. The man with the revolver saluted, and I heard him begging the occupants to pardon him, and directing them to dismount. A man and woman got down. They were again saluted and requested to go to the sidewalk. They did so.

The man crossed and stood by me. He was very tall and thin, middle-aged, with a shaven, wasted face. 'I want to get down to Armagh today,' he said to no one in particular. The loose bluish skin under his eyes was twitching. The Volunteers directed the chauffeur to drive to the barricade and lodge his car in a particular position there. He did it awkwardly, and after three attempts he succeeded in pleasing them. He was a big, brown-faced man, whose knees were rather high for the seat he was in, and they jerked with the speed and persistence of something moved with a powerful spring. His face was composed and fully under command, although his legs were not. He locked the car into the barricade, and then, being a man accustomed to be commanded, he awaited an order to descend. When the order came he walked directly to his master, still preserving all the solemnity of his features. These two men did not address a word to each other, but their drilled and expressionless eyes were loud with surprise and fear and rage. They went into the hotel.

I spoke to the man with the revolver. He was no more than a boy, not more certainly than twenty years of age, short in stature, with close curling red hair and blue eyes – a kindly-looking lad. The strap of his sombrero had torn loose on one side, and except while he held it in his teeth it flapped about his chin. His face was sunburnt and grimy with dust and sweat. . . .

When I spoke he looked at me, and I know that for some seconds he did not see me. I said:

'What is the meaning of all this? What has happened?'

He replied collectedly enough in speech, but with that ramble and errancy clouding his eyes.

'We have taken the city. We are expecting an attack from the military at any moment, and those people', he indicated knots of men, women and children clustered towards the end of the Green, 'won't go home for me. We have the Post Office, and the Railways, and the Castle. We have all the city. We have everything.'

[134] Easter Monday, 1916 outside the GPO; from the autobiography of Ernie O'Malley, *On Another Man's Wound*.

(Ernie O'Malley (1898–1957) was a seventeen-year-old medical student at the break of the Rising. He joined the Republicans soon after, fighting mainly in the Mendicity Institute on the Quays. He later fought in both the War of Independence and the Civil War (against the Treaty); was badly wounded and reprieved from a death-sentence after a forty-one-day hunger strike.)

Easter Monday, a holiday, was warm and many people went to the races, to the Hill of Howth, Killiney, or to the mountains. I walked across the city over the Liffey to the South Side, intending to visit the older portions of Dublin; up by Winetavern Street, through the Coombe, and back around by Dublin Castle walls. I looked at the statue of Justice on the upper Castle Gate. She had her back to the city, and I remembered that it had frequently been commented on, satirically.

I passed by Trinity College; the heavy oaken doors were closed. In O'Connell Street large groups of people were gathered together. From the flagstaff on top of the General Post Office, the GPO, floated a new flag, a tri-coloured one of green, white and orange, the colours running out from the mast.

'What's it all about?' I asked a man who stood near me, a scowl on his face.

'Those boyhoes, the Volunteers, have seized the Post Office. They want nothing less than a Republic,' he laughed scornfully. 'They've killed some Lancers; but they'll soon run away when the soldiers come.'

Thin strands of barbed wire ran out in front of the Post Office. Two sentries in green uniforms and slouched hats stood on guard with fixed bayonets. They seemed cool enough. Behind them the windows had been smashed. Heavy mail bags half-filled the spaces, rifle barrels projected, officers in uniform with yellow tabs could be seen hurrying through the rooms. Outside, men were carrying in heavy bundles – 'explosives, I bet, or ammunition,' said a man beside me. Others unloaded provisions and vegetables and carried the food inside. On the flat roof sentries patrolled to and fro. Men on motor bicycles, uniformed and in civilian clothes, arrived frequently and the sentries made a lane for them through the crowd.

I walked up the street. Behind Nelson's Pillar lay dead horses, some with their feet in the air, others lying flat. 'The Lancers' horses,' an old man said, although I had not spoken. 'Those fellows,' pointing with his right hand toward the GPO, 'are not going to be frightened by a troop of Lancers. They mean business.' Seated on a dead horse was a woman, a shawl around her head, untidy wisps of hair straggled across her dirty face. She swayed slowly, drunk, singing:

Boys in Khaki, Boys in Blue,
Here's the best of Jolly Good Luck to You.
On the base of the Pillar was a white poster. Gathered around were groups of men and women. Some looked at it with serious faces, others laughed and sniggered. I began to read it with a smile, but my smile ceased as I read.

Poblacht na hÉireann
The Provisional Government
OF THE
IRISH REPUBLIC
To The People of Ireland

Irishmen and Irishwomen

In the Name of God and of the dead generations from which she received her old traditions of nationhood, Ireland, through us, summons her children to her flag and strikes for her freedom.

. . . In every generation the Irish people have asserted their right to national freedom and sovereignty, six times during the past three hundred years they have asserted it in arms. . . . We declare the right of the people of Ireland to the ownership of Ireland and to the unfettered control of Irish destinies, to be sovereign and indefeasible. . . . The Republic guarantees religious and civil liberty, equal rights and equal opportunities to all its citizens . . .

Signed on behalf of the Provisonal Government.

Thomas J. Clarke

Sean Mac Diarmada	Thomas MacDonagh
P.H. Pearse	Eamonn Ceannt
James Connolly	Joseph Plunkett

Clarke, I had known through a friend of ours, Major MacBride, who used to come across the city to buy cigars in his little shop. Pearse I had seen for the first time a few minutes before. A man in the crowd had shouted out his name as a quiet-faced figure in uniform with a strange green, soft hat had passed slowly out through the front door of the GPO. He had talked with an officer underneath the portico beside a fluted pillar. His face was firm and composed. Connolly I had heard speak at meetings. I had seen MacDonagh in the University where he lectured on English, gayer than the other lectures. Plunkett was editor of the *Irish Review*, back numbers of which I had read. They did not mean anything – only names.

[135] Easter Monday, inside Trinity College; by John Joly, in *Blackwoods Magazine*, July 1916.

(John Joly, who published this account anonymously, was Professor of Geology at Trinity College; and also a brilliant scientist and inventor. Although a firm supporter of the British Empire, his account lays much of the blame for the Rising on misgovernment by the English authorities.)

Easter Monday, April 24, 1916 – not yet one fortnight old as I write – looked a day of peaceful thoughts if ever there was one. It was cool, bright weather. The Dublin hills stretched away to the south-west, a picture of immovable repose in the afternoon light.

Down the Dundrum road a band of the Veteran Volunteers – the 'G.R.'s – came swinging along at a steady pace, their faces towards the City. An officer on horseback led them. As he passed us, we recognised in him Major Harris of the Officers' Training Corps of the University of Dublin. He stopped us. 'Have you heard that the Sinn Feiners have risen in Dublin, and seized the General Post Office and Stephen's Green, and shot several of the police?' The Veterans passed on their way to the city, leaving us bewildered. Some of them were to meet death within an hour . . .

I was in Trinity College by four o'clock. I had already been in the city that same morning visiting a friend. There were then no signs of the fatal events proceeding elsewhere. The Post Office was actually being seized at the time I was sitting with my sick friend. But now how different! Carriage traffic had almost ceased, and crowds hurried, partly in terror, partly in curiosity, about the streets. An occasional shot was heard. But it soon became evident that the Rebels were virtually in possession of the city.

I left Trinity cautiously by one of the side gates. I was anxious to ascertain, if possible, the magnitude of the movement and to get some idea of the numbers engaged in it. I visited the General Post Office, the central building in Sackville Street. It was a wreck. Glass littered deeply the path and pavement in front of it. Armed men stood behind its shattered windows. Useless barricades had been piled up within – mail bags, evidently filled with letters, to keep out bullets! Chairs and tables through which bullets would pass almost as easily! And, peering out from their defences, the unhappy warriors threatened with their rifles the scared crowd which alternately approached and ran away. At one window a mere boy was still knocking out the glass with the butt of his rifle. Above the building floated a huge green banner with the inscription in white letters, 'Irish Republic'. Truly *Der Tag* had come! But oh, how pitiful! A fantastic chimera, and death the sure and certain wage!

The Rebels were moving about freely in the streets. All seemed armed with rifles. The police had entirely disappeared. They had done all they could, and some had offered their lives in a vain endeavour to save the city. St Stephen's Green, which I next visited, was closed. A sort of barrier had been placed within the large gate facing the foot of Grafton Street. Behind it stood, with set face and in Sinn Fein uniform, an armed man. He held his rifle at the ready. But neither military nor police contested his supremacy. . . . That the College had not already been captured was most inexplicable. It was obviously the most central and commanding position in the city. There was the additional attraction of the military stores of the OTC depot. In this were kept some hundreds of service rifles and many thousands of rounds of ammunition. The loot of the buildings would supply many requirements of those in possession. And once captured nothing but the wholesale destruction of buildings, containing the most precious heirlooms of the ancient University, would suffice to dislodge the enemy. I visited the Provost. He faced the position with which he had been so suddenly confronted with calmness. . . .

The Anzacs had been above on the roof of the College since an early hour. Owing to the strict order received from the Irish Command not to fire until attacked, many chances of 'potting' Rebels had been missed. But later in the morning this order had been withdrawn. Already before daylight a despatch-rider of the enemy had been brought down by the fire of the Anzacs. It was wonderful shooting. He was one of three who were riding past on bicycles. Four shots were fired. Three found their mark in the head of the unfortunate victim. Another of the riders was wounded and escaped on foot. The third abandoned his bicycle and also escaped. This shooting was done by the uncertain light of the electric lamps, and at a high angle downwards from a lofty building. The body was brought in.

Later I saw him. In no irreverent spirit I lifted the face-cloth. He looked quite young; one might almost call him a boy. The handsome waxen face was on one side concealed in blood. Poor boy! What crime was his? That of listening to the insane wickedness and folly preached by those older and who ought to be wiser than he. And was not he, after all, but one of those who carry to its logical conclusion the long crusade against English rule which for generations has kept peace from Irish hearts?

[136] Inside the GPO, Easter Week; from *Remembering Sion*
by Desmond Ryan.

(Desmond Ryan (1893–1964), son of a famous Irish nationalist
who edited the Gaelic League's newspaper, had worked as
Pearse's secretary before 1916. After his release from internment,
he became a journalist and wrote several memoirs of the 1916
Rising and its leaders, including this one.)

Marched according to orders to Liberty Hall with small
company in which I drilled, little expecting to be so soon in arms
against the armed forces of Great Britain. Great excitement
prevailed and the surrounding area was desolate in appearance.
The door is locked. Congestion of traffic has whetted our
curiosity as we marched through the average holiday crowds
and soldiers strolling with their girls past College Green.
Admitted to Larkin's palace we swarm upstairs. The Volunteers
are 'out' and Ireland is rising. It is evident from the excited
shouts to keep 'a watch on the railway line' and 'fill all vessels
with water.' Rifles and flushed faces. A feeling of momentary
sickness, then wonder. An excited youth informs our commander that there are no longer Volunteers or Citizen Army, so
Mr Connolly had said when the row started and the Volunteers
had been addressed in front of the Hall, only the Army of the
Irish Republic. Commandant Pearse sends down a message to us
to proceed to the GPO. We hurry downstairs and at the double
across Abbey Street. 'Hurrah for the Volunteers!' shouts an aged
working man. 'Hammer the s—— out the ——!' We rush across
Princes Street catching a glimpse of a girl crying and hurrying
along, a well-dressed young man beside her. Kids cheer from
doorways. A dim crowd up towards the Rotunda. The GPO
windows loom before us, men inside with rifles behind barri-
caded windows. Our commander's rifle-butt smashes through
glass and wood and breaks. Scramble in and over, shots ring
deafeningly in our ears, a cry, 'the Lancers!' and a volley from
within to stop those troops who retire, leaving two dead horses
behind. Hurry. Locks blown in, men rushed to the roof, to second
storey. Sacks, books, typewriters are stuffed in all hitherto not
strengthened windows. Men watch grimly behind. Pearse and
his brother appear and survey the scene calmly within, though
the latter looks a trifle sad. Vessels are filled with water

everywhere. Cooking is carried on where the GPO staff left off. The great door leading into Princes Street is eventually covered with a rough barricade. A young officer dashes in cheering, a smile on his flushed features. Later he is hurried by, the lower part of his face severely injured with a bomb explosion, his hands, chin and neck streaming blood. He is ordered at the revolver's point – for he grows obstinate – when his wounds are dressed and shock subsides – to hospital. Blood is new to us and we only learn later that he has recovered. Inside organisation proceeds. Parties come and go. The crowd outside cheers the hoisted Republican flags and the Proclamation. Pearse speaks without. Connolly, a grim, manly figure in green Commandant's uniform, grasps his hand: 'Thank God, Pearse, we have lived to see this day!' An orderly desolation has settled down within. A dazed DMP man sits in the yard, florid, his head between his hands . . .

[From the roof we can see] soldiers walk unmolested and unarmed within five yards of our guns. Nightfall. Meals of tea, rice and rumours. We laugh. No sleep. Heavy firing in distance, in Four Courts direction. No sleep. Dawn rises over the city.

Tuesday. – Roof still. Smaller crowds in streets. Rumours of Ireland ablaze. Cork, Kerry and Limerick are up and the Curragh line is held both sides. We don't care much. We get used to the bullets. 'Hurrah! Who'd miss it? Is so-and-so "out"? Who was killed? Good man, a pity. Keep under cover!' Inquiries as to advance of troops from different quarters. Our men are to be seen manning shops opposite. Organising of inside and outside defence proceeds. Telephone in good order but the wire is a nuisance when one moves across the parapet. A barricade blocks Earl Street. Looting begins. A fire opposite is put out. Another starts. Get used from then to fires. General preparations to resist siege and, if need be – make last stand. Rain falls and drenches us to the skins. We get waterproofs. News of P(earse) from the gent. in the fur coat (the Yank): 'He's in good form.' (P. and B. inspect the positions next day.) No sleep. Hunger, a past and dead sensation. Night. . . . Queer faces in the sky. . . . Wireless flashes from the DBC Restaurant. Get used to stray bullets and feel good. Drunken man singing is killed by stray shots. Kids singing below: 'We are the Volunteers, we'll whack the British Army.' Fires proceed, dawn, sleepless but happy. When *will* we be wounded?

Wednesday. – Roof still, with an old visit below. Stoics. Firing from the quays to Abbey Street. Tap-tap-tap. Liberty Hall is gone. Artillery and machine-guns at work. Get used to it. Next sensation please! Bullets overhead and down the street. Promise of relief. Ordered below later where we see our friends. Willie: 'That fire cannot be stopped. It will catch the whole block.' Pearse calm. James (Connolly): 'Boys, they're beaten!' Fall asleep while the fires glare in. Ten hours solid rest. Good outside reports.

Thursday. – The blaze spreads along opposite block – house to house. On guard at windows. Boom! The place shakes. Gets stale with repetition. Frequent stands to arms. Snipers and heavy artillery new and prevalent excitements. Connolly wounded in sortie. Armoured car report, and rumour of contemplated advance through Imperial (Hotel's) ruins of troops. Pearse addresses us: 'Her name is splendid among the names of cities!' Fires behind in Henry St. Linenhall ablaze. A terrible and depressing night. But the songs ring out and another dawn comes.

Friday. – Morning lull. Is it arbitration? Fire gains. The street in ruins. Hasty barricade in front in three rows of coal sacks. Constant stands to arms. Keen sniping from upstairs. Men on roof struck with shrapnel. Desperate fight against the fire which has now burst out upon the GPO roof. Fire wins. One constant stand to arms and tension. The women have departed in the morning. One darkened, roaring, leaping blaze in front, above, behind. Debris crashes in. Communications entirely cut. Expectation of general assault. Rations secured. Men shoot two of themselves by mistake. Order to retreat. Dash across the bullet-swept and flame-lit street. Men fall. Henry Place to Moore St. Plunkett rallies men past a fire-swept barricade: 'Don't be cowards! Advance!' Past and into houses. All night borings and snatches of rest. Old meals. Sleep. Fires raging. Nelson looks down on blazing GPO.

Saturday. – Waiting under cover. Rumours as to fire in new position. Preparations for final charge in rear and front of barricade closing our exit. 'Postponed six hours' *perhaps*, countermanded. Waiting, waiting, waiting. Negotiations opened by English. [*sic*] Departure of Pearse as firm as a rock. Tears in MacDermott's eyes. Two o'clock surrender. March out. Plunkett and MacD(ermott) beside us. Corpses on pavement, ruins around us, fires smouldering still. The Last March. Officers

Inside the Dublin GPO, Easter Week 1916, just before its evacuation: James Connolly is on the stretcher, Patrick Pearse standing in profile, left, above him. A contemporary reconstruction painted by Thomas Kiersey of British Army cover us with huge revolvers as we turn into O'Connell Street, lined with troops. The disarming. We lay down everything. . . .

On the worst night of all, when the fires glared in on the ground floor of the GPO, Pearse came and sat beside me. He was seated on a barrel, his slightly flushed face crowned by his turned-up military hat. He watched the flames leaping and curling fantastically in the stillness, broken periodically by rifle volleys. Around him men slept on the floor, Connolly amongst them. Others were on guard behind loop-holed sandbags. . . . The volleys rolled away, and Pearse watched the flames. 'All the boys were safe,' he said, with a sigh of relief. Then he suddenly turned and asked me, casually but with a certain abruptness: 'It was the right thing to do, wasn't it?' 'Yes. Failure means the end of everything, the Volunteers, Ireland, all!' And the tone showed the agony of his mind, but an agony flaming to final conviction. Outside the flames grew brighter and there was a terrific burst of gunfire away in the darkness. Pearse paused and continued with deep enthusiasm and passionate conviction in his words: 'Well, *when* we are all *wiped out*, people will blame us for everything, condemn us, but only for this protest the war would have ended and nothing would have been done. After a few years, they will see the meaning of what we tried to do. . . . Emmet's two-hour insurrection is nothing to this! . . . They will talk of Dublin in future as one of the splendid cities like they speak to-day of Paris! Dublin's name will be glorious for ever!'

[137] The aftermath of the Rising – looting in Grafton Street and Sackville Street; from *The Sinn Fein Rebellion as I saw it* by Mrs Hamilton Norway.

(Mrs Hamilton Norway was the wife of the Irish Postmaster-General whose headquarters, the Dublin GPO, had been at the centre of the Rising. She spent Easter Week in the (now, sadly, demolished) Hibernian Hotel in Dawson Street, with her husband and seventeen-year-old son, the future novelist Nevil Shute.)

Yesterday afternoon, when the firing in Grafton Street was over, the mob appeared and looted the shops, clearing the great provision shops and others. From the back of this hotel you look down on an alley that connects with Grafton Street, – and at the corner, the shop front in Grafton Street, but with a side entrance into this lane, is a very large and high-class fruiterer. From the windows we watched the proceedings, and I never saw anything so brazen! The mob were chiefly women and children, with a sprinkling of men. They swarmed in and out of the side door bearing huge consignments of bananas, the great bunches on the stalk, to which the children attached a cord and ran away dragging it along. Other boys had big orange boxes which they filled with tinned and bottled fruits. Women with their skirts held up received showers of apples and oranges and all kinds of fruit which were thrown from the upper windows by their pals; and ankle-deep on the ground lay all the pink and white and silver paper and paper shavings used for packing choice fruits. It was an amazing sight, and nothing daunted these people. Higher up at another shop we were told a woman was hanging out of a window dropping down loot to a friend, when she was shot through the head by a sniper, probably our man; the body dropped into the street and the mob cleared. In a few minutes a hand-cart appeared and gathered up the body, and instantly all the mob swarmed back . . .

In Sackville [*now O'Connell*] Street was a very large shop called Clery's; for some reason the looters were afraid to start on it, and old women passed up and down gazing longingly at fur coats and silken raiment and saying sorrowfully, 'Isn't Clery's broke yet?' and 'Isn't it a great shame that Clery's is not broke!' Humour and tragedy are so intermixed in this catastrophe. A very delicate elderly lady who is staying here said to me this morning, in answer to my inquiry as to how she had slept: 'I could not sleep at all. When the guns ceased the *awful silence* made me so nervous!' I know exactly what she meant. When the roar of the guns ceases you can *feel* the silence.

Monday 2 p.m.

I have just returned from walking round the GPO and Sackville Street with H. and some of the officials. It passes all my powers of description, only one word describes it, 'Desolation.' If you look at pictures of Yprès or Louvain after the bombardment it will give you some idea of the scene.

We looked up through the windows of the GPO and saw the safe that was in H.'s room still in the wall, and the door does not appear to have been opened or the safe touched, but the whole place has been such an inferno one would think the door must have been red-hot. Among all the *débris* the fire was still smouldering, and we could not penetrate inside. I picked up a great lump of molten metal, a fantastic shape with bits of glass embedded in it. It is bright like silver, but they tell me it is lead. It is quite curious. . . .

Behind the GPO was the Coliseum Theatre, now only a shell; and on the other side of the street was the office of the *Freeman's Journal*, with all the printing machinery lying among the *débris*, all twisted and distorted; but, worst of all, behind that was a great riding school, where all the horses were burnt to death.

[138] Part of Patrick Pearse's court martial speech in 1916.

(The trials by military tribunal of the 1916 leaders were held in secret at Richmond Jail three days after their surrender. This speech by Pearse was not published till 1946. Pearse, Thomas McDonagh, and Arthur Clarke were the first batch of prisoners to be executed in the courtyard of Kilmainham Jail on 3 May 1916.)

My object in agreeing to unconditional surrender was to prevent further slaughter of the civilian population of Dublin and to save the lives of our gallant fellows, who, having made for six days a stand unparalleled in military history, were now surrounded and (in the case of those under the immediate command of headquarters) without food. I fully understand now, as then, that my own life is forfeit to British law, and I shall die very cheerfully if I can think that the British Government, as it has already shown itself strong, will now show itself magnanimous enough to accept my single life in forfeiture and to give a general amnesty to the brave men and boys who have fought at my bidding. In the second place I wish it to be understood that any admissions I make here are to be taken as involving myself alone. They do not involve and must not be used against anyone who acted with me, not even those who may have set their names to documents with me. (The Court assented to this.)

I admit I was Commander-General Commander-in-Chief of the forces of the Irish Republic which have been acting against you for the past week and that I was President of the Provisional Government, I stand over all my acts and words done or spoken in these capacities. When I was a child of ten I went down on my knees by my bedside one night and promised God that I should devote my life to an effort to free my country. I have kept that promise. . . .

I repudiate the assertion of the prosecutor that I sought to aid and abet England's enemy. Germany is no more to me than England is. I asked and accepted German aid in the shape of arms and an expeditionary force, we neither asked for nor accepted German gold, nor had any traffic with Germany but what I state; my aim was to win Irish freedom; we struck the first blow ourselves but I should have been glad of an ally's aid.

I assume I am speaking to Englishmen who value their own freedom, and who profess to be fighting for the freedom of Belgium and Serbia. Believe that we too love freedom and desire it. To us it is more desirable than anything else in the world. If you strike us down now we shall rise again and renew the fight. You cannot conquer Ireland; you cannot extinguish the Irish passion for freedom; if our deed has not been sufficient to win freedom then our children will win it by a better deed.

[139] The execution of James Connolly in Kilmainham; from *Portrait of a Rebel Father* by Nora Connolly.

(James Connolly (1868–1916), born to poor Irish parents in an Edinburgh slum, came to Dublin in 1896, and was one of the chief organizers of Larkin's strike in 1913. His Irish Citizens' Army, founded to protect strikers from civil brutality, joined forces with Pearse and McDonagh's Irish Volunteers during the 1916 Rising. Connolly, who was badly wounded in the GPO, was taken to the military hospital in Dublin Castle after his surrender, and was one of the last prisoners to be executed. His death, while tied to a chair in front of a firing squad, horrified most Dublin opinion.)

On Tuesday [May 9] I went with mother. There were soldiers on guard at the top of the stairs and in the small alcove leading to Papa's room. They were fully armed and as they stood guard they had their bayonets fixed. In the room there was an RAMC officer with him all the time. His wounded leg was resting in a cage. He was weak and pale and his voice was very low. Mother asked was he suffering much pain. 'No, but I've been court-martialled today. They propped me up in bed. The strain was very great.' She knew then that if they had court-martialled him while unable to sit up in bed, they would not hesitate to shoot him while he was wounded. . . .

I saw father next on Thursday, May 11, at midnight. A motor ambulance came to the door. The officer said father was very weak and wished to see his wife and eldest daughter. Mama believed the story because she had seen him on Wednesday and he was in great pain and very weak, and he couldn't sleep without morphine. Nevertheless she asked the officer if they were going to shoot him. The officer said he could tell her nothing. Through dark, deserted sentry-ridden streets we rode. I was surprised to see about a dozen soldiers encamped outside Papa's door. There was an officer on guard inside the room. Papa turned his head at our coming.

"Well, Lillie, I suppose you know what this means?"

'Oh, James, it's not that – it's not that.'

'Yes, Lillie. I fell asleep for the first time tonight and they wakened me at eleven and told me that I was to die at dawn.' Mamma broke down and laid her head on the bed and sobbed heart-breakingly. Father patted her head and said: 'Don't cry, Lillie, you'll unman me.'

'But your beautiful life, James. Your beautiful life!' she sobbed.

'Well, Lillie, hasn't it been a full life and isn't this a good end?' I was also crying. 'Don't cry, Nora, there's nothing to cry about.'

'I won't cry, Papa,' I said.

He patted my hand and said: 'That's my brave girl. . . .'

He tried to cheer Mama by telling her of the man who had come into the Post Office during the Rising to try and buy a penny stamp. 'I don't know what Dublin's coming to when you can't buy a stamp at the Post Office. . . .'

The officer said: 'Only five minutes more.' Mama was nearly overcome – she had to be given water. Papa tried to clasp her in his arms but he could only lift his head and shoulders from the bed. The officer said: 'Time is up.' Papa turned and said good-bye to her and she could not see him. I tried to bring Mama away but I could not move her. The nurse came forward and helped

her away. I ran back and kissed Papa again. 'Nora, I'm proud of
you.' Then the door was shut and I saw him no more. . . .

(Later) We saw Father Aloysius who had attended him in
Kilmainham. 'How did they shoot him . . . how could they shoot
him?' asked Mama. 'He couldn't sit up in his bed.'

'It was a terrible shock to me,' said Father Aloysius . . . 'I'll
always thank God as long as I live that He permitted me to be
with your father until he was dead. Such a wonderful man – such
a concentration of mind. They carried him from his bed in an
ambulance stretcher down to a waiting ambulance and drove
him to Kilmainham Jail. They carried him from the ambulance
to the jail yard and put him in a chair. . . . He was very brave and
cool. . . . I said to him, 'Will you pray for the men who are about
to shoot you?' and he said: 'I will say a prayer for all brave men
who do their duty.'

[140] 'Sixteen Dead Men'; from *The Collected Poems of
W.B. Yeats.*

(W.B. Yeats composed two of his most celebrated poems a few
weeks after the execution of the 1916 leaders – 'Easter 1916' with
its famous refrain, 'A terrible beauty is born', and this short
ballad. They were originally printed only for friends, to avoid
political controversy. He wrote at the time to Lady Gregory: 'I
had no idea that any public event could so deeply move me.')

O but we talked at large before
The sixteen men were shot,
But who can talk of give and take,
What should be and what not
While those dead men are loitering there
To stir the boiling pot?

You say that we should still the land
Till Germany's overcome;
But who is there to argue that
Now Pearse is deaf and dumb?
And is their logic to outweigh
MacDonagh's bony thumb?

How could you dream they'd listen

That have an ear alone
For those new comrades they have found,
Lord Edward and Wolfe Tone,
Or meddle with our give and take
That converse bone to bone?

[141] A Dublin ballad by Dermot O'Byrne; from *An Anthology of 1916* by Edna Fitzhenry.

Well, the last fire is trodden down,
Our dead are rotting fast in lime,
We all can sneak back into town,
Stravague about as in old time,

And stare at gaps of grey and blue
Where Lower Mount Street used to be,
And where flies hum round muck we knew
For Abbey Street and Eden Quay.

And when the devil's made us wise
Each in his own peculiar hell,
With desert hearts and drunken eyes
We're free to sentimentalize
By corners where the martyrs fell.

[142] O'Connell Street after the Rising; from Kate O'Brien's autobiography, *My Ireland*.

How beautiful it looked. Sometimes now when I consider the pitiful mess of rebuilt O'Connell Street from the Bridge to Nelson's Pillar I smile back sadly to that other time, when this present stretch of absolutely comical commercial vulgarity was a huge, swept-away arena of tragedy, in black and white. Wide open to the sky, to the wondering question of any stranger, and to the cold mockery of Anna Livia herself, the gashed and silent piece of ground was like some giant permanent set, vaster than in any imaginable Roman or Palladian theatre, and seeming to commemorate a finished play rather than to wait for actors. That was what we beheld, with pity and awe, of the old street our fathers used to praise. And if some of them might have cursed

Sinn Fein for having brought about the destruction of their Sackville Street, I wonder what they would have said to what free prosperity has set up in its place?

[143] The Chief Secretary's verdict on the Rising, 1932; from Augustine Birrell's *Things Past Redress*.

(Augustine Birrell (1850–1933) held the post of Chief Secretary to Ireland in Asquith's government from 1907 to 1916. He was widely blamed for failing to foresee the outbreak of the Rising, and was forced to resign; he failed to grasp its historical impact until the end of his life.)

The Dublin rebellion in Easter Week, 1916, which terminated my connection with Ireland, has been so much written about and reported upon, that very little need be said about it. Labour troubles, fostered by the state of the slums in Dublin, which might be called a disgrace to civilization and Christianity, did such words possess any significance, and fermented also by exceedingly bad labour conditions, had a great deal to do with the outbreak . . .

As a 'rebellion' it was a ridiculous failure from the first, but as an event in Irish history it was horrible and heart-breaking, and being accompanied by house-to-house fighting, sniping and murdering, it stains the memory.

It was a supreme act of criminal folly on the part of those who were responsible for it, for it never had a chance, and was really nothing more than a Dublin row.

[144] 'Was he out in Easter Week?'; from *Inishfallen, fare you well* by Sean O'Casey.

Things had changed, but not utterly; and no terrible beauty was to be born. Short Mass was still the favourite service, and Brian Boru's harp still bloomed on the bottles of beer. But the boys were home again from prison-camp and prison cell. First the venial sinners from Frongoch; then the mortal sinners from Wakefield, Reading, Dartmoor, and other jails. . . . Nothing could be too good for the boys. When one spoke, all had to remain silent. They led at all meetings, dominated committees, won at cards, got everything anyone had to give, and were everywhere forced to lay down the law on all philosophy, patriotism, foresight, prophecy, and good manners. Was he out in Easter Week? became the touchstone of Irish life. And it was those who hadn't been out themselves who roared silence at anyone venturing to send a remark into a conversation led by a lad home from a prison or a concentration camp; for the lads, themselves, were exceedingly modest about it all, and were often embarrassed by their hangers-on, who forgot that most of Dublin, willy-nilly, was out in Easter Week; that there weren't many Dublin houses without bullet-holes in them; and that casualties were heavier among those who weren't out than among those who were. So for a long time, Easter Week became the Year of One in Irish history and Irish life.

❧ Life, Customs and Morals ❧
in Dublin

[145] The wild Irish; from *Topographia Hibernica* by Giraldus Cambrensis, quoted in *Strongbow's Conquest of Ireland* by F.P. Barnard.

(Much of the early history and records of Dublin deal with the protection of the city from 'uncivilized' (literally non-city-dwelling) Irish tribes outside the walls. This is the first hostile Norman account which set the pattern and formed what one Irish historian has called 'the poisoned source' of Norman and English attitudes to Ireland.)

I have thought it not superfluous to lay before the reader a brief description of this people as regards both their persons and their minds: that is to say the external and the internal peculiarities they present.

In this country children are not, as elsewhere delicately brought up; for everything over and above the homely and somewhat scanty nourishment they receive from their rude parents is left to nature. They are laid in no cradle, nor swathed in swaddling clothes; their tender limbs know not the use of the warm bath, neither are they adjusted with the help of art. Yet Nature, as if to show what her unaided power can do, fails not to rear and mould them through infancy and childhood, until in the fulness of time she leads each to man's estate conspicuous for a tall and handsome form, regular features, and a fresh complexion.

But although adorned to the full with such natural gifts as these, still the barbarous fashion of their garments, their shaggy beards, and their ignorance reveal the arrant savage. For little do they wear in the way of woollen clothing, and that little black (which is the colour of the sheep of the country) and of ungainly cut: their habit being to apparel themselves in small closely-fitting hoods extending over the shoulders and down to the elbow, generally made of parti-coloured scraps sewn together. Under this instead of a coat they have a gown. Woollen trews complete their attire, being breeches and hose in one, usually dyed some tint.

In riding they use no saddles, high boots, or spurs; but simply carry a rod crooked at the end, with which they both urge on and guide their horses. Reins indeed they have, yet they perform the

An 'uncivilized' Irish chief banquets in the forest;
from John Derricke's *Image of Ireland*

double duty of bit and bridle: thus the horses, which feed on
nothing but grass, can browse at any time.

They go to battle without armour, which they regard as an
encumbrance: and in fact think it a sign of valour and an honour
to fight without such protection. Of weapons they use but three
kinds: short spears and pairs of darts – and in this they follow the
custom of the Basques –, while they have learnt also from the
Norwegians and Ostmen (of whom later) the use of the great
battle-axe, and excellently well wrought and tempered their
axes are. They wield them with one hand only instead of both,
laying the thumb along the upper side of the haft and so directing
the blow. From the stroke of one of these neither the cone-shaped
helmet is sufficient to guard the head, nor a shirt of ring-mail the
body. Thus in our own time it happened that a soldier had his
thigh cut right through with one stroke of an axe, encased though
it was all round in good steel, the amputated leg falling to the
ground on one side of the horse, and its dying owner on the other.
When arms fail they cast stones, with which they can inflict much

damage on an enemy, as they are handier and readier at slinging than any other nation.

Verily a wild and inhospitable race: living only on the produce of their beasts, and living like beasts themselves. A race but little advanced from the primitive pastoral life. For whereas the stages of human progress are from the forest to the field, from the field to the town, and so to civic polity, this people despising agricultural labour, having little taste for the refinements of civilization, and showing a strong aversion from political institutions, knows not how to relinquish the sylvan and bucolic habits to which it has always been accustomed. . . .

Moreover they do not employ their time in the manufacture of linen, cloth, or any other ware, nor in the development of a single mechanic art. They are simply the slaves of ease and sloth: freedom from motion they esteem the height of luxury, freedom from restraint the summit of wealth.

[146] The Ostomen; from Holinshed's *Chronicles*.

(The Ostomen – or Easterlings – were the pre-Norman inhabitants of Dublin of Viking stock. Unlike the Irish, they are recognized by Giraldus as 'civilized' men. After the Norman conquest, they migrated en masse to the north side of the Liffey to found the settlement of Oxmantown, but were gradually assimilated to the Norman settlers.)

These Ostomen were not Irishmen, but yet of long continuance in Ireland. Some saie they came first out of Norwaie, and were called Ostomen, that is to saie Easterlings, or Easterne men, bicause that countrie lieth East in respect of England and Ireland. Some thinke they were Saxons and Normans; but whatsoever they were, they were merchants and used the trade of merchandize, and in peaceable maner they came into Ireland; and there being landed they found such favour with the Irishrie, that they licenced them to build haven townes wherein they might dwell & use their traffike. These men builded the ancientest and most part of the cities and towns upon or neere the sea side within that land; as namelie Dublin, Waterford, Corke, Limerike, and others. And albeit they in processe of time grew to be mightie and strong, and for their safetie did build townes and castels: yet they durst not to dwell among the Irish people, but still continued and kept themselves within their owne townes and forts, and thereof they are and were called since townesmen. And of them were these, being the inhabitants of Dublin, which came to meet the earle [*Strongbow*], and were thus slaine.

[147] Fortifying the city: a Royal Charter; from Sir John Gilbert's *Calendar of Ancient Records of Dublin*.

(This document shows some of the main items of trade used in thirteenth-century Dublin. Taxes levied were used to fortify and build up the medieval city walls. As one Dublin joke runs, the Dublin millennium celebrates 1,000 years of paying taxes.)

XV – 1250, May 30. Bisham. Henry III.: Permission to levy at Dublin, during three years, tolls as follows, for fortifying and enclosing the city: – of every crannoc of wheat, one farthing; of every crannoc of flour one farthing; of every butt of wine, two pence; of every butt of honey, four pence; of every weigh of wool, one penny; of every dacre of hides, one penny; of every dacre of hides of stag, goat, or horse, one halfpenny; of every great ship, sixteen pence; of every smaller ship, eight pence; of every piece of English or foreign cloth, one halfpenny; of every piece of Irish cloth, one farthing; of every crannoc of woad, two pence; of every crannoc of salt, one farthing; of every bend of iron, one halfpenny; of every mease of herrings, one farthing; of every ox, cow, or horse, one penny; of eight sheep, one penny; of every hog or pig, one farthing; of one hundred boards, one farthing; of one hundred horse-shoes, one halfpenny; of every weigh of tallow, butter, or grease, one halfpenny; of one hundred pounds of spice, two pence; of one hundred weight of wax, two pence; of one hundred pounds of alum, two pence; of every mill-stone, one halfpenny; of one hundred ells of linen cloth, one penny; of one hundred ells of canvas, one penny; of every load of lead, two pence; of every crannoc of beans, one farthing; of one dozen of kitchen ware, one halfpenny; of one hundred pounds of metal, one penny; of one hundred pounds of hogs' lard, one penny; of one hundred pounds of tallow, one penny; of three shillings' worth of merchandise, one farthing; of one hundred lamb-skins, one halfpenny; of one hundred squirrel-skins, one penny; of one hundred pounds of pitch, one halfpeny; of every horse-load of iron, one halfpenny; of one dozen cords of Linden wood, one farthing.–

[148] An Irish chieftain resists adopting English dress; from *The Government of Ireland under Sir John Perrot.*

A Parliament is now summoned to be held at Dublin (1585) where the nobility, clergy and commons being assembled, order was taken, that none were permitted to go in Irish attire (as in former times they used), but to sort themselves in such habit after the English manner, as was answerable to their several ranks and qualities. . . . He (Sir John Perrot) bestowed upon Tirlough Luineach (O'Neill), the principal lord of Ulster, and on some others, chief of the Irish, gowns and other robes fit for that place, and their degrees; which they embraced like fetters: of which being weary, one of them came to the Deputy and besought him, that one of his chaplains, which he called priests, might go with him along through the streets, clad in his Irish 'trouses': for then, quoth he, the boys will laugh as fast at him, as they now do at me, whereat though the Deputy could have smiled, yet casting a frown upon his countenance, told him, there was no cause he should think any laughed at him, for wearing those which were fit ornaments for the place he now held, and did present in Parliament; but if any did so, it was at his ill wearing of the same, which want of civil custom caused. Therefore since use would make that seemly, which was now ridiculous, he advised him to view the difference of being fit for all assemblies, and only fit for the woods and barbarous places; but, quoth the Deputy, if any idle or ill-affected person shall put the contrary into your head, believe it to be done out of an ill-meaning to the State, and worse unto your person, for contempt of order and decency will in the end be your downfall.

[149] A sixteenth-century Gaelic poet laments the betrayal of Irish ways; from Constantia Maxwell's *Irish History from Contemporary Sources.*

(This poem by Laoiseach Mac an Bhaird, contrasting an

'anglicized' Irish chieftain with his hardier rebel brother, shows that the English policy of 'taming' the Gaelic lords with clothes and luxuries at Court had at least some success.)

O man who follows English ways, who cut your thick-clustering hair, graceful hand of my choice, you are not Donnchadh's good son!

If you were, you would not give up your hair for an artificial English mode – the fairest ornament of the land of *Fódla!* – and your head would not be tonsured.

You think the yellow head of hair unfashionable, *he* detests both locks and going bald after the English style; your characters are different indeed.

A man who never loved English ways is Eóghan Bán, beloved of noble ladies. To English ways he never gave his heart: a savage life he chose.

Your mind is nothing to Eóghan Bán, a man who would give breeches for a trifle, who asked no cloak but a rag, who had no wish for coat and legging.

He would hate to carry at his ankle a jewelled spur on a boot, or stockings in the English style; he will have no locks upon him.

A blunt rapier that would not kill a fly, the weight of an awl sticking out behind as one goes to a hill of assembly – the son of Donnchadh sees no beauty in that!

Little he cares for a mantle gold-embroidered, or a high ornamental collar, or a gold ring that would only be irksome, or a satin scarf down to the heels.

He has no longing for a feather bed, he had rather lie upon rushes. Pleasanter to Donnchadh's good son is a hut of rough poles than the *táille* of a tower.

A troop of horse at the brink of a gap, a fierce fight, a struggle with foot soldiers, these are some of the desires of Donnchadh's son – and seeking battle aginst the foreigners!

How unlike are you to Eóghan Bán – they laugh at your foot on the stepping-stone. Pity that you have not seen your fault, O man who follow English ways.

[150] The State of Dublin in 1620; from Luke Gernon's *Discourses*, quoted in *Ireland 1607–1782* by James Carty.

(Luke Gernon, an English judge from Munster, is one of the first settlers to dismiss English xenophobia and paint a kindly picture of the Irish.)

Ireland is at all poynts like a young wench that hath a green sickness . . . She is very fayre of visage, and hath a smooth skinn of tender grasse. . . .

How shall I describe her towns . . . Dublin is the most frequented, more for conveniency than for majesty. There resides the Deputy and the Council. . . . The buildings are of timber and of the English form, and it is resembled to Bristol, but falleth short. . . .

Your will expect to know the state of our State. It is not very magnificent, nor to be disregarded. There is a presence where they stand at all times uncovered, and a cloth of State under which the Deputy sitteth. When that he sitteth at meat, there sit of men of quality as many as the table will contayne. When he goeth abroad in solemn manner, all whom it concerns do attend him. Before him go the gentlemen, captynes, knights, and officers, all on foot. Then cometh the Deputy riding in state, and before him a knight bareheaded carrying the sword. After the Deputy, the nobles, the Council, and the Judges all in foot-clothes. His guard consists of fifty tall men, they wear not red coates, but soldier's cassocks, and halberts in theyr hands. On principal festivals, the herald goes before him in a coat of arms. So much of Dublin I may call it her Whyte hall. . . .

Let us converse with the people. Lord, what makes you so squeamish? Be not afraid. The Irishman is no Cannibal to eat you up, nor no lowsy Jack to offend you.

The man of Ireland is of a strong constitution, tall and big-limbed, but seldom fat, patient of heat and cold, but impatient of labour. Of nature he is prompt and ingenious, but servile, crafty and inquisitive after news, the symptoms of a conquered nation. Their speech hath been accused to be a whining language, but that is among the beggars. I take it to be a smooth language well comixt of vowels and of consonants and hath a pleasing cadence.

The better sort are apparelled at all points like the English only they retain their mantle, which is a garment not indecent. His brogues are single-soled, more rudely sewed than a shoo but more strong, sharp at the toe, and a flap of leather left at the heels to pull them on. His hat is a frieze cap close to the head with two

A group of Irish soldiers (one wearing the
frieze mantle and brogue shoes described
by Luke Gernon) drawn by Albrecht
Dürer

lappetts, to button under his chinne. And for his weapon he
wears a skeyne which is a knife of three fingers broad, of the
length of a dagger and sharpening towards the point with a rude
wooden handle. . . .

The women of Ireland are very comely creatures, tall, slender
and upright. Of complexion very fayre and cleare-skinned (but
freckled) with tresses of bright yellow hayre, which they chain up
in curious knots and devises. They are not strait-laced nor plated
in their youth, but suffered to grow at liberty so that you shall
hardly see one crooked or deformed. . . . I never saw fayrer
wenches nor fowler calliots, so we call the old women. Of nature
they are very kind and tractable.

[151] The hospitable Mayor of Dublin, 1577, and how the Dublin citizens muster for their defence; from the *Description of Ireland* by Richard Stanyhurst in Holinshed's *Chronicles*.

There hath beene of late yeares a worshipfull gentleman, named Patrike Scarsefield, that bare the office of the maioraltie in Dublin, who kept so great port in this yeare, as his hospitalitie to his fame and renowme resteth as yet in fresh memorie. One of his especiall and entire friends entring in communication with the gentleman, his yeare being well neere expired, mooved question, to what he thought his expenses all that yeare amounted? Trulie Iames (so his friend was named) quoth maister Scarsefield, I take betweene me and God, when I entered into mine office, the last saint Hierome his daie (which is the morrow of Michaelmasse, on which daie the maior taketh his oth before the chiefe baron, at the excheker within the castell of Dublin) I had three barnes well stored and thwackt with corne, and I assured my selfe, that anie one of these three had bene sufficient to have stored mine house with bread, ale, and beere for this yeare. And now God and good companie be thanked, I stand in doubt, whether I shall rub out my maioraltie with my third barne, which is well nigh with my yeare ended. And yet nothing smiteth me so much at the heart, as that the knot of good fellowes that you see here (he ment the sergeants and officers) are readie to flit from me, and make their next yeares abode with the next maior. . . .

And in verie deed it was not to be marvelled: for during his maioraltie, his house was so open, as commonly from five of the clocke in the morning, to ten at night, his butterie and cellars were with one crew or other frequented. To the haunting of which, ghests were the sooner allured, for that you should never marke him or his bedfellow (such was their buxomnesse) once frowne or wrinkle their foreheads, or bend their browes, or glowme their countenances, or make a sowre face at anie ghest, were he never so meane. . . .

Some of his friends, that were snudging peniefathers, would take him up verie roughlie for his lavishing & his outragious expenses, as they tearme it. Tush my maisters (would he saie) take not the matter so hot. who so commeth to my table, and hath no need of my meat, I know he commeth for the good will he beareth me; and therefore I am beholding to thanke him for his companie: if he resort for need, how maie I bestow my goods better, than in releeving the poore? . . .

For the better training of their youth in martiall exploits, the citizens use to muster foure times by the yeare: on Black mondaie, which is the morrow of Easter daie, on Maie daie, saint Iohn Baptist his eeve, and saint Peter his eeve.

The Blacke mondaee muster sproong of this occasion. Soone after Ireland was conquered by the Britons, and the greater part of Leinster pacified, diverse townesmen of Bristow flitted from thense to Dublin, and in short space the civitie was by them so well inhabited, as it grew to bee verie populous. Whereupon the citizens having over great affiance in the multitude of the people, and so consequentlie being somewhat retchlesse in heeding the mounteine enimie that lurked under their noses, were woont to rome and roile in clusters, sometime three or foure miles from the towne. The Irish enimie spieng that the citizens were accustomed to fetch such od vagaries, especiallie on the holie daies, & having an inkling withall by some false clatterfert or other, that a companie of them would haue ranged abrode, on mondaie in the Easter weeke towards the wood of Cullen, which is distant two miles from Dublin, they laie in stale verie well appointed, and laid in sundrie places for their comming. The citizens rather minding the pleasure they should presentlie inioy, than forecasting the hurt that might insue, flockt unarmed out of the civitie to the wood, where being intercepted by them that laie hooving in ambush, they were to the number of five hundred miserablie slaine. Whereupon the remnant of the citizens deeming the unluckie time to be a crosse or a dismall daie, gave it the appellation of Black mondaie.

The citie soone after being peopled by a fresh supplie of Bristollians, to dare the Irish enimie, agreed to banket yearelie in that place, which to this daie is observed. For the maior and the shiriffs with the citizens repaire to the wood of Cullen, in which place the maior bestoweth a costlie dinner within a mote or a rundell, and both the shiriffs within another: where they are so well garded with the youth of the civitie, as the mounteine enimie dareth not attempt to snatch as much as a pastie crust from thense.

[152] An Elizabethan soldier complains of the price of Dublin ale in 1610; from Barnaby Rich's *New Description of Ireland*.

Barnaby Rich (1540–1617) was a professional Elizabethan soldier, who had fought in Essex's Irish campaign in the 1570s. He settled in Dublin for the next forty-seven years, supplementing a small pension with a string of popular tracts and romances – one of which gave Shakespeare the plot for *Twelfth Night*).

I might speak here of friars [and] Jesuits ... well known to be his Majesty's vowed and protested enemies, that are yet entertained, upholden and maintained in Dublin, not without great contributions allowed unto them by the Papistical sort of the citizens, that will grudge and murmur to give a soldier a night's lodging . . . and they do not only show an unwillingness to his Majesty in these trifling matters, but they do likewise make manifest their ingratitude by many other means. And whereas their corporation hath been dignified by several kings and princes of England with many large privileges, and that they have the whole trade and traffic amongst themselves, no man to buy or sell within their liberties, unless he be a freeman . . . There is neither merchandise, nor any manner of commodity that is brought from Spain, from France, from Flanders . . . but they will have the whole bargain to themselves, not suffering any man that is not free, to buy for his own provision, no, not so much as a drinking glass, but it must be had from them, and by that means he shall be enforced to pay double the price. . . .

I am now to speak of a certain kind of commodity that outstretcheth all that I have hitherto spoken of, and that is the selling of ale in Dublin, a quotidian commodity, that hath vent in every house in the town every day in the week . . . there is no merchandise so vendible (saleable), it is the very marrow of the commonwealth in Dublin: the whole profit of the town stand upon alehouses and selling of ale. . . . They buy malt in Dublin, at half the price that it is sold for in London, and they sell their drink in Dublin at double the rate that they do in London: and this commodity the aldermen's wives and the rest of the women brewers do find so sweet, that Master mayor and his brethren are willing to wink at, and to tolerate those multitude of alehouses, that themselves do even know to be the very nurseries of drunkenness . . . and many other vile abominations.

[153] Sunday in Dublin, 1725, by D— S—; quoted in *Irish Cavalcade* by M.J. McManus.

(The author of this anonymous pamphlet may be the great Dean Swift himself, although as M.J. McManus notes, during Swift's life any witty or scurrilous piece of uncertain parentage appearing in Dublin was ascribed to him 'as if by a standing affiliation order'.)

Sunday, *Six in the Morning*. Old infirm letchers plagued in their beds with impracticable wishes, wrangling with their diseases and age, and repining because nature has not altered her course and exempted them from the common fate – Rakes and bullies breaking up from their nocturnal debauches, and retiring to their quarters – Petty equipages, as chaises, chairs and hackney-horses getting ready to carry declining shop-keepers and their wives to adjacent villages to divert melancholy thoughts of bankruptcy – Tailors, stay-makers, manteau-makers and milliners busy in breaking the Fourth Commandment – News-writers inventing stories of rapes, riots, robberies, etc., to fill up the Monday's newspapers – The Ministerial and anti-Court writers racking their inventions for argument and matter for their next week's essays, to transmit to London.

Seven o'clock. Officers of the army, lawyers' clerks, mercers' journeymen, and city apprentices swallowing their mercurials and water-gruel – Twelve-penny harlots rapping at pawn-brokers' doors to redeem their wearing-apparel – Servantmaids by the help of false keys pilfering their mistress's teas and sugars – Reduced officers rallied by their laundresses and denied a clean shirt – Demi-clergymen, i.e., parish-clerks, putting on their stiff bands and grave countenances – Foot-soldiers and bullies distribuing curses, black eyes and swollen faces amongst their doxies – Brandy shops opening for the reception of thieves and pickpockets – Beggars putting on their rueful countenances and crutches and managing their sores and ulcers to move compassion.

Eight o'clock. Barbers vastly busy embellishing their customers

– Bawds with band-boxes, borrowed smocks, and scoured manteaus in motion about Aungier Street – Apothecaries and their apprentices trotting thro' the streets with purges and potions – Lap-dogs cleaning and dressing to go to church with their ladies.

Nine o'clock. Pampered clergymen vouchsafe to think of arising and the duty of the day – French artificers quit their garrets and exchange their greasy woollen nightcaps for swords and laced ruffles, declare for a walk to Stephen's Green and a dinner eleemosynary at a dirty alehouse – Insolvent debtors shake hands with bailiffs and appear out of the Verge with gay countenance – Poor people employed in erasing the wrinkles out of their wearing apparel and other symptoms of their having been under date and tribulation – Gentlemen's housekeepers opening their pipes upon the lower servants.

Ten o'clock. Wives, maids and widows washing, wiping, scrubbing, picking, prinking, pinning, parching, painting, hooping, lacing and scolding . . . Kept mistresses as lazy in their beds as lifeguardsmen in their quarters – Informers plaguing poor alehousemen, barbers and nosegay-women – Hackney writers, Connaught fortune-hunters, and English solicitors carefully cogging the heels of their stockings, and darning their shirt-collars in order to issue forth from the noisy instances of their landladies to borrow half-a-crown or beg a dinner – . . . Bakers and pastrycooks robbing their customers' pies and puddings – Vintners and victuallers looking out their worst wines and liquors for the accommodation of such as are to dine with them gratis.

Eleven o'clock. Fine fans, rich brilliants, white hands, envious eyes and gay snuff-boxes displaying in most parish churches – Many excellent stolen sermons preaching by some clergymen who won't take pains to make worse of their own – Folks of fashion humbling themselves in rich lace and tissue and enduring the fatigue of Divine Service with wonderful seeming patience – Drunken beggars battling and breaking one another's heads in the public streets about dividing the charity of ostentatious fools and old women – Hackney coachmen and chairmen lifting up their eyes to Heaven for wet weather – Dabs and portions of beef, pork, and mutton roasting in pack-thread strings in the apartments of married cobblers, porters, penny-postmen and poor harlots.

Twelve o'clock. . . . City wives at their dram-bottles or criticising upon one another's dress and behaviour at church before dinner – Parish officers and young tradesmen vastly noisy over the dumplings in tavern kitchens – . . . Begging cripples bestowing prayers and benedictions in the streets upon their benefactors – . . .

One o'clock. Politicians dropping their two-pences upon the coffee-house bars and returning home to dinner – Hackney coaches flying about the streets with whole families, new-married couples, uncles, aunts and cousins to dine with their friends and relations . . . – All the common people's jaws in and around this great metropolis in full employment.

Two o'clock. The sexes ogling and stealing glances at one another as they sit at dinner together – Church bells and tavern bells keep time with one another – Some politicians upon the Catholic bench at the end of Stephen's Green bring the Spanish arms to Gibraltar and Great Britain and do wonders for the Pretender – Those on the Court Bench at the other end let loose a powerful army of Moors upon them and drive them out of their late conquests in Barbary . . . Pickpockets taking their stands at the avenues into public walks.

Three o'clock. Pawn Brokers' wives dressing themselves with their customers' wearing apparel, rings and watches – Prebendaries, petty canons and choristers, with much reluctancy, quit their couches, wives and bottles for cathedral exercises . . . – City cheesemongers and grocers snoring in churches and meeting-houses – The paths of Rathfarnham, Finglass and Donnybrook found much more pleasant than those of the Gospel – Citizens marching in threes, fours and fives thro' the town, in quest of sour wine and cider – Waiters at taverns and coffee-houses making vast preparations to cut a figure in the Beau Monde – Looking-glasses and — in great favour with the ladies – Women servants, half naked, at their broken bits of looking-glasses, vainly attempting, by the power of soap and labour, to alter the colour of their skins.

Four o'clock. Drunken bullies, beaus and gamesters religiously in their beds, as remembering that the Sabbath was appointed for a day of rest – People of quality picking their teeth and talking of modes and mortgages . . .

Five o'clock. A general church and meeting-house delivery for the City of Dublin – Vintners begin to yawn and quit their afternoon naps and welcome in their guests – All the pretty prating mouths sitting at tea-tables, like coroners' inquests upon the murdered reputations of their neighbours – Hired servants meeting and saluting one another in the streets, abusing the families that entertain them, and advancing the old doctrine of 'more places than parish churches' – Single men who have had their dinner given them at ale-houses begin to call to pay.

Six o'clock. People of quality and distinction drove out of the Green by milliners, manteaumakers, tire-women, sempstresses, clearstarchers, poulterers, staymakers, French peruke makers, dancing-masters, drapers, gentlemen's gentlemen, tailors' wives, starch old maids, and butchers' daughters Assignations and malicious whisperings at the Ring in the Park – Night-walkers washing their smocks against the close of the day – Vintners' wives and daughters dressed up behind their bars, to decoy young fellows into large reckonings – Match-makers and fortune-hunters in full employment – Beggars converting their coppers into true sterling.

Seven o'clock. Fools and powdered fops admiring themselves in coffee-houses – City apprentices complaining to fond mothers of their masters – Foot-soldiers drunk at their posts with brandy – The Ministry severely censured in ale-houses – Few lawyers at evening lectures – Men, women and children returning from the fields drunk and hungry – Dusty chaises with shores in high-crown hats limping thro' the streets of Dublin – People of quality beginning to pay spiteful visits to one another.

Eight o'clock. Cold beef and pudding most vigorously attacked in taverns and other public-houses – Servants in gentlemen's and tradesmen's kitchens carousing the liquors stolen from their masters – Young shopkeepers, beau journeymen and lawyers' clerks sneaking into town upon broken-kneed horses . . . Hired infants, who have been lent out to beggars, restored to their real parents – Men of quality visiting their wives' chamber maids in the absence of their wives from home.

Nine o'clock. Young rakes conversing with their mothers' maids in taverns – City dames vouching for one another, for the good company they have passed the afternoon in – . . . Journeymen shoemakers taking off their wearing apparel, as holding it by no longer tenure than the opening of the pawnbrokers' shops the next morning – Children, servants, old women, and others of the same size of understanding, pleasing and terrifying themselves with stories of witches, devils and apparitions. –

[154] Dublin society in the 1750s, and the virtuous Dublin ladies; manuscript of a letter from Chief Baron Willes in the British Museum.

The morning is generally spent in riding out or taking the Air in a Coach . . . and a bad morning in visiting, for no Gentleman ever visits in an afternoon, Most Gent being supposed (& generally are engaged) at dinner either at home or abroad with company. There is scarce such a thing as meeting a Gent & asking him to take a family dinner today, the fashion is a mutual Course of entertainment where you meet with a Table as well covered at a private Gentlemans house taking the magnificence of plate & the Garnish of ornaments & servants as at a Man of Quality or of large Fortune. The people generally dine late, Never before 4 & generally 5. I don't think considering the fashion of the place that is a prudent hour, for no Gent except of the profession of the Law ever does any business after dinner. It was the custom till within these few years that where you dined you supped, But now the Company parts generally from 8 to 10. Unless the master of the house or some of the company are hard drinkers & choose to sit later at the bottle. There is one good custom that any Gent takes up his hat & goes away when he pleases without taking Notice of the master of the House And tis reckoned rather unpolite to press anyone to stay. If there is a Lady, Generally there is a dinner & cards where you dine, If not there is scarce a Gent or Lady who has not one or more Cards for a Rout or Routs Every night in the Week.

The generality of the play is rather too high for the general circumstances of the people, The lowest players hazarding the winning or losing 3 or 4 Games a night. There are some that turn playing at cards into Gaming & lose considerable Sums. And indeed high play is too much the fashion of this kingdom . . . This usual rota of diversions, together with plays every night in Winter & publick Concerts, & in parliament Winter one Ball & one Drawing Room night at the Castle every week, And in

Dublin society amuses itself in the Rotunda pleasure-gardens,
late eighteenth century; from Walker's *Hibernian Magazine*, 1790

Summer time the publick Gardens Make altogether such a
round of Diversions, And the Time is so fully employed in them
That it gives too trifling and disipated Ideas to the minds of
Young People And is too apt to make them fancy that they were
born into this world for no other purpose but like the great
Leviathan to take their pastime therein.

But there is one thing I must say for the Honour of the Irish
ladies, Tis very uncommon to hear of any scandal upon their
Reputations Both Single & married Ladies in general behave
with great Virtue, and I do attribute it to Virtue rather than to
prudence & caution in concealing an Intrigue, Because Dublin is
like a large Market town in England where everyone knows & is
known by everybody, and there is scarce anything done by
anybody But it is publickly known. . . .

[155] The fighting Dubliners; from *Ireland Sixty Years Ago* by J.E. Walsh.

At the period we refer to [*the late eighteenth century*], any approach to the habits of the industrious classes by an application to trade or business, or even a profession, was considered a degradation to a gentleman, and the upper orders of society affected a most rigid exclusiveness. There was, however, one most singular pursuit in which the highest and lowest seemed alike to participate, with an astonishing relish – viz., fighting – which all classes in Ireland appear to have enjoyed with a keenness now hardly credible even to a native of Kentucky. The passion for brawls and quarrels was as rife in the metropolis as elsewhere, and led to scenes in Dublin, sixty or seventy years ago, which present a most extraordinary contrast to the state of society there at the present day.

Among the lower orders, a feud and deadly hostility had grown up between the Liberty boys, or tailors and weavers of the Coombe, and the Ormond boys, or butchers who lived in Ormond-market, on Ormond-quay, which caused frequent conflicts; and it is in the memory of many now living that the streets, and particularly the quays and bridges, were impassable in consequence of the battles of these parties. The weavers descending from the upper regions beyond Thomas-street, poured down on their opponents below; they were opposed by the butchers, and a contest commenced on the quays which extended from Essex to Island bridge. The shops were closed; all business suspended; the sober and peaceable compelled to keep their houses; and those whose occasions led them through the streets where the belligerents were engaged, were stopped ; while the war of stones and other missiles was carried on across the river, and the bridges were taken and retaken by the hostile parties. It will hardly be believed that for whole days the intercourse of the city was interrupted by the feuds of these factions. The few miserable watchmen, inefficient for any purpose of protection, looked on in terror, and thought themselves well acquitted for their duty if they escaped from stick and stone. A friend of ours has told us that he has gone down to Essex-bridge, when he has been informed that one of those battles was raging, and stood quietly on the battlements for a whole day looking at the combat, in which above a thousand men were engaged. At one time, the Ormond boys drove those of the Liberty up to Thomas-street, where rallying, they repulsed their assailants and drove them back as far as the Broad-stone, while the bridges and quays were strewed with the maimed and wounded. On May 11th, 1790, one of these frightful riots raged for an entire Saturday on Ormond-quay, the contending parties struggling for the mastery of the bridge; but nightfall having separated them before the victory was decided, the battle was renewed on the Monday following. It was reported of Alderman Emerson, when lord mayor, on one of those occasions, that he declined to interfere when applied to, asserting that 'it was as much as his life was worth to go among them.'

These feuds terminated sometimes in frightful excesses. The butchers used their knives, not to stab their opponents, but for a purpose then common in the barbarous state of Irish society, to *hough* or cut the tendon of the leg, thereby rendering the person incurably lame for life. On one occasion after a defeat of the Ormond boys, those of the Liberty retaliated in a manner still more barbarous and revolting. They dragged the persons they seized to their market, and dislodging the meat they found there, hooked the men by the jaws, and retired, leaving the butchers hanging on their own stalls.

The spirit of the times led men of the highest grade and respectability to join with the dregs of the market in these outrages . . . and the young aristocrat, who would have felt it an intolerable degradation to associate or even be seen with an honest merchant, however respectable, with a singular inconsistency made a boast of his intimate acquaintance with the lawless excesses of butchers and coal-porters. The students of Trinity College were particularly prone to join in the affrays between the belligerents, and generally united their forces to those of the Liberty boys against the butchers. On one occasion, several of them were seized by the latter, and to the great terror of their friends, it was reported they were hanged up in the stalls, in retaliation for the cruelty of the weavers. A party of watchmen sufficiently strong was at length collected by the authorities, and they proceeded to Ormond-market: there they saw a frightful spectacle – a number of college lads in their gowns and caps hanging to the hooks. On examination, however, it was found that the butchers, pitying their youth and respecting their rank, had only hung them by the waistbands of their breeches, where they remained as helpless, indeed, as if they were suspended by the neck.

[156] The Dublin footpads; from *Ireland Sixty Years Ago* by J.E. Walsh.

The footpads of Dublin robbed in a manner, we believe, peculiar to themselves. The streets were miserably lighted – indeed, in many places hardly lighted at all. So late as 1812, there were only twenty-six small oil lamps to light the immense square of Stephen's green, which were therefore one hundred and seventy feet from one another. The footpads congregated in a dark entry, on the shady side of the street, if the moon shone; if not, the dim and dismal light of the lamps was little obstruction. A cord was provided with a loop at the end of it. The loop was laid on the pavement, and the thieves watched the approach of a passenger. If he put his foot in the loop, it was immediately chucked. The man fell prostrate, and was dragged rapidly up the entry to some cellar or waste yard, where he was robbed, and sometimes murdered. The stun received by the fall usually prevented the victim from ever recognizing the robbers. We knew a gentleman who had been thus robbed, and when he recovered, found himself in an alley at the end of a lane off Bride-street, nearly naked, and severely contused and lacerated by being dragged over the rough pavement.

[157] The eloquence of the Dublin beggar; from John Gamble's *Sketches of History, Politics and Manners taken in Dublin in the Autumn of 1811.*

The address of an Irish beggar is much more poetical and animated than that of an English one; his phraseology is as peculiar as the recitative in which it is delivered; he conjures you, for the love and honour of God, to throw something to the poor famished sinner – by your father and mother's soul to cast an eye of pity on his sufferings – he is equally liberal in his good wishes, whether you give him anything or not; 'may you live a hundred years – may you pass unhurt through fire and water – may the gates of Paradise be ever open to receive you'; are common

A Dublin beggar plies his trade by Capel Street bridge: note
the State lottery office in the background, another prominent
feature of Dublin eighteenth-century life; detail from an
aquatint by James Malton, 1797

modes of expression, which he utters with a volubility that is inconceivable.

[158] Eloquence at the Viceroy's supper party in the early 1800s; from *Jack Hinton, the Guardsman* by Charles Lever.

Amid a shower of smart, caustic, and witty sayings, droll stories, retort and repartee, the wine circulated freely from hand to hand; the presence of the Duke adding fresh impulse to the sallies of fun and merriment around him. Anecdotes of the army, the bench, and the bar, poured in unceasingly, accompanied by running commentaries of the hearers, who never let slip an opportunity for a jest or a rejoinder. To me the most singular feature of all this was, that no one seemed too old or too dignified, too high in station or too venerable from office, to join in this headlong current of conviviality: austere churchmen, erudite chief-justices, profound politicians, privy councillors, military officers of high rank and standing, were here all mixed up together into one strange medley, apparently bent on throwing an air of ridicule over the graver business of life, and laughing alike at themselves and the world. Nothing was too grave for a jest, nothing too solemn for a sarcasm. All the soldier's experience of men and manners, all the lawyer's acuteness of perception and readiness of wit, all the politician's practised tact and habitual subtlety, were brought to bear upon the common topics of the day with such promptitude and such power, that one knew not whether to be more struck by the mass of information they possessed, or by that strange fatality which could make men so great and so gifted, satisfied to jest where they might be called on to judge.

Play and politics, wine and women, debts and duels, were discussed not only with an absence of all restraint, but with a deep knowledge of the world and a profound insight into the heart, which often imparted to the careless and random speech the sharpness of the most cutting sarcasm. Personalities too were rife: no one spared his neighbour, for he did not expect mercy for himself; and the luckless wight who tripped in his narrative or stumbled in his story, was assailed on every side, until some happy expedient of his own, or some new victim being discovered, the attack would take another direction, and leave him once more at liberty.

[159] An American tourist looks at splendour and misery in Dublin in the first years of the nineteenth century; from *Ancient & Modern Dublin* by William Curry.

'This city,' says the Tourist, 'presents the most extraordinary contrast of poverty and magnificence to be met with in Europe. As you approach it, you find the suburbs composed of hovels, the sides of which are partly stone and partly earth, the roofs of turf, the whole dimensions of each not exceeding twelve or fourteen feet square. These miserable caves may or may not have a hole for a window, and an aperture on the top, to let out the smoke, if the luxury of fire can be afforded. Around the door the dirty children are huddled – not one half are decently clad; some of them still evince notions of civilization by slinking into a house, or turning their bare parts against a wall. I saw hundreds whose whole dress, consisting of a mass of rags, of all colours and all sorts of fabrics, will not furnish one piece of cloth eight inches square – and these tatters seemed to be sewed together only to prevent them deserting each other. Having passed the suburbs, the dwellings improve; and, on reaching Sackville-street, you imagine yourself in one of the most elegant cities in Europe. In walking over the city, the Irish Parliament House, (now the Bank,) the Exchange, the quay along the Liffey, and several of the public squares, excite the stranger's admiration. There is no part of London which can compare with the centre of Dublin in beauty and magnificence. But, in turning the eye from the architectural splendour which surrounds him, upon the crowds which flow along the streets, the stranger will be struck with the motley nature of the throng. Here is a lass almost buoyant with satin and feathers; there is a trembling girl of eighteen, purple from cold, shrinking from shame, and drawing around her the poor rags which, with all her care, scarce cover her body; here is an *exquisite*, perfuming the air as he passes, with rings on his fingers, diamonds on his brooch, and a gemmed quizzing-glass at his side; there is an honest fellow who cannot afford a hat, whose feet, summer or winter, know not the luxury of shoe or stocking, and whose whole wardrobe consists of two articles, viz. a tattered jacket, and about half a pair of small-clothes; and, not to multiply pictures, while the Lieutenant dashes by in a coach and four, the stranger gazes at the gallant and costly pageant, while he empties his pocket to satisfy the throng of beggars who pray him, in the name of God, to give them a penny.'

Happily for the citizens and the traveller, the last remark does not now apply, as beggars are not allowed on the streets; the Mendicity Society [*see next extract*] providing what is at least sufficient to keep them from starvation. Should the American Tourist have again occasion to visit the metropolis he would find the state of things much improved.

[160] William Cobbett visits the Dublin workhouse; from *Not by Bullets and Bayonets* by Molly Townsend.

(William Cobbett, the famous radical journalist and MP, visited Dublin in 1834 when he was seventy-one. A long-standing champion of the Irish Catholic Cause, he received a rapturous welcome. His harrowing account of the Dublin poor was published as an Open Letter to an English farm labourer. The Mendicity Institute on Ussher's Island (blithely referred to in Curry's guide-book (see previous extract) as relieving the problem of Dublin's beggars) was originally one of Dublin's great private houses – Moira House. Its bricked-up entrance still survives on the Quays.)

MARSHALL,

I have this morning seen more than one thousand of working persons, men and women, boys and girls, all the clothes upon the bodies of all of whom were not worth so much as the smock-frock that you go to work in; and you have a wife and eight children, seven of whom are too young to go to work. I have seen the *food* and the *cooking* of the food, in a LARGE HOUSE, where food is prepared for a part of these wretched people. Cast-iron coppers, three or four times as big as our largest brewing copper, are employed to boil *oatmeal* (that is, *ground oats*) *in water*, or *butter-milk*, or *skim-milk*; and this is the food given to these poor creatures. . . . The LARGE HOUSE, of which I have spoken to you above, is called the MENDICITY. The word *mendicant* means *beggar*, and the word MENDICITY means *beggary*. So that this, which was formerly a nobleman's mansion, is now the *house of beggars*. From this house there are sent forth, every day, *begging carts*, drawn by women, who go from house to house to collect what is called '*broken victuals*.' These carts are precisely, in shape and in size, like my *dog-hutches*, except that the begging carts have a sort of *copper* at top to put the victuals in at, and a locked-up door at one end, to take the victuals out of. Now mind what I am going to say: the bones, bits of rusty bacon, rind of bacon, scrapings of dishes and plates, left cabbage, left turnips, peas, beans, beets, and the like odds and ends, that Mrs Kenning throws into our *hog-tub*, form a mass of victuals *superior in quality* to these *mendicity-collections*; and in proof of which I state the following facts: that the carts, when they come in, have their contents taken out and examined by persons appointed for the purpose, who separate all that can become food from the mere rubbish and filth, that is, by servants at the houses, tossed into the carts amongst it; and a gentleman has, in evidence given by him before commissioners here, stated, that out of *seventy odd hundred weight* taken out of the carts the examiners found *only nine hundred weight* that could by any *possibility* become human food, the *bones* in these nine hundred weight not being included. . . .

In another place I saw the most painful sight of all: *women*, with heavy hammers, *cracking stones* into very small pieces, to *make walks in gentlemen's gardens!* These women were as ragged as the rest; and the sight of them and their work, and the thoughts accompanying these, would have sunk the heart in your body, as they did mine.

[161] Dining-out in Dublin in the 1840s; from W.M. Thackeray's *An Irish Sketchbook*.

And so having reached Dublin, it becomes necessary to curtail the observations which were to be made upon that city; which surely ought to have a volume to itself: the humours of Dublin at least require so much space. For instance, there was the dinner at the Kildare Street Club, or the Hotel opposite, – the dinner in Trinity College Hall, – that at Mr –, the publisher's, where a dozen of the literary men of Ireland were assembled, – and those (say fifty) with Harry Lorrequer himself, at his mansion of Templeogue. What a favourable opportunity to discourse upon the peculiarities of Irish character! to describe men of letters, of fashion, and university dons! . . . But the author who wishes to dine again at his friend's cost, must needs have a care how he puts him in print.

Suffice it to say, that at Kildare Street we had white neckcloths, black waiters, wax-candles, and some of the best wine in Europe; at Mr –, the publisher's, wax-candles, and some of the best wine in Europe; at Mr Lever's, wax-candles, and some of the best wine in Europe; at Trinity College – but there is no need to mention what took place at Trinity College; for on returning to London, and recounting the circumstances of the repast, my friend B–, a Master of Arts of that university, solemnly declared the thing was impossible: – no stranger *could* dine at Trinity College; it was too great a privilege – in a word, he would not believe the story, nor will he to this day; and why, therefore, tell it in vain?

I am sure if the Fellows of Colleges in Oxford and Cambridge were told that the Fellows of T. C. D. only drink beer at dinner, they would not believe *that*. Such, however, was the fact: or may be it was a dream, which was followed by another dream of about four-and-twenty gentlemen seated round a common-room table after dinner; and, by a subsequent vision of a tray of oysters in the apartments of a tutor of the university, sometime before midnight. Did we swallow them or not? – the oysters are an open question.

[162] Brass-plate Dublin; from *Seven Winters* by Elizabeth Bowen.

(The novelist Elizabeth Bowen was born at 15 Herbert Place by the Grand Canal, and spent the first seven winters of her childhood there.)

Between the middle of Dublin and Herbert Place lies a tract of Georgian streets and squares. We had a choice of two routes into the city. From the foot of our steps we could turn right, then go along Lower Baggot Street; or we could turn left, take the curve round St Stephen's Church and after that go along Upper Mount Street and the south side of Merrion Square; to this route was added the charm of going through Leinster Lawn, between the Museum and the National Gallery; one then followed that secretive passage, under the high flank of Leinster House, through to the circular lawn on the other side and the gates opening on to Kildare Street.

(When I was with my father, the glory of the Royal Dublin Society was upon us and we took the indoor short cut, through the Leinster House rooms.)

The perspectives of this quarter of Dublin are to any eye, at any time, very long. In those first winters they were endless to me. The tense distances that one only slowly demolished gave a feeling of undertaking to any walk. Everything in this quarter seemed outsize. The width of the streets, the stretch of the squares, the unbroken cliff-like height of the houses made the human idea look to me superhuman. And there was something abstract about this idea, with its built-up planes of shadow and light.

At the same time, the complexion of these façades humanly altered from day to day. The neighbourhood seemed infused with a temper or temperament of its own, and my spirits, on morning or afternoon walks, corresponded with this in their rise and fall. . . . Some days, a pinkish sun-charged gauze hung even over the houses that were in shadow; sunlight marked with its blades the intersections of streets and dissolved over the mews that I saw through archways. On such days, Dublin appeared to seal up sunshine as an unopened orange seals up juice. The most implacable buildings were lanced with light; the glass half-moons over the darkest front doors glowed with sun that, let in by a staircase window, fell like a cascade down flights of stairs. . . .

The post-Union exodus of the bright-plumaged people had not (as I saw) been followed by real decay. The Irish Bar and the eminent Dublin doctors kept South Dublin witty and sociable. Judges and specialists now lived round Merrion Square. The front doors were painted, the fanlights and windows polished, the great staircases possibly better swept and the high-ceilinged double drawing-rooms heated and lit for *conversazioni*. In the winters of my childhood this second society was still in full, if not at its fullest, force. The twentieth century governed only in name; the nineteenth was still a powerful dowager. Between England and Anglo-Ireland a time-lag is, I think, always perceptible. Any transition into Edwardian dashingness would have been seen in the Castle set. But the Castle seasons left my father and mother cold. The world my parents inhabited, and the subworld of its children, was still late-Victorian. Their friends were drawn from the Bar, from Trinity College, from among the prelates of the Church of Ireland or landed people quietly living in town.

In fact, the climatic moodiness of South Dublin (a bold Italianate town-plan in tricky Celtic light) must have existed only in my eye. All here stood for stability. The front doors were, as I say, fresh painted – crimson, chocolate, chestnut, ink-blue or olive-green. One barrister friend of my father's had a chalk-white front door I found beautiful. And each door – to this my memory finds no single exception – bore its polished brass plate. Daughter of a professional neighbourhood, I took this brass plate announcing its owner's name to be the *sine qua non* of any gentleman's house. Just as the tombstone says '*Here Lies*' the plate on the front door (in my view) said '*Here Lives.*' Failure to write one's name on one's door seemed to me the admission of nonentity. The house-holder with the anonymous door must resign himself to being overlooked by the world – to being passed by by the postman, unfed by tradesmen, guestless, unsought by friends – and his family dwelt in the shadow of this disgrace.

The fact that I could not read made these plates with writing still more significant. The first time I did see a town front door of unmistakable standing *without* a plate, I remember being not only scornful but hostile. Why should the dweller here envelop himself in mystery? On that occasion, my mother explained to me that plates were not, after all, the rule. If not, why not? I said hotly: how very silly. How else was one to know who lived in a house? In the light of this fixed idea (which I still think a good one) I remember my first view of London – street after street of triste anonymity. So no one cares who lives in London, I thought. No wonder London is so large; all the nonentities settle here. Dublin has chosen to be smaller than London because she is grander and more exclusive. All the important people live in Dublin, near me.

[163] Dublin, after the 'crossness'; from *In Search of Ireland* by H.V. Morton.

(H.V. Morton was one of the first travel-writers to describe Dublin after the establishment of the Free State; and his delightful book, first published in 1930, is still in print. The 'crossness' is, of course, the War of Independence or Anglo-Irish War which began with the Rising of 1916 and was ended by the Treaty of 1921; followed by the Civil War between the Free State army and the Republicans which ended only in 1923. All in all, Dublin had had seven years of fighting.)

Why has Dublin been called 'dear dirty Dublin'? This surely is an ancient libel. The roads outside Dublin are apparently dirty on the evidence of the omnibus wheels, to which are attached small hanging brooms of stiff bristles. These brooms tickle the tyres when the wheels are in motion and brush off the mud. But the city itself is as clean as a Dutch dresser.

In the streets stand amongst the taxicabs many of the oldest horse-cabs on earth, objects of remarkable antiquity which surely, by some virtue of the Irish temperament, continue to function, and there is also that strange but famous vehicle, known to the English as a 'jaunting-car', but called in Ireland an 'outside-car'. I imagine that the outside-car is to Dublin what the few remaining hansom cabs are to London – a sentimental refuge for Americans. When you hire one of them and sit sideways to the world, Dublin smiles indulgently at you from the pavement. I went round behind a spanking bay pony while the jarvey pointed out the sights with his whip.

In O'Connell Street he indicated a line of shattered buildings, and remarked that they had been destroyed during the 'crossness'.

'You mean,' I said, 'the fighting.'

'Och, sure,' he replied, 'it was the crossness, I said.'

I thought this description quite the kindest and most generous I had ever heard!

Sentries, smart in green uniforms and brown leggings, marched before the Government building, which flies the tricolour of the Free State. A hefty young man, armed with a revolver, stood on the steps. In a barrack square we saw a company of young soldiers at bayonet drill, practising a lunge and parry, which looked to me something new in warfare.

The crowds in the Dublin streets are vastly different from English crowds. You do not see the haggard money look which is becoming characteristic of all large English cities. There is more laughter. There is no painful rushing about. There is a cheerful ease about Dublin, a casual good temper, which makes it difficult to realize the dark times through which this city has passed. There are certain apparent superficialities which, however, possess a deep significance. The English red has vanished from the streets; the pillarboxes are green. So are the envelopes in which telegrams are delivered. So are the mail vans. And the names of the streets are written in Gaelic, which not one in a thousand Dubliners can read! Still this proves a change in ownership and a striving to be Irish.

When we came to the end of the journey the jarvey said, when I asked how much he wanted:

'I'll leave it to yourself.'

A Frenchman would have taken my enormous bribe with a surly doubtfulness, but he was quite frankly overpaid, and showed it with Irish candour. 'God bless ye,' he said. 'And now what about a bit of a drive to-morrow?'

Bibliography

BAGWELL, RICHARD, *Ireland under the Stuarts*, London, 1909
BARNARD, F.P., *Strongbow's Conquest of Ireland*, London, 1888
BARRINGTON, SIR JONAH, *Personal Sketches of His Own Times*, Dublin, 1827
– *The Rise and Fall of the Irish Nation*, Dublin, 1833
– *Historic Memoirs of Ireland*
BEHAN, BRENDAN, *Brendan Behan's Island*, London, 1962
BIRRELL, AUGUSTINE, *Things Past Redress*, London, 1932
Blackwoods Magazine, July 1916
BOWEN, ELIZABETH, *Seven Winters*, Dublin, 1942
– *The Shelbourne*, London, 1951
CAMPBELL, REVD THOMAS, *A Philosophical Survey of the South of Ireland*, Dublin, 1777
CARLETON, WILLIAM, *Autobiography*, ed. D. Masson, London, 1896
CARLYLE, THOMAS, *Reminiscences of My Irish Journey in 1849*, London, 1882
CARTE, THOMAS, *An History of the Life of James, Duke of Ormonde*, London, 1735
CARTY, JAMES, *Ireland 1607–1782, A documentary record*, Dublin, 1951
CHART, D.A., *The Story of Dublin*, London, 1907
CHURCHILL, WINSTON, *My Early Life*, London, 1930
CLARKE, AUSTIN, *A Penny in the Clouds*, London, 1962
CONNOLLY, NORA, *Portrait of a Rebel Father*, Dublin, 1935
COOPER, GEORGE, *Letters on the Irish Nation*, Dublin, 1799
CROKER, JOHN WILSON, *The Croker Papers 1808–57*, ed. R. Pool, London, 1967
CURRAN, W.H., *Sketches of the Irish Bar*, Dublin, 1855
CURRY, WILLIAM, *A New Picture of Dublin*, London, 1820
– *Ancient & Modern Dublin*
DE BOVET, ANNE, *Three Months in Ireland*, London, 1891
DELANY, MARY, *Autobiography and Correspondence of Mary Granville, Mrs Delany*, ed. Lady Llanover, London, 1861
DE QUINCEY, THOMAS, *Autobiographic Sketches*, London, 1890
Desiderata Curiosa Hibernica, Dublin, 1772
DE VERE, AUBREY, *Recollections*, London, 1897
Dublin Historical Record, The, Vol. 20, Dublin, 1964
Dublin Penny Journal, The, Dublin, 1840
EVERETT, KATHERINE, *Bricks and Flowers*, London, 1949

FITZHENRY, EDNA, *An Anthology of 1916*, London, 1935

GAMBLE, JOHN, *Sketches of History, Politics and Manners taken in Dublin in the Autumn of 1811*, Dublin, 1811

GERARD, FRANCIS, *Picturesque Dublin*, London, 1898

GILBERT, SIR JOHN, *The History of the City of Dublin*, Dublin, 1854–59

– *Calendar of Ancient Records of Dublin*, Dublin, 1889–1907

– *The History of the Parliament House*, Dublin, 1896

GOGARTY, OLIVER ST JOHN, *As I was going down Sackville Street*, London, 1937

– *It isn't This Time of Year at all*, New York, 1954

Government of Ireland under Sir John Perrott, The [by E.C.S.] London, 1626.

GRATTAN, HENRY, *The Life and Times of Henry Grattan by his son*, London, 1839–46

GREGORY, AUGUSTA, *Our Irish Theatre*, London, 1914

– *Seventy Years, the autobiography of Lady Gregory*, New York, 1976

GWYNN, STEPHEN, *Dublin Old and New*, London, 1938

HALL, MR and MRS S.C., *Ireland, its Scenery, Character, etc*, London, 1841

HANDEL, G.F., *Autograph Letters of Handel and Jennens*, ed. Edward, 6th Earl of Howe, Christie's Catalogue, London, 1973

HARDY, FRANCIS, *Memoirs of the Earl of Charlemont*, London, 1812

HARRIS, FRANK, *The Life of Oscar Wilde*, London, 1937

HERBERT, J.D., *Irish Varieties*, Dublin, 1836

HOLINSHED, RALPH, *Chronicles of England and Ireland*, London, 1808

HOLLOWAY, JOSEPH, *Joseph Holloway's Abbey Theatre*, ed. Roger Hogan and Michael J. O'Neill, Illinois, 1967

HOPKINS, GERARD MANLEY, *Letters of Gerard Manley Hopkins to Robert Bridges*, London, 1935

HYDE, DOUGLAS, *The Literary History of Ireland*, London, 1899

Illustrated London News, The, London, May 1882 and August 1847

JEFFREYS, NATHANIEL, *An Englishman's Descriptive Account of Dublin*, London, 1810

JOYCE, JAMES, *Portrait of the Artist as a Young Man*, New York, 1916

– *Ulysses*, Paris, 1922

– *Selected Letters of James Joyce*, ed. Richard Ellmann, Oxford, 1975

KELLY, LINDA, *The Kemble Era*, London, 1980

KENNEDY, TOM (ed.), *Victorian Dublin*, Dublin, 1980

LEVER, CHARLES, *Charles O'Malley*, Dublin, 1842

– *Jack Hinton, the Guardsman*, Dublin, 1847

LOCKHART, J.G., *The Life of Sir Walter Scott*, London, 1847

LONGFORD, CHRISTINE, *A Biography of Dublin*, London, 1936

MACBRIDE, MAUD GONNE, *A Servant of the Queen*, London, 1938

MCCARTHY, MURIEL, *All Graduates and Gentlemen*, Dublin, 1980

MACREADY, WILLIAM CHARLES, *Reminiscences*, ed. Sir F. Pollock, London, 1875

MACDONAGH, MICHAEL, *The Life of Daniel O'Connell*, London, 1903

MACLYSAGHT, EDWARD, *Irish Life in the Seventeenth Century*, Dublin, 1939

MCMANUS, M.J., *Irish Cavalcade*, London, 1939

MACNEILE DIXON, W., *Trinity College, Dublin*, London, 1902

MADDEN, R.R., *Ireland in '98*, London, 1888

MALTON, JAMES, *A Picturesque and Descriptive View of Dublin*, London, 1792–99

MAXWELL, CONSTANTIA, *Irish History from Contemporary Sources*, London, 1923

– *Dublin under the Georges*, London, 1936

– *History of Trinity College, Dublin, 1591–1892*, Dublin, 1942

MOORE, GEORGE, *Parnell and his Island*, London, 1886

– *Hail and Farewell (Ave, Salve, Vale)*, London, 1900

MORTON, H.V., *In Search of Ireland*, London, 1930

MULVANEY, T.J., *The Life of James Gandon*, London, 1847

NEWBOLT, HENRY, *Froissart in Britain*, London, 1900

NORWAY, MRS JAMES HAMILTON, *The Sinn Fein Rebellion as I saw it*, London, 1918

O'BRIEN, JOSEPH, *Dear, Dirty Dublin, A city in distress, 1899–1916*, California, 1982

O'BRIEN, KATE, *My Ireland*, London, 1962

O'BRIEN, WILLIAM, *Recollections*, London, 1905

O'CASEY, SEAN, *Pictures in the Hallway*, London, 1942

– *Drums under the Windows*, London, 1945

– *Inishfallen, fare you well*, London, 1949

O'KEEFFE, JOHN, *Recollections*, London, 1826

O'MALLEY, ERNIE, *On Another Man's Wound*, London, 1936

ORRERY, LORD, *The Orrery Papers*, ed. the Countess of Cork and Orrery, London, 1903

PILKINGTON, LETITIA, *The Memoirs of Letitia Pilkington*, London, 1748

Recollections of Dublin Castle and Dublin Society, Anon, Dublin, 1902

RICH, BARNABY, *New Description of Ireland*, London, 1610.

RYAN, DESMOND, *Remembering Sion*, Dublin, 1934

SAMUELS, ARTHUR, *The Early Life and Correspondence of Edmund Burke*, London, 1923

SHELLEY, PERCY BYSSHE, *Letters to Elizabeth Hitchener*, London, 1908

SHERIDAN, THOMAS, *The Life of Doctor Swift*, London, 1770

STARKIE, WALTER, *Scholars and Gypsies*, London, 1963

STEPHENS, JAMES, *The Insurrection in Dublin*, London, 1916

SWIFT, JONATHAN, *The Correspondence of Jonathan Swift*, ed. Elrington Ball, London, 1911–14

THACKERAY, WILLIAM MAKEPEACE, *An Irish Sketchbook*, London, 1843

TOWNSEND, MOLLY, *Not by Bullets and Bayonets*, London, 1983

TOWNSHEND, DOROTHEA, *The Life and Letters of the Great Earl of Cork*, London, 1904

VICTORIA, QUEEN, *The Collected Letters of Queen Victoria*, ed. G.E. Buckle, London, 1926

WALSH, J.E., *Ireland Sixty Years Ago*, Dublin, 1847

WESLEY, JOHN, *Wesley, His Own Biographer*, London, 1891

WILLES, CHIEF JUSTICE BARON, Add MSS 29 252, British Museum, London

WINSTANLEY, JOHN, *The Poems of John Winstanley*, London, 1748

YEATS, WILLIAM BUTLER, *The Collected Poems of W.B. Yeats*, London, 1950.

Index

Numbers in *italics* refer to illustrations

INDEX OF PLACES

Abbey Street, 242, 284, 286, 294
Abbey Street Theatre, 239–40, 242;
    see also Abbey Theatre
Abbey Theatre, 45, 122, 215,
    241–51, *250*
Adelphi Theatre, 239
All Hallows, Abbey of, 165
Aras an Uachtaran (Vice-regal
    Lodge), 128, 131, 132–4, 135,
    136, 149
Arran Bridge, 37
Arran Quay, 155
Assembly Hall, Dublin Castle, 182
Ath Cliath (Dublin), 27, 28

Back-Lane, 102
Bank of Ireland, 131, 179, 182, 321
Battery, the, 261
Beaux Walk, St Stephen's Green,
    198, *200–1*
Belvedere House (Belvedere
    College), 145–6, 211, 249
Black Pool (Linn Dubh), 27, 28
Blackrock, 44
Bloody Bridge, 37
Bluecoat School, 37
Bride Street, 318
Broad-stone, 317

Capel Street bridge, *319*
Carlisle Bridge, 43, 147; *see also*
    O'Connell Bridge
Carmelites' Church, Whitefriars
    Street, 33
Castle Market, 101
Castle Yard, 58–9, 70
Castleknock, 32
Cavendish Row, 148
Chapel Izod, 127, *136*
Charlemont House (Municipal Art
    Gallery), 143–4
Chichester House, 182
Christ Church Cathedral, 28, 30,

31, 32, 33, 77–83, *80*
City Hall, 28
Clery's Store, 273, 289
Clontarf, 30, 32, 143
Coliseum Theatre, 290
College Green, 34, 41, 182–97
Cook Street, 31
Coombe, the, 98, 279, 316
Coote Lane, 41
Cork Hill, 76
Corn Market, 102
Cullen Wood, 308
Custom House, 38, 42, 43, 151–4,
    153, 155, 158, 169

Dáil Eireann, 225–6; *see also*
    Leinster House
Dalkey road, 248
Dawson Street, 44, 288
Deanery House, 91–2
Delville, 66
Donnybrook, 44, 312
Dr Mosse's Lying-in Hospital,
    137–40, *139*; *see also* the Rotunda
Dublin Bay, 27, 206, 221, 256–7
Dublin Castle, 31, 33, 34, 35,
    56–76, *57*, *71*, 106, 107, 149, 157,
    182, 273–4, 277, 279, 291
Dublin harbour, 27, 255, 256–7, 261
Dublin mountains, 32, 42, 131
Dun Laoghaire (Dunlcary), 44,
    224, 258–60, *259*, 261; *see also*
    Kingstown

Earl Street, 285
Eden Quay, 294
Ely House, 211–14
Essex Bridge, 37, 43, 316

Fifteen Acres, 128
Finglass, 312
Fishamble Street, 31, 235; theatre,
    240

Fitzwilliam Square, 43, 230–1
Fitzwilliam Street, 42
Forty Foot, the, 261
Four Courts, *frontis*, 38, 42, 44, 46, 155–6, 227, 285
Francis Street, 98
Frederick Street, 219
French Walk, St Stephen's Green, 198

Gardiner's Mall, 137
Gate Theatre, 137
George I, statue of, 206
George's Lane, 137
Glasnevin, 44, 66
GPO, *see* Post Office
Grafton Street, 44, 216, 283, 288–9
Grand Canal, 324
Great Brunswick Street, 239
Great Denmark Street, 145
Guinness brewery, 111, 113–14

Harold's Cross, 106
Henrietta Street, 40
Henry Place, 286
Henry Street, 158, 286
Herbert Place, 324
Hibernian Hotel, 288
High Street, 29
Holy Trinity Church, 77; *see also* Christ Church Cathedral
House of Commons, *see* Parliament House
House of Lords, 43, 182, 192–3, 194
Howth, 27, 44, 209, 268–70; Hill of, 206, 258, 279
Hume Street, 211
Hurdle Ford, 27

Imperial Hotel, 286
Irish Foreign Office, 199
Irish National Gallery, 198, 276, 324
Island Bridge, 316
Iveagh House, 199

Jesuit University College (Newman House), 203, 204–5
Joseph's Lane, 101

Kildare Street, 41, 219, 325
Kildare Street Club, 131, 219, 323, 324
Killiney, 27, 44, 279
Kilmainham Hospital, 36, 41, 115, 116–17
Kilmainham Jail, 117–24, *119*, 290–3
King's Hospital, 115
Kingstown (Dun Laoghaire), 194, 206, 248, 258–60, *259*

Lazy-hill, 255
Leeson Walk, St Stephen's Green, 198
Leinster, 30
Leinster House, 41–2, 220–6, *223*, 324
Liberties, the, 98–114, 316–17
Liberty Hall, 273, *275*, 284, 286
Library Square, 177
Liffey, *frontis*, 27, 28, 29, 30, 36, 54, 113, 155–6, 321; bridges, 32, 37, 40, 147, 316, *319*
Linenhall, 286
Linn Dubh *see* Black Pool
Lower Baggot Street, 324
Lower Dominick Street, 40
Lower Mount Street, 294

Marino, Clontarf, 143
Market-House, 107
Marlborough Street Chapel (later St Mary's Pro-Cathedral), 158–62, *160–1*
Marsh's library, 40, 97
Martello Towers, 256, 261–7
Maynooth Castle, 87
Meath Street, 98
Mendicity Institute, 279, 322; *see also* Moira House
Merchants Quay, 32
Merrion Row, 276, 277
Merrion Square, 42, 196, 220, 227–31, *228*, 324, 325
Merrion Street, 42
Military Hospital, 131
Model School, 131
Moira House, 322

Monkstown, 68
Moore Street, 286
Mountjoy Square, 43
Municipal Art Gallery, 143

Neal's Music-hall, 235
Nelson's Pillar, 43, 274, 280
Newman College, 203
Newman House, St Stephen's
 Green, 204
Nicholas Street, 102
North Great George Street, 105
North Wall, Dublin harbour, 255

O'Connell Bridge, 40, 43, 147
O'Connell Street, 40, 45, 137,
 147–50, 273–4, 279–80, 288–9,
 294, 327; *see also* Sackville Street
Ormonde Bridge, 37
Ormonde Market, 37, 316, 317
Ormonde's Quay, 37
Oxmantown, 301
Oxmantown, Green, 34, 37

Pale, the, 30; *see also* Normans
Palmerston Road, 231
Parliament House, College Green,
 38, 41, 43, 138, 176, 182–97, *185*,
 187, *197*, 225–6, 321; *see also*
 Bank of Ireland
Peacock Theatre, 249
Phoenix Park, 36, 115, 117, 127–36,
 136, 203, 215
Pigeon house, 256
Portobello Gardens, 239
Post Office, 43, 46, 149–50, 217,
 277, 279–81, 282, 284–90, *287*
Princes Street, 284, 285
Pro-Cathedral, *see* St Mary's Pro-
 Cathedral and Marlborough St
 Chapel

Quays, the, 42, 46, 115, 155–7, 224,
 241, 279, 286, 316, 322

Ranger's Lodge, Phoenix Park *see*
 Aras an Uachtaran
Rathfarnham, 70, 72, 312
Richmond Prison, 194, 197, 290–1

Ringsend, 255
Rotunda, 137–42, *139*, 239, *315*
Royal Barracks, 157
Royal Dublin Society, 226, 325
Royal Exchange, 75–6, 141–2, 321
Royal Hospital, Kilmainham, 36,
 41, 115, 116–17
Rutland Square, 148

Sackville Street (later O'Connell
 Street), 40, 141, 147–50, 151,
 159, 282, 288–9, 295, 321
St Andrew's Church, 43
St Anne's House, near Dublin, 215
St Audoen's Church, 31, 32
St Catherine's Church, 100, 106,
 107, *109*
St John, Priory of, 116
St Martin's Church, 31
St Mary's Abbey, 33, 40
St Mary's Pro-Cathedral, 43,
 158–62, *160–1*
St Michael and St John, Church of,
 236
St Michan's Church, 30
St Nicholas' Church, 31, 43
St Patrick's Cathedral, 30, 31, 63,
 84–96, *86*, *95*, 97, 99, 112, 214
St Stephen's Church, 324
St Stephen's Green, 34, 36–7,
 198–218, *200–1*, 276–9, 282–3,
 312, 318
St Werburgh's Church, 31
Sandycove, 261–7
Santry, 70
School-House Lane, 101–2
Scotsman's Bay, 261
Shelbourne Hotel, 205–11, 216
Slieve Roe, 61
Smithfield, 224
Smock Alley Theatre, 93, 236–8
South Dublin, 165–231, 326
South Wall, Dublin harbour, 255,
 256
State Lottery Office, *319*
Steyne, the, 28
Strongbow Monument, 78
Sugar Loaf mountain, 27
Sutton, 268

Tailor's Hall, 102–3
Temple Bar, 148
Templeogue, 323
Theatre Royal, 239
Thomas Court, Great Abbey of, 98
Thomas Street, 104–7, 225, 316, 317
Three Rock Mountain, 61
Trinity College, 34, 41, 74, 97,131, 165–81, *178*, 245, 279, 281–3, 317, 323, 324, 326

University College, 203, 216, 249
Upper Ely Place, 211

Upper Mount Street, 324
Ussher's Island, 322

Vice-Regal Lodge, Phoenix Park, *see* Aras an Uachtaran

Weaver's Hall, 98
West Essex Street, 236
Westland Row, 194
Westmoreland Street, 75
Whitefriars Street, 33
Wicklow mountains, 59; *see also* Dublin mountains
Wine Tavern Street, 31, 279
Wood Quay, 32

GENERAL INDEX

AE (George Russell), 246
Albert, Prince, 131
ale, 309
Altamont, Lord, 192
archaeology, 28–9
architecture, 29, 32, 34, 39–44, 321, 325
Ardilaun, Lady (Olive), 214–15
Ardilaun, Lord, *see* Guinness, Sir Benjamin
Asgill, Sir Charles, 129
Avellanus, 53

'Back Lane Parliament', 102
Bagwell, Richard, 115–16
Ball, Elrington, 89
Baltinglas, Lord, 182
Barnard, F.P., 54–6, 77–8, 299–301
Barrett, Dr Jacky, 177, 179–80
Barrington, Sir Jonah, 69–72, 140–2, 143, 185–8, 191
Barry, Sir David, 63
Beerbohm, Max, *208*
beggars, 318, *319*, 320, 322
Behan, Brendan, 217
Behan, Kathleen, 217–18
Belvedere, Earls of, 145
Beresford, John, 151–2
Berkeley, Bishop, 175
Birrell, Augustine, 211–13, 295

Black Death, 32–3
Blacker, Colonel William, 147–9
Bond, Oliver, 224
Boru, Brian, 30
Bovet, Anne Marie de, 111–14
Bowen, Elizabeth, 210–11, 324–6
Boyle, Archbishop, 116
Boyle, Richard, Earl of Cork, *86*, 87–9, 199
Boyle, Roger, 1st Earl of Orrery, 182
Boyne, Battle of, 38
Brabazon, William, 98
Bramhall, John, 182
brass plates, 326
brawling, 316–17
Brocas, S.F. and H., *frontis*, *139*
Broughton, Sir Thomas, 83
Bruce, Robert, 32
Buckle, G.E., 131
buildings, *see* architecture
Burgh (Surveyor-General), 40
Burke, Edmund, 144, 155, 170–1, 236–7
Burke, Thomas, 134–6
Burlington, Lord, 41
Butler, James, Duke of Ormonde (1610–88), 35–6, 37, 115–16, 127–8
Butler, Simon, 102

Butt, Isaac, 229
Buttevant, Viscount, 63

cabs, 327
Cambrensis, Giraldus, 77–8,
   299–301
Camden, Lord, 72
Campbell, Dr Thomas, 138, 175
Carleton, William, 109–11
Carlyle, Thomas, 132–3
Carte, Thomas, 127
Carty, James, 304
Cassells, Richard, 41–2, 137, 138,
   199, 202
Castide, Henry, 79
Castlemaine, Lady, 127–8
Castlereagh, Lord, 193
Catholicism, 93–4, 95, 97–8, 63, 74,
   143–4, 158–62, 165–6, 194, 322
Caulfield, James, Earl of
   Charlemont, 140, 143–4
Cavendish, Lord Frederick, 134–6
Ceannt, Eamonn, 281
Chambers, Sir William, 42, 151
Charlemont, Earl of, *see* Caulfield,
   James
Charles I, 127
Charles II, 35, 36, 115, 116, 127
Chart, D.A., 194
Chesterfield, Lord, 67
Christianity, 27, 30, 31, 33–4, 166
Churchill, Winston, 133–4
city planning, 34–44
city walls, 302–3
Civil War, English, 35
Civil War, Irish, 46, 279, 327
Clare, Lord, 192–3
Clarence, Duke of, 82–3, 113
Clarke, Arthur, 290
Clarke, Austin, 249–51
Clarke, Thomas J., 281
Clayton, Robert, Bishop of Cork,
   198, 199
Clayton, Mrs Robert, 198–9
Clements, Nathaniel, 128
Clontarf, Battle of, 30
Clyn, John, 32–3
Cobbett, William, 322–3
Connolly, James, 45, 46, 281, 284,
   285, 286, *287*, 288; execution,
   291–3
Cooper, George, 155–6
Coote, Charles, Earl of Mountrath,
   182
Cork, Earl of, *see* Boyle, Richard
Cork and Orrery, Countess of, 199
Cowper, Earl of, 135
Crampton, Sir Philip, 132
Croker, John Wilson, 74–5
Cromwell, Oliver, 35
Crosbie, Richard, 221–4, *223*
Cruikshank, George, *106*
Cuaran, Olaf, 30
Cumberland, Duke of, 74
Curran, W.H., 227
Curry, William, 149–50, 321–2
Curtis, Robert, 116
Cushing, Thomas, 184

Danes, 28–30, 78
Davies, Sir John, 64
Delany, Dr, 66, 91, 137
Delany, Mrs, 66–7, 137–8, 198–9
Derricke, John, *57*, *300*
Desmond, Earl of, 78
Dillon, Eilis, 230–1
Disraeli, Benjamin, 74, 133
Donegal, Lord, 74
Donoughmore, Lord, 74
dress, 303, 304, 305–6
Dublin, Battle of, 28
Dublin Penny Journal, 180
Dublin United Tramways
   Company, 273
Dublin Verse Speaking Society, 249
Dun, Sir Patrick, 116
Dunton, John, 64–6, 255
Dürer, Albrecht, *306*

Easter Rising, 46, 217, 276–95
Elizabeth I, 34, 165
Ellmann, Richard, 267
Emerson, Alderman, 317
Emmett, Robert, 105–8, *109*, 288
Eóghan Bán, 304
Essex, Earl of, 309
Eustace, Sir Maurice, 182

Everard, Sir John, 64
Everett, Katherine, 214–16

Famine, 131, 132, 156
Fay, W.G., 245, 247
Fellows of Trinity College, 37, 41, 166–7, 168–9, 171, 324
Fenians, 133, 134–6; *see also* United Irishmen
Fenton, Catherine, 87
Fenton, Sir Geoffrey, 87
Fingal, Earl of, *see* Plunkett, Sir Christopher
FitzGerald, Lord Edward, 43, 69, 104–6, *104*, 220, 224–5, 226
FitzGerald, James, 20th Earl of Kildare and 1st Duke of Leinster, 41, 42, 43, 104, 138
FitzGerald, Sir John, 168
FitzGerald, 'Silken Thomas', 33
FitzGerald, clan, 77
Fitzhenry, Edna, 294
Fitz-Robert, G., 56
Fitzthomas, Maurice, 83
Fitzwilliam of Merrion, Lord, 42, 176
footpads, 318
Ford, William, 194, 195
Franklin, Benjamin, 184
Free State, 46, 326–7; Parliament, 225–6
Freeman's Journal, 128, 162, 290
Froissart's *Chronicles*, 79–82, *80*

Gaelic League, 57, 284
Gamble, John, 318
Gandon, James, 39, 42–3, 151–4, *153*, 155, 220
Gardiner, Luke, 39–40, 42
George, Duke of Cambridge, 132
George II, statue of, 98
George IV, 74–5, 147–9, 258; monument to, 258, *259*
Gerard, Francis, 198
Gernon, Luke, 304–6
Gilbert, Sir John, 182–4, 221–5, 302
Gladstone, William, 134, 219
Gogarty, Oliver St John, 45, 180, 211–14, 261–7

Goldsmith, Oliver, 170
Gonne, Maud, 216, 217–18, 242, 268–70
Goodwin, Peter, 116
Granard, Lord, 116
Grattan, Henry, 69, 176–7, 186–91, *187*, 194, 242
Great Plague, 32–3
Gregory, Lady (Augusta), 45, 243–5, 247, 248–9
Guinness, Sir Benjamin, 96, 207, 214–15
Guinness, Sir Edward Cecil, 113
Gwynn, Stephen, 128

Hall, Anna Maria, 104
Hampton, Sir Christopher, 63
Handel, G.F., 93, 235–6
Hardy, Francis, 144
Harrington, Lord, 129
Harris, Frank, 229–30
Hartington, Lord, 135
Henry II, *54*, 54–5, 77
Henry III, 302
Henry VII, 82–3, 84
Henry VIII, 34, 98
Henry, Dr R.M., 246
Herbert, J.D., 99–100
Hibernian Magazine, 95, *178*, *315*
Hogan, Roger, 244
Holinshed's *Chronicles*, 53–4, 58–9, 78–9, 82–3, 84–7, 301–2, 307–8
Holloway, Joseph, 244–5
Hopkins, Gerard Manley, 203
Howe, Earl of, 235
Hugenots, 98–100
Hyde, Douglas, 44–5, 56–7

Invincibles, 134
Irish, attitudes to, 299–301, 305–6
Irish Citizen's Army, 291
Irish Independent, 273
Irish Literary Renaissance, 44–5, 207
Irish Literary Society, 44, 45
Irish Literary Theatre, 45, 242
Irish National Theatre, 45, 247
Irish Republican Army, 46; *see also* Irish Volunteers

Irish Transport and General
Workers' Union, 273–4
Irish Volunteers, 1780s: 140–2, 144,
187, 220, 222; 1916: 276–88, 291

James II, 37–8, 115–16, 156,
167–9
Jebb, Dr, 140
Jeffreys, Nathaniel, 256–7
Jennens, Charles, 235
John, King of England, 31, 56, 77,
156
John de Sainte Paule, 78
John of Evesham, 78
Johnson, Mrs Hester (Stella), 94,
96
Johnson, James, 111
Johnson, Samuel, 127, 138, 199
Joly, John, 281–3
Joyce, James, 45, 145–6, 204–5,
211, 218, 261–7

Kean, Edmund, 238
Kelly, Linda, 237
Kemble, John Philip, 237
Kemble, Miss, 239
Kennedy, Tom, 230
Kent, William, 41
Kiersey, Thomas, *287*
Kildare, 8th Earl of (the 'Great'),
82, 84–7
Kildare, 9th Earl of, 33
Kildare, 16th Earl of, 87
Kildare, 17th Earl of, 182
Kildare, 20th Earl of, *see*
FitzGerald, James
Kilmainham pact, 134

Land League, 118
language, Irish, 305, 328
Lansdowne, Lord, 66
Larkin, James 45, 46, 122, 273–4,
275, 284
Laud, Archbishop, 88
Laurence, St, Archbishop of
Dublin, 78
Lefanu, Emma, 104
Lefanu, Sheridan, 104
Leinster, Duchess of, 225

Leinster, 1st Duke of, *see*
FitzGerald, James
Leinster, 2nd Duke of, 220
Lever, Charles, 72–4, 128–30, 177,
320
Lockhart, J.G., 94
Loftus, Adam, 165
Loftus, Dr Dudley, 182
Logue, Cardinal, 243
Longford, Christine, 99
Longford, 6th Countess of, 99
Lorrequer, Harry, 323
Lovaine, Lord, 75
Lovell, Lord, 83
Lutterel, Colonel, 169

Mac an Bhaird, Laoiseach, 303–4
MacBride, John, 268
MacBride, Maud Gonne, *see*
Gonne, Maud
Mac Diarmada, Sean, 281
MacDonagh, Michael, 194
MacDonagh, Thomas, 281, 290,
291, 293
MacHugh, Fiach, 62
MacLysaght, Edward, 255
McManus, M.J., 67, 156, 310–13
MacMorrough, King of Leinster,
82
Mac Murchadha, Dermot, King of
Leinster, 165
MacNeile Dixon, W., 166–9
Macready, William Charles, 238–9
Madden, R.R., 105, 107
Mahaffy, Sir John Pentland, 180–1
Malton, James, *71*, *153*, *172–3*,
198, *200–1*, 220–1, *319*
Marlborough, Duke of, 133
Marsh, Narcissus, Archbishop of
Armagh, 41, 97
Martyn, Edward, 45, 209, 242, 243
Maxwell, Constantia, 59, 100, 147,
165–6, 303–4
Maxwell, W.H., 106
Meath, Bishop of, 169
Meath, Earl of, 98
Mendicity Society, 322
Mervyn, Sir Audley, 182
Miley, Revd Dr, 162, 196

Mitchel, John, 156–7
Montgomery, Viscount, 182
Moore, Arthur, 189, 190
Moore, George, 45, 207–10, *208*,
    211–14, 219, 241–3
Moore, Dr Michael, 167
morals, 310–13
Morton, H.V., 225–6, 326–8
Mosse, Bartholomew, 137–40
Mulvaney, T.J., 151–4
Murphy, William Martin, 273,
    274

Neill, Ui, 30
Newbolt, Sir Henry, 79
Newman, Cardinal, 203
Normans, 30–3, 54–7, 63, 77–82,
    299, 301, 302
Norway, Mrs Hamilton, 288–90
Nottingham, Robert le, 32

O'Brien, Kate, 216–17
O'Brien, King of Thomond, 82
O'Brien, William, 117–21
O'Brien, William Smith, 195
O'Brien clan, 32
O'Byrne, Dermot, 294
O'Casey, Sean, 45, 46, 122–4,
    273–4, 295–6
O'Clery, Lughaidh, 59–62
O'Connell, Daniel, 156, 158–62,
    160–1, 194–6, *197*, 225, 227–9,
    228
O'Connor, King of Connaught and
    Erne, 82
O'Daly, Angus, 56–7
O'Donnell, Hugh Roe, 59–62
O'Hagarty, Edmond, 195
O'Keeffe, John, 98, 174
'Old English', 63
O'Malley, Ernie, 279–81
O'Neal, King of Meath, 82
O'Neill, Henry, 61
O'Neill, Hugh, 59
O'Neill, Michael J., 244
O'Neill clan, 39, 303
Ormonde, Duke of, *see* Butler,
    James
Ormonde, 3rd Earl of, 81–2
Ormonde, 7th Earl of, 84–7

Orpen, William, *275*
Orrery, 1st Earl of, *see* Boyle,
    Roger
Orrery, 5th Earl of, 199
O'Shea brothers, 219
Ostomen, 301–2
O'Sullivan, Denis, 245
O'Sullivan, Seamus, 45, 267
O'Toole clan, 32, 33
Ould, Sir Fielding, 137
Ourgham, Sir Thomas, 82

Pado, Sir Jonathan, 82
Palladian architecture, 27, 39, 41,
    42
Parliament, Irish, 41, 42, 43, 69,
    143, 182–97, 303
Parnell, Charles, Stewart, 44,
    117–21, *119*, 123, 134
Pearce, Sir Edward, 39, 41, 42, 43,
    182
Pearse, Patrick, 281, 284, 285, 286,
    287, 288, 290–1, 293
Pellasier, Dr, 171
Perrott, Sir John, 303
Petty, Sir William, 182
Phoenix Park murders, 134–6, *136*
Pilkington, Letitia, 90–3
Pitt, William, 189, 193, 256
Playboy of the Western World, The
    243–6
Plunkett, Sir Christopher, Earl of
    Fingal, 63–4
Plunkett, Joseph, 281
Pole, John de la, 83
Pollock, Sir F., 238
Pool, R., 74–5
Pope, Alexander, 89, 199
poverty, 318, *319*, 321–3
Protestants, 34, 35, 37–8, 41, 43,
    44, 116, 165

Quincey, Thomas de, 192–3

Reformation, 33–4, 63, 165
Repeal Association, 194–5
Restoration, the, 35, 182
Reynolds, Thomas, 158, 224
Rich, Barnaby, 309
Richard II, 79–82

Richmond, Duke of, 72
Roberts, George, 245
Robinson, Sir William, 36
Roden, Lord, 70, 74
Romanesque style, 31
Rowan, Hamilton, 102–3
Russell, Lord John, 156–7
Rutland, Duke and Duchess of, 224
Ryan, Desmond, 273, 284–8

Samuels, Arthur, 155, 170, 236
Santry, Lady, 67.
Scarsfield, Patrick, 307
Schomberg, General, 38
Scortchbill, Henry, 78
Scott, Sir Walter, 94
Sechnaill, Mael, 30
Shackleton, Dick, 170
Shaw, Bernard, 246
Shelley, Percy Bysshe, 147
Sheridan, Revd Dr, 91
Sheridan, Richard Brinsley, 93
Sheridan, Thomas, 93, 236–7
Shute, Nevil, 288
Siddons, Sarah, 237–8
Sidney, Sir Henry, 57, 65, 78
Silkenbeard, Sitric, 30
Simnel, Lambert, 82–3
Simon, Sir Richard, 82
Sinn Fein, 282, 288, 295
Sirr, Major, *104*, 105, 192, 193
social life, 314, 320, 323, 325–6
Spencer, Earl, 135
Stanyhurst, Richard, 53–4, 58,
    78–9, 307
Starkie, Walter, 245–8
Steel, Tom, 196
Stephens, James, 45, 276–9
Stoker, Sir Thornley, 211–14
Strafford, Earl of, *see* Wentworth,
    Thomas
Strongbow, Earl of Pembroke, 54–
    6, 77–9, 299, 302
Swan, Major, 104
Swift, Dean, 40–1, 66, 89–97, *95*,
    99, 199, 310
Synge, J.M., 45, 122, 243–8

Talbot, Lord, 149
Talbot, Richard, 116

Tandy, James Napper, 102–3, 141
taxes, 302
Temple, Sir William, 182
Thackeray, W.M., 96, 205–7,
    239–40, 258–60, 323–4
theatre, 235–51
Tobin, Paddy, 246–8
Tone, Wolfe, 43, 102–3, 224
Townsend, Molly, 322–3
Townsend, Dorothea, 87–9
trade, 29, 31–2, 302
transport, 327
Travers, Mary, 229–30
Tyrconnell, Prince of, 59

Uffort, Robert, 78
Union, Act of, 43, 44, 143, 189–93
United Irish Rebellion (1798), 43,
    44, 63, 69–72, 104–8, 189, 224–5
United Irishman, The, 156
United Irishmen, 69, 102–3,
    118–21, 224; *see also* United Irish
    Rebellion

Vere, Aubrey de, 130–1
Vice-regal Court, 75–6
Victoria, Queen, 131–2
Vikings, 27–30, 300–1

Walker's *Hibernian Magazine*, 95,
    178, *315*
Walsh, J.E., 102, 176–7, 316–18
Warbeck, Perkin, 82, 84
Ware, Sir James, 182
Warwick, Earl of, 82–3
weavers, 98–100
Wentworth, Thomas, Earl of
    Strafford, 34–5, 36, 86, 87–9
Wesley, John, 117
Weston, Dr, 87
Whaley, Richard, 203
Wheatley, Francis, *185*
Whelan, Dr, 162
Whitelaw, Revd James, 100–2
Whitworth, Earl, 149
Wide Streets Commission, 43, 151
wild Irish, the, 299–301
Wilde, Oscar, 229
Wilde, Dr William, 229–30
Willes, Chief Baron, 68–9, 314

William of Orange, 38
Winstanley, John, 169–70
Wogan Brown, Dorothy, 246
women, 306

Yeats, W.B., 44, 45, 94, 207, *208*,
209, 210, 214–18, 241–5, 249–51,
250, 268, 293–4